Praise for *Think Better*

Excellent! A practical guide to the power of productive thinking that should be read by everyone.

Glenn Bishop
Director, Engineering, Yahoo! Europe

A treasury of powerful ideas for anyone who wants to boost their brand equity and contribute mightily to their company's success.

Andy Boynton. Ph.D.
Dean, Carroll School of Management,
Boston College and author, *Virtuoso Teams*

A perfect balance of theory and practice. Read it, and don't look back!

Roger J. Burns
Worldwide Partner, Mercer Human Resource Consulting

Not just a book to be read, but a manifesto for action.

Kevin Byron, Ph.D.
Senior Fellow, British Higher Education Academy

Possibly the most inspiring thinking process I have come across — you'll miss out if you don't use it!

Rob Devine
Leadership Consultant, Singapore

The best book I've ever read on innovative thinking—accessible, interesting, fascinating, with great examples and stories.

Gregg Fraley
author, *Jack's Notebook*

If you want to create the future for your team, organization or the planet, put down the crystal ball and pick up Think Better.

Colin Funk
Director, Leadership Learning Lab, The Banff Centre

An easy read that will train your brain without giving you a headache.

Paul Hoffert
Fellow, Harvard University and author, *The New Client*

I heartily recommend this lively, pragmatic and exceptionally insightful book for anyone looking to think better in business and in life.

Timothy S. Mescon, Ph.D.
Dean, Coles College of Business, Kennesaw State University

THINK
BETTER

THINK
BETTER

**(your company's future depends on it . . .
and so does yours)**

TIM HURSON

New York   Chicago   San Francisco
Lisbon   London   Madrid   Mexico City
Milan   New Delhi   San Juan   Seoul
Singapore   Sydney   Toronto

1-4-08

153.42
HUR

25.95

Copyright © 2008 by The McGraw-Hill Companies. All rights reserved. Printed in the United States of America. Except as permitted under the United States Copyright Act of 1976, no part of this publication may be reproduced or distributed in any form or by any means, or stored in a data base or retrieval system, without the prior written permission of the publisher.

1 2 3 4 5 6 7 8 9 0 DOC/DOC 0 9 8 7

ISBN-13: 978-0-07-149493-9
ISBN-10: 0-07-149493-6

McGraw-Hill books are available at special quantity discounts to use as premiums and sales promotions, or for use in corporate training programs. For more information, please write to the Director of Special Sales, Professional Publishing, McGraw-Hill, Two Penn Plaza, New York, NY 10121-2298. Or contact your local bookstore.

This book is printed on acid-free paper.

Illustrations by Jim Ridge

To my wife, my partner, my teacher,
my inspiration, and my best friend,
Franca Leeson

CONTENTS

PREFACE

Although I didn't realize it at the time, I began working on this book about 15 years ago. I was involved in an online discussion on the subject of creativity. One of the participants was adamant that creativity is an innate quality that cannot be taught: Either you have it or you don't. I had a different view. I had been in the creativity business my entire working life, starting as a scriptwriter on documentary films and eventually becoming creative director of my own marketing firm. I had read books by James L. Adams, Edward de Bono, and Roger von Oech and was convinced that creativity, like other thinking skills, is something that can be learned and developed. But I had no direct proof.

That discussion led me on a journey that refocused my life. I attended seminars, hunted for books, and experimented. Eventually, I came in contact with the Creative Education Foundation (CEF). CEF had been launched in 1954 by Alex Osborn, the advertising executive who pioneered the concept of brainstorming, and Sid Parnes, a brilliant young psychology professor. I joined the foundation mainly to get the 10 percent discount on its extensive book list. From its mailings, I learned that CEF held an annual conference called the Creative Problem Solving Institute (CPSI). I decided to go.

CPSI (pronounced "sip-see") consisted of numerous concurrent sessions, ranging from serious academic dissertations to arts-related programs to some pretty off-the-wall presentations. Its main offering, though, was a methodology that Osborn and Parnes had developed over the years called the Creative Problem Solving Process (CPS). Built on Osborn's original rules for brainstorming, CPS proposed that the main thing you have to do to be more creative is to *not* think, that the most productive thing you can do is simply to generate lists of ideas—ideas about causes of problems, ideas about where you want to go once you solve those problems, and ideas about how to get there. Once you've generated those ideas, no matter how far-fetched they may be, you return to your lists and *only then* apply critical thinking to evaluate them, choose the most promising ones, and develop them further. It seemed too simple.

I developed a kind of love-hate relationship with CPS. I thought it had potential, but for me, it focused too much on the generation of ideas and not enough on the rigorous, critical evaluation of them. I needed to learn more. I benefited greatly from long and fascinating conversations with Sid Parnes, who became my mentor and a dear friend, as well as with many other CPS practitioners. I also explored a variety of engineering-based problem-solving systems, among them a methodology called Integrated Definition (IDEF), which was used by NASA. I culled some of the more rigorous approaches from those systems and wove them into the core CPS process. In facilitating strategy sessions with clients, I experimented with and modified what I had learned. Slowly, what began to emerge was a new model for thinking more productively: a disciplined, repeatable way for people to generate more ideas, better ideas, more of the time.

The result of that work is the think^x Productive Thinking Model that my colleagues and I use to facilitate corporate innovation sessions and train people to think more creatively and effectively. The think^x model is built firmly on the foundation of the Osborn-Parnes Creative Problem Solving Process, with numerous additions based on my own experience and the invaluable insights and contributions of my colleagues, especially my business partner, Kristen Peterson.

In my work with businesses and not-for-profit organizations, I have seen the think^x model and its underlying principles foster profound changes in the way individuals and organizations operate. This book gives me the opportunity to introduce the model and its potential benefits to a wider audience.

The premise of *Think Better* is that success in our business, professional, and personal lives is less a matter of what we know than of how we think. If we can develop the thinking skills to generate more options and then evaluate those options more effectively, we can all live richer, fuller lives—and so can the people around us.

Everybody talks about creativity and innovation these days, but very few actually know how to put them into practice. The think^x model shines a bright light on the productive thinking strategies that people we celebrate for their creativity have been using for centuries. I think you'll find that productive thinking is a game changer. It brings the skills to think better out of the closet and presents them in a way that makes them easy for anyone to grasp and use—so they can think better, work better, and do better in every aspect of their lives.

The good news is that productive thinking is a skill that anyone can learn and develop. Regardless of your starting point, you *can* learn to use your mind better. It's not much different from driving a car. Two people can drive the same vehicle. One does so adequately, getting reasonable mileage and performance. The other drives it superbly by applying learned skills to get the best mileage and performance possible. Will some people always be more creative than others? Of course. But whatever vehicle you start with, whether it's a BMW or a Skoda, you can learn to use it better.

Think Better is not an academic study. My company, think^x intellectual capital, works with real organizations that face real-world issues. One of the difficulties in trying to illustrate the concepts in this book is the type of work we do for our clients. For almost any organization, it is impossible to separate issues of innovation from issues of competitiveness. As a result, much of the work we do involves proprietary information that is inappropriate to reveal. In providing examples and illustrations in the following pages, I have tried as much as possible to use actual cases without revealing confidential information or the names of the companies involved.

Think Better is divided into 14 chapters and an appendix.

Chapter 1, "Why Think Better," presents a case for how we can all benefit from thinking better and introduces the concept of the unexpected connection, which is threaded throughout the book.

Chapter 2, "Monkey Mind, Gator Brain, and the Elephant's Tether," discusses the barriers to productive thinking and the reasons we don't think very creatively—or effectively—most of the time.

Chapter 3, "*Kaizen* vs. *Tenkaizen*," introduces and contrasts the concepts of productive thinking and reproductive thinking and suggests how they can be applied to organizational change.

Chapter 4, "Stay in the Question," discusses the tendency to jump too quickly to conclusions rather than taking the time to explore questions fully.

Chapter 5, "The Miracle of the Third Third," contrasts good and bad brainstorming and explains why the most creative ideas usually come toward the end of brainstorming sessions rather than at the beginning.

Chapter 6, "Productive Thinking by Design," provides an introduction to and overview of the six-step think^x model.

Chapters 7 through 12 provide detailed explanations of each of the six steps of the model, with examples and case studies.

Chapter 7, "Step 1: What's Going On?" explores the issue or issues that need resolution.

Chapter 8, "Step 2: What's Success?" establishes criteria for success.

Chapter 9, "Step 3: What's the Question?" defines the real problem to be solved.

Chapter 10, "Step 4: Generate Answers," proposes initial ideas for solutions.

Chapter 11, "Step 5: Forge the Solution," transforms the initial ideas into powerful solutions.

Chapter 12, "Step 6: Align Resources," identifies and assigns resources to implement the solution.

Chapter 13, "Productive Thinking Redux," recaps the model and offers several tips about using its various steps and tools.

Chapter 14, "Training vs. Entraining," suggests four essential criteria for developing productive thinking skills and embedding productive thinking in organizational cultures.

The back matter includes a glossary of productive thinking terms and key tools as well as a comprehensive example of the Productive Thinking Model in action.

I hope that by the end of the book you will have a solid appreciation of productive thinking. I hope, too, that you will be motivated to put it to the test so that you can experience for yourself how this simple but powerful model can help you understand more clearly, think more creatively, and plan more effectively.

The think^x Productive Thinking Model is straightforward to learn, practical to implement, and it works. With the right attitude, the right approach, and the right skills, we can all think better!

ACKNOWLEDGMENTS

There are many people to thank for this book.

First, I want to thank all my consulting partners and associates at think^x intellectual capital for their support and enthusiasm. First and foremost, they are my friends. They have also been evangelists and ambassadors who have spread the word about productive thinking by delivering facilitation, training, and coaching to clients around the world. Without these people the think^x Productive Thinking Model would have no legs. I owe a huge debt of gratitude to them all. In the United States they are Paul Groncki and Clare Dus (New York), Janeen Whalen (Los Angeles), Russ Schoen (Chicago), Steve Fox (Boston), Stanley Young (Sacramento), and Julieta Parra-McPherson (Omaha). In Europe they are Patrizia Sorgiovanni and Scott Middleton (London), Tim Dunne and Maggie Dugan (Paris), and Matteo Catullo and Paolo Sbuttoni (Milan). In Canada they are Dan Bigonesse, Alison Cohen, Marc Hurwitz, Glenn Pothier, and John Sedgwick.

I have had the good fortune to meet hundreds of people who have inspired me with their intelligence, their creativity, their compassion, and their courage. Neither this book nor the work leading up to it would have been possible without their examples.

George Langler and Ralf Hotchkiss, whose story appears in Chapter 1, both influenced me in ways they can never know. No expression of appreciation could be adequate. Rafe Martin, Tom Friedman, Tom Stoyan, Robin Wall, Michael Jacot, Ken McLeod, and Peter Lloyd each taught me that thinking better is a function of using both mind and heart. Cindy Krysac, girl physicist, taught me the value of persistence. Doug Scott taught me how to write. My good friend Roger von Oech, whom I first met in a book, later online, and eventually by phone—but whom I have yet to meet in the flesh—taught me that serious writing can be fun writing. My former business partner Eric Young taught me the importance of thinking it through and writing it down. My uncle Harry Hurwitz, the most energetically creative person

I have ever known, taught me that we are all inexhaustible wells of new ideas.

Thanks to Maria Shinoto for her invaluable assistance in helping me understand the Japanese *kanji* construction for the term *tenkaizen*, which plays an important role in my thinking. Thanks also to Robert Bick for urging me to develop the Productive Thinking Model and for helping me explore its concepts during the early stages.

Very few of the ideas in this book would have been possible without the hundreds of hours of conversations I have had with a very special group of people: the professionals who teach at the many global creativity and innovation conferences with which I am involved. These people have shared their insights and experiences with me and also become fast friends. For both of those gifts, I wish to thank Guy Aznar, René Bernèche, Laura Barbero, Alan Black, Kevin Byron, Jean Bystedt, Colette Chambon, Jeanne Chatigny, Ted Coulson, Nancylyn Davis, Dave Dilts, Mark Dodsworth, Lee Dunne, Newell Eaton, Bob Eckert, Gregg Fraley, John Frederick, Guido Galimberti, Bill Hartwell, Kitty Heusner, Magellan Horth, Anthony Hyatt, Clara Kluk, Hedria Lunken, Joe Miguez, Oliver MacDonald, Tom McMullen, Allie Middleton, Sandra Minnee, Liz Monroe Cook, Len Mozzi, Nancy Myers, Murli Nagasundaram, Kobus Neethling, Charlene Pasco, Jon Pearson, Frank Prince, Sjra Puts, Kanes Rajah, Doug Reid, Leslie Seabury, Tim Switalski, Guingo Sylwan, Andy Van Gundy, Harry Vardis, Jonathan Vehar, Ken Wall, Win Wenger, Jack Wolf, and Olwen Wolfe.

Very special thanks for the lessons they have taught me to Sid and Bea Parnes and to Jacquie Lowell, without whose invitation I would not have entered this wonderful community. Thanks to Jim Ridge, whose illustrations for this book bring productive thinking to life. Who would have imagined that a chance meeting in Buffalo, New York, could produce such a wonderful collaboration! *Think Better* would be much the poorer without Jim's creativity and dedication.

I also wish to thank my four children, Emily, Branwen, Peter, and Max Hurson, who put up with me for the year or so it's taken to write this book. You've been a wonderful support.

Finally, I need to express my deepest possible gratitude to four extraordinary women, each of whom helped give birth to *Think Better*.

First, my business partner, Kristen Peterson, who said she would do anything it took to free up my time so I could write this book. She did that and more. Without her support, her strength, and her stamina, neither the think^x model nor *Think Better* would exist. Thank you, Kristen.

Second, my editor, Leah Spiro, who was relentless in forcing me to be clear. The passages in *Think Better* that are lucid are probably the result of Leah's sharp pencil. Those that are opaque are almost certainly ones in which I didn't follow her advice.

Third, my literary agent, Cathy Hemming. I will never cease to be grateful for the lovely bit of serendipity that brought us together. Cathy had faith that there was a book in me somewhere. I cannot express how much that faith means to me.

Last and most, my wife, Franca, who is infinitely more creative and intelligent than I could ever hope to be. She sweated through this book every bit as much as I did. She was my second editor, my organizer, my supporter, my advisor, at times my goad, and always, always my friend. Thank you, Franca.

PART 1

PRODUCTIVE THINKING IN
CONTEXT

Why Think Better

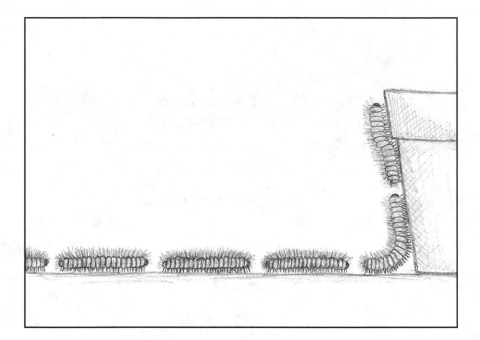

Imagination is the beginning of creation:
you imagine what you desire,
you will what you imagine,
and at last you create what you will.

George Bernard Shaw

This book is about creating the future. It's about a way to see more clearly, think more creatively, and plan more effectively. It's about thinking better, working better, and doing better in every area of your life. All of us have the potential to think better. The first step is to free ourselves from the unproductive thinking patterns that hold us back.

There's an interesting little insect known as the processionary caterpillar that can teach us a lot about the stifling habits of everyday thinking. Processionaries got their name because of their distinctive behavior. When they leave their nests to forage for food, they travel in a line, like elephants in a circus, head to tail, head to tail. The lead caterpillar spins a fine trail of silk as it crawls along. The next caterpillar in line walks along the silk trail and adds its own. Processionaries can form trains hundreds of creatures long as they march through the forest.

There's nothing particularly distinctive about the lead caterpillar: It just happens to be at the front. It walks along for a while, pausing and raising its head occasionally, trying to sense which way the nearest food source is, and then continues the trek. If you remove the lead caterpillar, the second in line will take up the scouting duties without hesitation. The trailing caterpillars don't seem to care about the change in leadership.

Processionaries fascinated one of the world's great naturalists, Jean Henri Fabre, who is considered by many the father of modern entomology. He spent years studying them, both in his green house and in their natural environment. Fabre was an observer. He took nothing as given, nothing for granted, made no assumptions. He once wrote that his scientific credo was "the method of ignorance. I read very little. . . . I know nothing. So much the better: my queries will be all the freer, now in this direction, now in the opposite, according to the lights obtained."[1]

Fabre was curious to see how powerful the processionaries' instinct to follow the leader could be. What would happen if he arranged the caterpillars in a circle? Would their instinct to follow force them to keep going round and round in an endless loop? On January 30, 1896, Fabre constructed an experiment in which he coaxed a chain of caterpillars around the rim of a large pot filled with earth. As soon as enough caterpillars had ascended to form a ring, he brushed away the ones at the end of the chain. He then nudged the lead caterpillar behind the trailing caterpillar to close the circle. Instantly, there was no more leader. Each caterpillar in the circle simply followed the threads laid down by those ahead of it, ignoring a cache of the caterpillars' favorite food that Fabre had placed within about 12 inches of the circle.

Six days later, on February 5, the caterpillars were still circling. Only after many started to collapse from exhaustion and starvation did the circle begin to break, allowing a few caterpillars with the strength to do so to escape. According to Fabre's calculations, the caterpillars had made over 500 circuits of the pot and traveled over a quarter of a mile. That's equivalent to a person walking about 90 miles, or completing three and a half marathons, without food, drink, or rest. Fabre concluded his description of the experiment with these words: "The caterpillars in distress, starved, shelterless, chilled with cold at night, cling obstinately to the silk ribbon covered hundreds of times, because they lack the rudimentary glimmers of reason which would advise them to abandon it."[2]

If you've ever had the feeling that you have been in a procession of caterpillars—on your job, in your community, or at home—read on.

At some time in our lives we've all been processionary caterpillars, mindlessly following a trail of silk for no reason except that it's laid out before us. It's all too easy to be a part of the procession and not even realize we're in the parade. It's not the exceptional day that we find ourselves in the procession. It's most days. We go through our lives following the patterns we've grown comfortable with. We do things because that's the way they're done. Our routines seem so natural that it doesn't even occur to us that we're following patterns at all. We overlook opportunities, fail to see warning signs, or just plod along because we've kept our eye, not on the target, but on the routine. It happens to all of us.

As with the caterpillars in Fabre's experiments, sometimes the only thing that saves us is that things go so drastically wrong that we're forced out of our processions. Our pattern has been so counterproductive that the circle we've created can no longer sustain itself. It breaks apart. With no more circle, we're forced to find new ways of doing things. We change only when we're forced to.

How different are we from the processionary caterpillar?

● ● ●

At its heart productive thinking is about freedom. It's a way of escaping from the tyranny of the silken track. Sometimes, of course, there's real value in following the procession. It can be useful and efficient to do things the way they've always been done. Clearly, social conventions, thinking conventions, and best practices have very important and power-ful places in our lives. They represent a type of thinking I call reproductive thinking, which I'll discuss in more detail in Chapter 3. In many areas of our lives there is nothing wrong with reproductive thinking. After all, the behavior of the processionary caterpillar has been a successful survival mechanism for millions of years.

At its heart, productive thinking is about freedom. It's a way of escaping from the tyranny of the silken track.

Nevertheless, as Fabre observed, there are times when reproductive thinking can be counterproductive and even disastrous. As I will try to demonstrate throughout this book, all of us have the potential to think better, more productively, and more creatively. What we need is the incentive. The silken track is alluring: It's safe, it's easy, and in many cases it works just fine. Rarely will you be criticized for sticking to it. No wonder most people are content to play follow the leader. Thinking better is hard work. It can be risky. And it can certainly make you unpopular. So why bother?

I think there are three good reasons.

There's Plenty of Room for Improvement

Nothing is perfect. The word is full of things we can do better.

I once heard the systems thinker Dr. George Ainsworth-Land[3] tell a story that changed my life. Land worked as a consulting psychologist to school systems throughout the country. In preparation for one assignment, he was given a tour of an Arizona high school by its principal. On their walk through the halls, they saw two boys fighting in front of their lockers. One of the boys was the aggressor, pounding furiously on the other boy, who was trying to defend himself. The principal grabbed both boys by the collar, marched them into his office, sat them down, calmed them down, then turned to the aggressor, and asked, "Why were you hitting Brian like that?"

The boy looked up and said, "Because I couldn't think of anything else to do."

I couldn't think of anything else to do. What a statement! How much misery do we cause and endure in our personal lives, our business lives, our community lives, and our geopolitical lives because we can't think of anything else to do, because we can't find better options, because we act and react according to our timeworn limited—and limiting—patterns? How much better would our lives, our businesses, our world be if only we could think of better things to do, if only we could increase our options, if only we could truly think productively?

Wouldn't it be great if we could avoid the processionary caterpillar syndrome in which we do things just because we can't think of better things to do? As you'll see later in the book, the productive thinking process uses a series of trigger questions to stimulate thinking about issues. One of the "stems" we use to construct those questions is "Wouldn't it be great if . . . ?" I've listed six challenges in each of three areas: global challenges, business challenges, and personal challenges. Read through them and count how many you think it would be great to answer yes to:

Global challenges
Wouldn't it be great if . . .
we could find a cure for AIDS?
we could produce clean, reliable, renewable energy?
we could eliminate famine?
we could preserve freshwater supplies?
we could reduce air pollution?
we could end war?

Business challenges
Wouldn't it be great if . . .
my company could be quicker to market with new ideas?
I got more recognition for my ideas and contributions?
I could take the guesswork out of hiring good people?
my company could learn more about our markets and competitors?
I could have more time to be productive and creative?
my company could develop a breakthrough product or service?

Personal challenges
Wouldn't it be great if . . .
I could make more time for myself?
my family could settle differences better?

I could find a way to earn what I need by doing something that gives me satisfaction?

my family could communicate better?

my family could make the most of the time we spend together?

I could find ways to be of greater service to my community?

If you answered yes to just one of these questions, you have a good reason to learn how to think better.

The Indian philosopher Nisargadatta Maharaj once said, "Everything is perfect just as it is—and there's plenty of room for improvement." I don't know anyone who doesn't believe that his or her life or the lives of others couldn't be improved. Wouldn't it be great if we could think of ways to do so?

The good news is that every one of these questions and countless thousands more can be addressed by thinking better: more clearly, more creatively, more productively.

We can all do better. The first step is to start thinking better.

It's Not What You Know but How You Think

In 1969 Peter Drucker coined the term *knowledge economy* in his book *The Age of Discontinuity*. His thesis was that modern society had transformed from a reliance on manual workers to a reliance on knowledge workers. By the early 1990s many large global companies had begun to transform themselves into knowledge-based organizations. Corporate boardrooms and corridors were abuzz with people talking about the information age and intellectual capital. Drucker, as usual, was right.

Today a high school student in Albania can access essentially the same base of information as a chief executive officer in Atlanta. It has become increasingly difficult for the creators of information to husband it. In many industries protecting intellectual property has become a practical impossibility. Within hours of their release and sometimes even before their release, major movies are available as free downloads on the Internet. Music industry executives are apoplectic about piracy. Social security numbers and personal bank records seem to slip effortlessly from the confines of the information fortresses designed to protect them.

More than any other commodity, information is everywhere. Not only can almost anyone access almost anything at almost no cost, but unlike corn and wheat, information doesn't have to be consumed to be used. Quite the opposite: The more it's used, the more it grows. Access to information is no longer the great differentiator. In the transformation economy what matters is how you think. Today the only significant economic differentiator for organizations is how well they can *use* that exponentially growing bank of information: how effectively they can sift through it, evaluate it, transform it into new knowledge, and maximize its economic potential. If it isn't already, the ability to think better will soon become the most significant competitive advantage companies and individuals can claim. Thinking better is what it's all about. And unlike manufacturing, accounting, or telemarketing, the thinking capacity of an organization can't be effectively outsourced.

> *The ability to think better will soon become the most significant competitive advantage companies and individuals can claim. Thinking better is what it's all about.*

Clearly, as innovation becomes the watchword for business leaders, those who think better will win. Companies that have paid lip service to the value of their intellectual capital will have to put their money where their heads are. But that won't be easy. Intellectual capital is slippery. Its value lies in its potential, but it's difficult to measure, sometimes even difficult to see.

Creative intellectual capital is also unpredictable. You don't know what it's going to produce. That can be uncomfortable for corporate leaders who've grown up believing that spreadsheets and systems can define reality. The old axiom "what's not measurable is not manageable" may not apply anymore.

One of my clients is a large U.S.-based food manufacturer. In the belief that innovation has to be an organizational priority, the company recently allocated several million dollars in plant, equipment, and people to launch its Imaginarium Innovation Center.[4] Several months before the scheduled opening, the budget was cut, the launch was downplayed, and a directive was released to all the people involved in the center stating that its initial activities were to be "understated and conservative." Somebody got cold feet.

Yes, thinking better can be scary. But not nearly as scary as the alternative.

Thinking Better Is a Skill

The third reason to think better is because you can. Productive thinking is a skill anyone can learn. In describing public speakers, Ralph Waldo Emerson observed, "All great speakers were bad speakers first." None of us starts out in life knowing how to think. It's a skill we learn. Some of us, through good fortune, encounter mentors and circumstances that teach us well. Some of us don't. But regardless of your basic equipment or the training you've encountered, you can learn to think better.

The Productive Thinking Model is a disciplined, repeatable process for thinking better, thinking more creatively, thinking more innovatively. It is based on over 50 years of cognitive research. And it can be learned. When I started exploring the Internet in the late 1980s, I joined a Usenet forum that focused on creative thinking. I remember thinking at the time that it was miraculous that I could exchange views with people all over the world. One of the threads of our conversation was about whether creativity is innate or can be taught. The debate was hot. Many of the people in the forum were convinced that either you had it or you didn't. I was equally sure that there must be ways to enhance whatever natural abilities people have. The debate in the forum was never resolved, but something clicked for me over those several weeks of exchanges. I discovered that consciously or not, people in all walks of life believe that thinking is innate: You don't learn how to think, you just do it, and some people are simply better at it than others. I couldn't buy that. It seemed to me that if athletes can be trained to run faster and musicians can be taught to play better, surely people can be taught to think better.

I'm happy to tell you that I was right. Over the years evidence has mounted that thinking, and specifically creative thinking, is a skill like any other. It can be taught, it can be developed, and it can be nurtured. Every brain, regardless of its intelligence quotient (IQ) or creative quotient (CQ), can be taught to think better: to understand more clearly, think more creatively, and plan more effectively. I know. I've seen it happen thousands of times.

I'm passionate about productive thinking because I know it can work. I know it can change lives. I know it can transform organizations. I know it can create a better world.

Finding the Unexpected Connection

Heraclitus, the sixth-century BCE philosopher, wrote, "The unexpected connection is more powerful than one that is obvious." The unexpected connection is the heart of the productive thinking process. Seeing old things in new ways—seeing the initially strange but later obvious connections between familiar things—is what AHA! is all about. The unexpected connection has brought us every innovation we've ever created, from early hominids' discovery that a bone could be a weapon to Apple's creation of the iPhone.

Archimedes made an unexpected connection as he sat in his bath and watched the water rise and fall with his movements. Suddenly, it occurred to him that he could use the concept of displacement to ascertain the purity of gold in King Hieron's crown. Myth has it that he was so excited by his insight that he jumped out of the tub and ran naked through the streets of Syracuse yelling, "Eureka!" which means "I've found it!"

John Snow, the father of modern epidemiology, made an unexpected connection that saved a city. In 1854 London experienced an extensive cholera epidemic. The situation was so severe that people began preparing themselves for another Black Plague. A man could wake up healthy in the morning and die before supper. Conventional wisdom held that the disease was spread by people breathing the miasma of sickness. Snow had been interviewing residents of one of the most heavily afflicted areas, Soho. Almost by chance, he observed a pattern. The houses with the greatest number of victims seemed to radiate like spokes of a wheel from a hub at the junction of Broad and Cambridge streets: The closer to the junction, the higher the death toll. On Broad Street, just off Cambridge, there was a water pump. Suddenly it became clear: The pump was the source, and contaminated water the likely cause. The pump was shut down, and the epidemic subsided almost instantly.

Philo T. Farnsworth made an unexpected connection when, as a fourteen-year-old farm boy, he watched his father working the fields of their Idaho homestead. As he watched the tractor furrowing lines in the dark earth, he wondered if it might be possible to scan and then reproduce a picture by using horizontal lines. Within seven years, in 1927, Farnsworth had built and demonstrated the world's first working television.

More recently, Jaap van Ballegooijen, chief engineer for Royal Dutch Shell, made an unexpected connection that allowed the company to extract millions of barrels of previously inaccessible oil. He saw his son turn around his flexible straw to finish the last drop of his milk shake and realized that it might be possible to use the same technique thousands of feet underground.

Unexpected connections don't occur only in the fields of science and technology. Bill Bowerman made an unexpected connection between a tennis shoe and a waffle iron. He literally put the two together, created a new type of sole, and launched Nike, the most successful shoe company in history.

Productive thinking is a way to shine a bright light on the potential connections that are waiting to be discovered all around us. Imagine increasing your chances of finding unexpected connections. Could you make your business better? Your family? Your world?

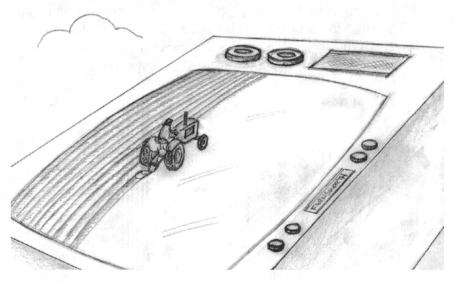

An unexpected connection

About 10 years ago I decided to go to a reunion of my alma mater, Oberlin College, in Ohio. Oberlin was small, with only about 2,500 students, but it was full of culture and life. A third of the students were music majors at its world-famous conservatory. One of Oberlin's real treats was that you could attend three concerts a day if you wanted to. I'd lost contact and hadn't returned since graduation.

On our last evening together we had a class dinner. I had the good luck to sit at the table of one of our honorees, George Langler, then in his eighties. Langler had been dean of students during my years at Oberlin, and though one of his main functions was to maintain order and discipline, he loved his students and had a powerful impact on many of them, including me.

After the meal a microphone was set up, and person after person walked up to tell Dean Langler stories. The last person to come to the mike didn't walk to it; he glided to it in his wheelchair. His name was Ralf Hotchkiss. Ralf had not been in our class originally. He was a year ahead of us. I remember as a freshman seeing Ralf riding around campus on contraptions he had built. Ralf was a bike enthusiast—and a character. You'd see him riding around on double-decker bikes, weird pentacycles, and bikes with passenger seats. It seemed that every week there would be a new bike incarnation. I think Ralf probably created the first-ever reclining bicycle. Ralf loved bikes. He also loved motorcycles. One summer Ralf had a terrible accident, fracturing his spine. It took nine months of surgeries and intense physical therapy for him to recover. But not fully: He had lost the use of the lower half of his body. He would never walk again, never ride a bike.

> *"Gee, Ralf, I don't see why not. We move pianos in and out of buildings all the time." –George Langler*

When he was well enough to consider returning to school, he put the thought of attending Oberlin out of his mind. He knew that a small school in the Midwest was unlikely to be able to accommodate someone with his mobility constraints. So he applied to Ohio State. They liked his academic record but didn't have any buildings that were wheelchair-accessible, so they couldn't accept him. He tried the University of Michigan. Same story. University of Illinois. Same story. As it happened, Ralf's sister had gone to Oberlin a year or two ahead of him. She urged him to reapply. After all, what could he lose? Ralf made the call and spoke to George Langler. Langler listened for a moment and then said "Gee, Ralf, I don't see why not. We move pianos in and out of buildings all the time. Let me call the buildings and grounds people and see if they can modify our portable ramps for your wheelchair. I'll get right back to you."

Ralf returned to school that fall, and Oberlin became the first institution in the United States to have an official policy of accommodating people with mobility disabilities. All because one man, Dean George Langler, sitting in an office in a small college in the Midwest, could see the unexpected connection between moving pianos and moving people. But the story doesn't end there. If you were alive in the late 1960s, you may remember what wheelchairs looked like then. If you're too young, look at the big, clunky upright things you see in airports and hospital waiting rooms. Fortunately, most wheelchairs don't look like that anymore. They're low-slung, with canted wheels and back supports. They're sturdy, light, and maneuverable. And they're all based on breakthrough designs created by Ralf Hotchkiss.

Ralf went on to found Whirlwind, a company that designs and manufactures the best wheelchairs in the world. Whirlwind has a special division that designs wheelchairs for third world countries, wheelchairs that are inexpensive, easy to maintain, can be lifted with one hand, and don't even need paved surfaces. Ralf changed the world, but without George Langler and his ability to see the unexpected connection between moving pianos and moving people, Ralf might never have had the chance.

Creating the Future

To create the future, you have to be able to imagine it. Productive thinking is a way to help you do that. It's not magic. It's a disciplined approach to thinking more creatively and more effectively. You can actually train yourself to think better. The more you practice it, the better you'll get. The better you get, the more opportunities you will have to make a better world, a better company, a better life.

The power of productive thinking lies its potential to increase your chances of finding, developing, and ultimately implementing unexpected connections. Although I've been helping people and companies discover unexpected connections for years, I am consistently astonished when they appear—sometimes in an instant, sometimes after months or even years of searching. They seem to be in limitless supply: an infinite number of AHAs waiting to be discovered.

Unexpected connections can be physically powerful. The moment of insight can actually jolt your body. People's AHA moments are often punctuated by triumphant Archimedes-like yells, by air punches and cries of "YES!", by laughter, and sometimes even tears. Yet once the unexpected connection is revealed, it seems so obvious, even mundane. People often shake their heads and say, "Well, of course. Why didn't we see that before?" That's one of the beauties of insight. Before a connection is made, there's nothing. A moment later, the connection seems like it's been there forever. It's been said that genius is simply a talent for seeing the obvious.

●　　●　　●

Chapter 2, "Monkey Mind, Gator Brain, and the Elephant's Tether," explains why unexpected connections elude us. The rest of this book shows how to find them.

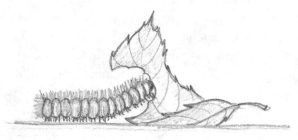

Monkey Mind, Gator Brain, and the Elephant's Tether

*It's not what you don't know that hurts you.
It's what you do know that ain't so.*

Will Rogers

This book is about thinking. So I'm going to ask you to do some thinking with me as you work through it. I use the word *work* deliberately. Because thinking is hard work. Henry Ford once said, "Thinking is the hardest work there is, which is the probable reason why so few engage in it."

There's an interesting biological yardstick called the RMR, which stands for resting metabolic rate. Your RMR is the amount of energy your body needs just to stay alive. Your brain, that mysterious cluster of ganglia, neurons, axons, dendrites, gray and white matter, lobes, synapses (and empty space!), represents about 2 percent of your total body mass (to get a sense of that ratio, imagine one teaspoon of sugar in a standard cup of coffee). Just to keep you alive, your brain requires a disproportionate amount of energy. At rest, it consumes about 20 percent of the oxygen you breathe and the calories you burn (imagine your coffee with 10 teaspoons of sugar!). That's more than your heart (10 percent), your lungs (10 percent), and your kidneys (7 percent). And that 20 percent gobbled up by your brain is just in a resting state. When you're really thinking, that proportion can go way up. Chess masters, for example, have been known to sweat out between 7 and 10 pounds of fluid during a two-hour chess match.

So thinking—truly focused thinking, which includes mental activities such as observing, remembering, wondering, imagining, inquiring, interpreting, evaluating, judging, identifying, supposing, composing, comparing, analyzing, calculating, and even metacognition (thinking about thinking)—is hard work. Which, as Ford said, is probably why so few people actually do it.

You may be saying to yourself, "Don't be silly. I'm thinking all the time. I never stop thinking. I think while I work, while I talk, while I drive. In fact, I'm thinking while I read these words." Well, it probably seems as though you're thinking all the time, but like the rest of your body, your brain uses a variety of strategies and tricks to minimize the energy it requires. And its most effective strategy for conserving brain energy is actually not to think at all. In fact, most of the time your brain is involved in just one of three activities: distraction, reaction, or following well-worn patterns.

Monkey Mind

Let's start with the most common thinking avoidance strategy: distraction. You haven't been reading this chapter for very long, but if you're honest with yourself, you'll probably admit that you lost focus several times during the last 400 or so words. We've all had the experience of reading even the most fascinating material and suddenly realizing that we have no idea what we just read. So we go back to the paragraph containing the last stuff we actually do remember and start again. That often works, of course, but not always. Haven't you also had the experience of getting to the same point you did the first time and suddenly realizing, once again, that you have no idea what you just read? Well, you're not alone. It happens to all of us.

Buddhist meditators call this phenomenon monkey mind. Others have called it runaway mind, stream of consciousness, chatterbox mind, or just plain daydreaming. I like the term *monkey mind* because it calls to mind the image of a troop of monkeys leaping frenetically from tree to tree, staying for just a moment on one thought branch before swinging, seemingly randomly, to another. Monkey mind is a fact. Your mind has a mind of its own, and it's awfully hard to control. Whether you're reading or listening to a lecture, driving your car, or drifting off to sleep, your mind has a tendency to take you for a ride, often to destinations very distant from the one you'd planned to visit.

Monkey mind isn't always a bad thing. Later in this book I'll show you how you can make use of monkey mind to come up with startlingly good creative ideas. But monkey mind isn't focused thinking. It's your mind controlling you, rather than you controlling it.

Gator Brain

The second avoidance strategy is instinctive reaction. Like monkey mind, instinctive reaction is deeply embedded in our being. All of us have essentially three brains. The largest and most recently evolved brain is the cerebral cortex. Let's call this the human brain, since it's one of the distinguishing features of our species. It's one of the things that defines being human. Among the functions of your cerebral cortex are rational thought, logical analysis, speech making, number crunching, associative thinking, and the imaging, analyzing, calculating, and various focused thinking activities I mentioned earlier. Sometimes this is called higher-order thinking. Though many animals also have cortical structures, they are much, much smaller and less robust than ours. Your cerebral cortex is about 2 millimeters thick and very wrinkled. If you were to flatten it out, it would cover an area equivalent to about four sheets of letter-size paper. Flatten out the cortical structure of a chimpanzee and it would cover one sheet. A monkey's would fit on a postcard, and a rat's on a stamp.[1]

This cerebral cortex, or human brain, is a very powerful piece of equipment. All our literature, our art, our architecture, our culture, our philosophy, our medicine, our technology, our science would not exist without the work of millions and millions of cerebral cortices throughout human history. The cerebral cortex is the part of our brain we like to think we think with. But despite its enormous power and potential, it turns out that your cerebral cortex may have a lot less influence on the way you behave than you'd like to believe.

The stem brain or gator brain processes and teacts to sensory input. It either fights, flees, feeds, mates or freezes.

The other two parts of your brain—the more primitive parts—are the limbic system, sometimes called the mammalian brain, and the stem brain. The limbic system is concerned primarily with generating emotional responses to sensory input: responses such as elation, attraction, fear, and anger. The stem brain, an even more primitive structure, processes and reacts to sensory input. I call the stem brain our *gator brain* because it's essentially the only brain an alligator has.

Alligators don't have much choice about how to react to sensory input. If a new creature comes into its territory, a gator has only a limited set of possible behaviors. It can fight, it can flee, it can try to feed on the intruder, it may try to mate with the intruder, or it can freeze. It does those things without thought, without emotion. They are purely instinctive. If the intruder is large or intimidating, the gator will flee. If the intruder is a same-sex gator, it will fight. If the intruder is small enough to be prey, the gator will attack and eat it. If the season is right and the intruder is a gator of the opposite sex, the gator will try to mate with it. And if the intruder appears to be none of the above, the gator will freeze until either the thing disappears from its perceptual screen or does something to trigger one of the other responses. That's it—the entire range of gator brain responses.

So what does this have to do with us? Well, as it turns out, a great deal of the way we relate to the world has to do with our own gator brain. We tend to react first (from our gator brain), develop an emotional response second (with our mammalian brain), and think last (with our human brain). Even when we finally do get around to thinking, the primary response of our human brain is often not a rational processing of information but a rationalization of our first two responses.

Here's how it works. Imagine you are in a supermarket. You've picked up a few last-minute items on your way home from work. Since you've picked up eight items or fewer, you move to the express checkout line. You glance at the basket of the person ahead of you and without having made a conscious decision to do so, you start counting the number of items in it. We've all done it. That's gator brain, that instinctive, reactive response to a potential threat—in this case to your ego rather than to your body—different only in degree from the intruder in the gator's swamp.

Now your mammalian or emotional brain takes over. If the shopper in front of you has more than eight items, you may get angry. You feel that you've been infringed on. You feel that your personal space, your psychic territory, has been invaded. The feeling comes before the rational thought. A moment later your cortical, human brain kicks in and labels both the person and your emotional response. He or she is thoughtless, obnoxious, presumptuous, arrogant. No wonder you're angry, having had to suffer such an inconvenience!

We experience this sequence of brain processes—from gator to mammalian to human—all the time. Not because we're weak or foolish or stupid but simply because the neural fibers that connect the different parts of the brain are of different lengths. When our senses pick up an electromechanical stimulus, whether light or sound or touch, a signal goes first to the stem. Then, a fraction of a second later, traveling a slightly longer pathway, it arrives at the limbic brain, and a fraction of a second after that it reaches the cortical regions.

That's why in emergency situations we are able to react without thinking—and without feeling. If you've ever had to slam on your brakes to avoid an accident, you know the experience: You act first, then you start shaking with the emotion of a near miss, then you get angry at and label the thing that almost caused the accident, whether the stupid driver who didn't signal his turn, the careless child who ran into the street, or your incompetent self for having been distracted. Like monkey mind, gator brain isn't a bad thing. It often keeps us out of trouble. Your gator brain has probably even saved your life a number of times.

But when it comes to focused thinking, gator brain, like money mind, can get us into trouble because gator brain treats strange, invading ideas in exactly the same way it treats strange, invading creatures. When encountering a new idea, your gator brain will see it either as a threat and therefore fight it or flee from it or as prey and therefore destroy it by devouring it. If your gator brain recognizes the invading idea as an old idea (like an alligator of the opposite sex), it may try to mate with it, simply reproducing and reinforcing the old idea. Finally, if the invading idea just doesn't fit at all, your gator brain's response is to freeze.

As any successful survival mechanism should be, gator brain is powerful. It is responsible for most of the decisions we make. We may think we think with our cortex, but often our "higher-function thinking" is merely a matter of rationalizing a decision the gator has already made. As the French psychologist Cloutaire Rapaille observed, "When it comes to making decisions, the reptilian always wins."

The Elephant's Tether

After monkey mind and gator brain, your brain's third energy-conserving strategy is patterning. Your mind consistently chooses to follow well-worn patterns rather than generate new thoughts, new interpretations, or new ways of doing things. Human beings are far more skilled at following old patterns than at thinking new thoughts. Most of the neural circuitry in our brains is devoted to recognizing, storing, and retrieving patterns, including patterns first set by our gator brain reactions. It's a good thing too because pattern recognition has been and continues to be one of our most important survival mechanisms. Our patterns are like tethers constantly pulling us back to the known, the familiar, the safe. They keep our minds in check, preventing them from drifting off aimlessly rather than focusing on the business of life. It's no exaggeration to say that without this remarkable ability to recognize patterns, human beings might still be swinging from trees. Here are a few examples of the positive power of patterning.

Arguably, one of the most important survival functions of the human brain is its ability to predict the future. When we encounter a situation, one of the first things our brains do is attempt to determine what is most likely to happen next. Imagine you're driving on a country road.

Yours is the through road, and there are several side roads intersecting it, each of which has a stop sign. As you near one of the crossroads, you notice a car approaching its stop sign at high speed. Your natural reaction might be to slow down, or to speed up to get through the intersection quickly, or to swerve. That's because your mind predicted the future. It called on its patterns of velocity (yours and that of the other car), direction, road conditions, photographs or stories of cars being T-boned, your knowledge of how you behave when you approach a stop sign, perhaps even your own past experience of failing to see a stop sign, and a host of other things to predict that in a moment your car and the other car will attempt to occupy the same space at the same time.

> *Your mind has a mind of its own, and it's awfully hard to control.*

What your mind did not do was calculate the vectors of the two cars, debate with itself about the reasons the other driver might not be slowing down, or think about how your insurance rate might go up. You simply reacted to a pattern that suggested an undesirable future, and you did so quickly. Even if it turns out that the other driver was just a "late braker" (at least according to your patterned standards), your patterned response was probably more useful than one that would have involved a careful calculation of speeds, distances, and masses. Why? Because by the time you had done all that data dissection, it would have been too late.

Some years ago I went into the garden shed of our house in Toronto. It was spring and time for the first lawn mowing of the year. Over the winter, the light bulb must have succumbed to the cold, so when I snapped the switch, nothing happened. As I looked into the dim shed, I saw a snake in the corner. My reaction was pure gator brain: not fight, not flight, but freeze. I was paralyzed. At least most of my body was paralyzed. My heart rate jumped instantly, and my pupils dilated much more quickly than normal in response to the involuntary release of epinephrine and norepinephrine triggered by gator brain's sense of emergency. Only after all that happened did I become aware of my next reaction: the emotion of fear. As my eyes grew accustomed to the gloom (I don't know if it took half a second or half a minute), I saw that it wasn't a snake but a garden hose.

You've probably had experiences that were not dissimilar, perhaps not with garden hoses, but it's likely you've seen indistinct shadow shapes as animals or people or heard innocent sounds that you interpreted as something malevolent. Shakespeare reminds us of this phenomenon in *A Midsummer Night's Dream* when Theseus says, "Or in the night, imagining some fear/How easy is a bush a supposed bear." Is there any such thing as a frightening shape? A frightening color? A frightening texture? Clearly not. But I didn't see shapes or colors or textures. I saw a snake. My brain instantly put together those shapes and colors and textures, matched them against its database of stored patterns, and came up with *snake*.. And it did so virtually instantaneously. The sequence was stimulus, pattern recognition, autonomic physical response, emotion of fear, name of fear. If my brain had gone into analytical mode, it wouldn't have given me the time to react appropriately. From the point of view of survival, speed is far more important than accuracy. My brain's survival function didn't care if the snake was male or female, dead or alive.

From a survival point of view, all it cared about was *snake*. One of the key advantages of patterning is that it can produce almost instantaneous responses. Rather than laboriously analyzing situations, your brain simply makes close matches. If the match is close enough, the patterned response swings into action. No thought is required. Our brains are wired to sacrifice accuracy for speed. For survival, that's very useful.

Patterning is also very practical. Imagine getting dressed in the morning. It's fairly typical for both men and women to wear 10 or 11 items of clothing to work each day. Assuming you've already laid out your clothing (you've decided what you'll wear), your next task is putting on the individual items. With 10 items of clothing, you have exactly 3,628,800 different choices about what to put on first, what to put on second, and so on. With 11 items, your choices multiply to almost 40 million. Even if you eliminated nonsensical choices such as putting your socks on over your shoes (by the way, young children who haven't learned getting-dressed patterns yet don't eliminate those kinds of choices), you'd still have over 15,000 reasonable sequences in which to put on your clothes. Making all those decisions consciously would take you several days. But once you've chosen what to wear, you don't make any decisions at all about getting dressed. You do it automatically. You follow your getting-dressed pattern, and with a few possible exceptions, you do it the same way every day of your life. Your patterns have conserved both time and energy and allowed you to get on with your life.

Patterning is also useful for learning and recall. Try this experiment: Recite the months of the year as fast as you can. You were probably able to do that in less than five seconds. Now list the months again, this time alphabetically. With the pattern, no problem. Without it, it's almost as though you are approaching the data for the first time. A fair question might be, Are you remembering the data or the pattern?

When it comes to learning and recall, patterns can be more important than data.

Clearly, patterning is useful, powerful, and pervasive. You rely on patterning every time you brush your teeth, shave, put on your makeup, comb your hair, drive to work, reach into your pocket to pull out the right coin, read the time on your watch, or dial the phone. You're using patterning right now as you read the words on this page. Patterning is used by athletes to develop and execute plays, by magicians to engage and entrance their audiences, and by Hollywood moviemakers to make scenes suspenseful or romantic or funny. Patterning is why you whisper in libraries, why you sing "Happy Birthday," and why you cry at the end of *It's a Wonderful Life*. Patterning helps us make sense of the world around us.

But your brain's ability to fill in the blanks so that things make sense for you is not without its drawbacks. Because we often see patterns more clearly than we see data, every day of our lives we make decisions that are based more on the past, on our patterns, than on what's in front of our noses.

In his book *How the Mind Works*, the linguist Steven Pinker gives a wonderful example of this. Pinker tells a simple three-sentence story: "Janie heard the jingling of the ice cream truck. She ran upstairs to get her piggy bank. She shook it till some money came out."[2]

By themselves these three sentences don't tell you much. But because of your patterns, without consciously thinking about it, you construct a meaning for the story that makes sense. You probably have some idea of how old Janie is. It's unlikely that you picture her as someone in her thirties; you probably assume she's 9 or 10. It's unlikely you think bills came out when she shook her piggy bank; you probably heard coins. And you certainly don't assume that she wanted the money to invest in Enron. None of this meaning is contained in the original three sentences, but because of your patterns, you impose meaning—*your* meaning—on the story.

Thus, although pattering is usually a good thing—it conserves thinking energy, predicts the future, tackles routine tasks quickly, facilitates learning, and helps make sense of the world—from a thinking point of view, patterning can be a problem. Patterning often causes us to assume that we see things that actually aren't there, like my seeing the snake or your seeing Janie as a 10-year-old. Or your probable interpretation of the following illusion by Oliver Selfridge.[3]

THE CHT

It is almost impossible not to see this as THE CAT.

The middle character in each cluster is neither an H nor an A. It is a hybrid of the two and is identical in both clusters, but it is almost impossible for an English reader not to see this agglomeration of shapes as THE CAT. No one reading this book can look at these shapes and say, "I have no idea what this means." And few people can force themselves to see the shapes as only one of the two letters, such as THE CHT.

Consider how patterning can also prevent us from seeing what is there. Among the many discoveries NASA made when it began sending people into space was that the astronauts' pens did not work well in zero gravity. The ink wouldn't flow properly. You can simulate the effect at home by trying to write with the business end of your pen pointing up. Pretty soon, the ink stops flowing and the pen won't write. To overcome the problem, NASA gathered several teams of mechanical, chemical, and hydrodynamic engineers; steeped them in the problem; and spent millions of research and prototype dollars to develop what became known as the space pen. The space pen was very effective. It worked in zero gravity, it worked on earth writing upside down, it even worked under water—a technological marvel. Our archrivals at the time, the Soviets, solved the problem as well, but much more cheaply and, arguably, more effectively: They supplied their cosmonauts with pencils. The NASA scientists were grounded in patterns based on high technology. Despite the fact that many of the engineers working on the problem probably used pencils themselves, they failed to see that there was an inexpensive, elegant, and reliable low-tech solution readily available. They saw the problem as "How might we make a pen write in zero gravity?" rather than simply "How might we write in zero gravity?"

Despite its enormous power and potential, it turns out that your cerebral cortex may have a lot less influence on the way you behave than you'd like to believe.

In the late 1960s three scientists working in a research laboratory in Lausanne, Switzerland, came up with an elegant solution to the problem of timing lab experiments accurately. They used electronic pulses, quartz crystals, and nixie tubes (the precursors of today's digital displays), all stuffed into a box about the size of a microwave oven. They demonstrated their accomplishment to management, which was delighted with the results. The instrument was inexpensive, accurate, and, because it had no moving parts, highly reliable in a wide range of environmental conditions, including temperature and pressure fluctuations, vibration, dust, and prolonged use. However, no one—not the scientists, not their managers, not the corporate executives—saw this box with flashing lights as a potential watch. It didn't fit their watch pattern. It wasn't small enough to be a watch. It had no hands, no face, no knurled knob to adjust the time. It never dawned on them that this piece of lab equipment might also be a watch.

But two electronics companies, one in Japan and one in the United States, were not encumbered by the Swiss notion of what a watch is. Within 10 years, Seiko and Texas Instruments transformed the world-wide market for watches. By the mid-1970s the Swiss dominance in wrist-watches imploded, falling from 75 percent of the world market to 25 percent, from 85 percent of the annual global profit to 10 percent. Dozens of household brand names disappeared and thousands of Swiss watch artisans no longer had jobs. All because of Swiss pattern thinking.

Will Rogers captured the perils of patterning perfectly when he said, "It's not what you don't know that hurts you, but what you do know that ain't so."

Patterns are hard to change. Some years ago my wife, Franca, decided she'd had it with the location of the cutlery drawer in our kitchen. It seemed that whenever one of us wanted to get something from that drawer, the other one would be standing in front of it. We had tolerated this minor inconvenience for years, but one day Franca decided to make a change. Indeed, the drawer's new location was significantly better: central, easy to reach, and with less congestion. It worked perfectly. Except for one thing. For months, whenever one of us wanted a utensil, we'd open the old drawer. This was always followed by a chuckle, before reaching for the new drawer. So persistent was our old-drawer pattern that we decided to post a piece of paper on which to record how often we reached for the wrong drawer. Even with the reminder of the paper, we still reached for the old drawer more often than not. It took over a year to break our old patterns, and even today, almost 10 years later, if I'm particularly distracted, I will reach for the old drawer. You've probably had similar experiences.

Why are patterns so hard to change? You'd think with all that wonderfully sophisticated neurocircuitry in our brains, we'd be able to accommodate a simple change. We can learn patterns quickly enough. Why does it take us so long to unlearn them?

Several years ago, Franca and I spent some time in Sedona, Arizona, one of the truly magical places on earth. The land around Sedona is known as red rock country for the rich red-tinted, timeworn, almost liquid-looking formations that seem to sprout organically from the valley floor. The red rocks are very soft. If you rub them with your hand, you'll pick up some of the particles of red dust that are constantly eroding from the surface.

Benny Bennington, a local guide, took us on several hikes through the back country, away from roads and telephone poles and other signs of civilization. On one of those trips we stopped for lunch on a slightly angled stretch of smooth rock. Not far from where we sat, a small rivulet had carved a channel in the rock. I asked Benny how long it might have taken for the channel to form. He made a broad guesstimate of anywhere from a couple of hundred to a couple of thousand years. Each time it rained during those years, the contours of the rock would force the runoff into the same channel. The water had no choice. Year after year, rainfall after rainfall washed down that channel, widening and deepening it slightly each time. The process of gradual erosion had started long before we arrived and would continue long after.

A few days later we traveled about 90 miles to the north and peered over the edge of the Grand Canyon. The same natural processes that had formed our little channel in the red rock were responsible for sculpting the mile-deep gorge into which we were about to descend. In the case of the Grand Canyon, the Colorado River had been doing its work for millions of years.

Suddenly it occurred to me that we were looking at a model of the human brain. Just as the Colorado had worn its channel through the rock, creating an inescapable mile-deep path for its water, so too have the thousands of repeated stimulus-response sequences created almost unbreakable thought patterns in our heads. Stimulus-response. Stimulus-response. Stimulus-response. Until it is virtually impossible for anything resembling that initial stimulus to produce anything but the patterned response. The reason it is so difficult to break our patterns is that we don't learn them just once; we learn them and then relearn them thousands of times. We create neural throughways so strong, so deep, and so intractable that it's almost impossible for us to think outside them. Our channels are so deep, we don't even see them as channels anymore. Like the Colorado River, our thoughts are trapped in channels of our own making.

Our patterns are who we are. We love them as we love our lives. After all, we've spent a lifetime nurturing them. No wonder they're so difficult to break! But what a world of possibilities might open up if we could.

The Swedish knock-down furniture phenomenon IKEA increased its store sales and profit almost overnight by breaking a pattern. IKEA's initial concept for its stores was to offer customers a supermarket for furniture. Customers walked in, picked up their shopping carts, and browsed through a carefully constructed maze of aisles, picking up the merchandise that fit their needs. They then wheeled their often brimming carts through supermarket-style checkout counters to make their payments. The system worked astonishingly well, making IKEA the largest and most profitable furniture company in the world.

Ingvar Kamprad—IKEA's founder, owner, and the *IK* in *IKEA*—wanted to find a way to increase sales and profits even more without making a significant investment. He challenged his people to reexamine the supermarket model (or pattern) to see if it could be improved. In observing customers at conventional supermarkets, they noticed a curious thing. Shoppers would often pick up a basket; go to the aisles they were interested in; pop a carton of milk, some eggs, some cereal, and a perhaps few other staples into their baskets; and then walk to the checkout line. On the way, they might hesitate over an impulse purchase—a bag of cookies or a case of soda on special—and then pass it by. Why? Because their baskets were already full. And why was that? Because supermarkets place baskets and carts only at store entrances. What would happen, asked the IKEA people, if we placed baskets and carts and bags throughout the store so that people would always have room for impulse purchases?

Human beings are far more skilled at following old patterns than at thinking new thoughts.

By breaking a pattern, IKEA substantially increased in-store sales and profits virtually overnight and at virtually no cost. Why haven't conventional supermarkets adopted this simple, proven strategy? As I said, patterns are powerful. They are hard to break even if the benefit of doing so is obvious. As John Kenneth Galbraith observed, "Faced with the choice of changing one's mind and proving there's no need to do so, almost everybody gets busy on the proof."

Like the distraction of monkey mind and the split-second reaction of gator brain, the tethering effect of following well-worn patterns can be a major barrier to thinking. In India, elephant wranglers, or mahouts, prevent elephant calves from wandering by chaining one of the animal's legs to a stake deeply embedded in the ground. Try as they might, the young elephants aren't strong enough either to break their chains or dislodge the stake. Attempting to do so is not only fruitless but uncomfortable as the chain tightens around their legs. Pretty soon they stop trying. As adults, elephants are kept in place with a length of woven hemp (much cheaper and more convenient than a chain) tied to a stake hammered into the ground with a few strokes. Full-grown elephants can pull away from their tethers easily, but they don't. They have a deeply ingrained pattern that tells them that escape is impossible. For the elephants, the pattern has become more powerful than the data.

This book is about harnessing monkey mind, taming the gator, and cutting the elephant's tether.

PART 2

PRODUCTIVE THINKING IN
PRINCIPLE

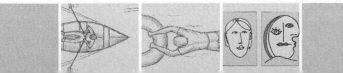

CHAPTER 3

Kaizen vs. Tenkaizen

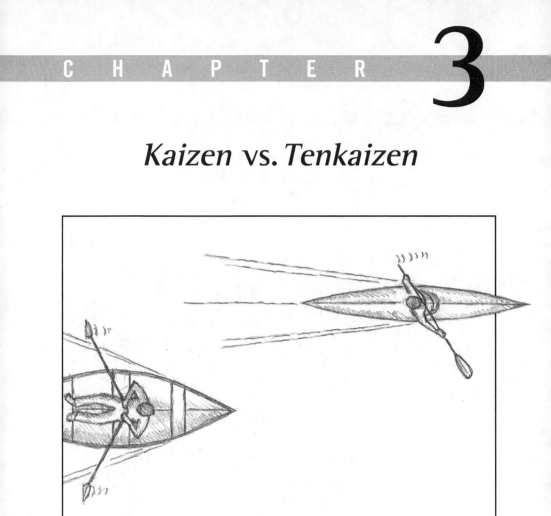

Good is the enemy of great.
Jim Collins

Reproductive Thinking and Productive Thinking

Reproductive thinking is a way to refine what is known; it aims for efficiency. Productive thinking is a way to generate the new; it aims for insight.

When you were a child, you probably had a thaumatrope. A thaumatrope isn't a childhood disease; it's a toy first popularized in Victorian England. It consists of a disk about the size of a small paper plate with a picture on either side. The disk is usually mounted on a dowel that you spin by rubbing your palms back and forth. The images on each side of the disk are different but complementary. If you get the disk spinning fast enough, the two images merge. A common Victorian-era thaumotrope showed a bird on one side and an empty birdcage on the other. When you twirled the disk, you saw the bird in the birdcage. It's a simple but fascinating effect. Although there is no actual picture of a bird in a cage, you see it as clearly as can be. You see a picture of something that isn't there.

Although there is still debate among theorists about how it works,[1] this basic visual phenomenon is the same happy neurophysical fluke that allows you to see movement in a progressive series of flip book drawings, interpret 24 still images per second as action in a movie, and perceive movement in electronic signs. This odd but useful phenomenon also stimulated the development of a school of psychology that changed the way we see the world.

In 1910 a young scientist named Max Wertheimer traveled from Vienna to Frankfurt by train. Wertheimer was a student of an embryonic fringe concept known as Gestalt, which posited that the way people perceive the whole of a thing is different from the way they perceive its parts. As he daydreamed and stared at the interior of the coach, Wertheimer noticed that reflections from the train's windows were creating a flashing pattern of light on the seat in front of him. Two separate points of light were alternating, on and off. When the timing was just right, the flashes gave the illusion of being not two separate lights but a single light traveling back and forth. What Wertheimer had discovered was a compelling demonstration of the basic Gestalt premise that what we perceive is not simply the sum of the things that stimulate our senses but something different—that in some way we act on the stimuli, just as they act on us.

Over the next several years, Wertheimer and his colleagues Wolfgang Köhler and Kurt Koffka built the framework for what would become known as Gestalt theory,[2] the principles of which have been applied to psychotherapy, philosophy, ethics, and even political theory. Wertheimer's concepts about new ways of thinking and problem solving, which developed in part through a famous series of conversations with Albert Einstein on the development of the theory of relativity, were published posthumously in Wertheimer's book *Productive Thinking*. Wertheimer's essential argument is that to think effectively, it is necessary to view problems as a whole rather than as the sum of their component parts. Wertheimer categorized problem solving as the result of either reproductive thinking, that is, solving problems based on what is already known, or productive thinking, that is, solving problems with new insights.[3]

The ideas in this book build on the work of many pioneers in the field of thinking: Wertheimer, Guilford, Torrance, Parnes, Osborn,[4] and many others. I hope that this recasting of productive thinking into a straightforward, practical, and disciplined framework for perceiving and acting on the challenges of life, whether business or personal, will help you think better, work better, and ultimately do better in every aspect of your life.

Reproductive Thinking

Reproductive thinking is essentially a matter of repeating the past: doing what you've done before and thinking what you've thunk before. You can visualize reproductive thinking on a continuum. At one end is mindless repetition, in the middle is conscious systematization, and at the other end is incremental improvement, or *kaizen* thinking.

Let's start with the crudest form of reproductive thinking, reactive gator-brain or elephant-tether nonthinking, in which a given stimulus produces a fixed, predictable response. The way you brush your teeth each morning, from unscrewing the cap of your toothpaste, to the way you dab the bristles of your toothbrush, to the length and strength and shape of the strokes you take—all of these are performed with the minimum possible exertion of brain power.

These kinds of patterns are not confined to personal habits. They can become even more powerful when transmitted from person to person. Ellen Langer in her book *Mindfulness* tells the story of learning from her mother how to prepare a roast. As a little girl she would watch as her mother cut off a small bit from one end of the meat before placing it in the roasting pan. As an adult, Langer followed the same routine until one day she wondered what the purpose of cutting off the end of the roast was. She asked her mother, who said she had no idea; she'd learned to do it from her own mother. Langer then asked her grandmother, who explained that when she was a young mother, the only roasting pan she'd had was too short for a standard roast, so she had to cut off the end to fit it into the pan. She'd long since gotten roasting pans in larger sizes and hadn't cut an end off since. Yet for years both Langer and her mother had mindlessly followed this routine.[5] At one time the thought that stimulated the action was relevant, but over time circumstances changed. Instead of disappearing, the thought fossilized into meaningless routine.

Kaizen *has its limits. No amount of incremental change will turn an adding machine into a spreadsheet.*

　　I've had countless experiences with organizations that have based entire systems on fossil ideas. Those organizations work on the "that's the way we do things around here" principle, not because people are actively opposed to new ideas but because the old ideas seem so natural. After all, they still work, more or less, so why challenge them? Why do we tend to schedule meetings for an hour even though most of them probably don't need anywhere near 60 minutes and some might require a lot more? Is the one-hour meeting the chronological equivalent to Langer's grand-mother's pan? Why is the plug for your computer behind your desk instead of on it? Why is it at foot height rather than hand height? Why do we cc so many people on our e-mails? Why do you *get* cc'ed on so many e-mails? Why do we use the term *cc* anyway? Do you even have carbon paper in your office? When you visit someone else's place of work, why do receptionists and security guards always ask you to take a seat? Because you look tired? Because they don't want you hanging around their desks? If you work in a large organization (unless it's Google, Apple, or the like), all your common meeting rooms are probably mini-boardrooms with tables surrounded by chairs. Why? Are you planning to have dinner? Come to think of it, why are all boardrooms modeled after private dining rooms? Why is the top row of your telephone keypad labeled 1 2 3, whereas the top row of your calculator is 7 8 9? Because both the telephone company and the calculator company say, "That's the way we do things around here."

Take a look around your home or work environment. See if you can identify how many things you, your family, or your colleagues do in the basic reproductive thinking mode. This may be harder to do than you think. These fossilized reproductive patterns are so strong and seem so "right" that we usually don't even notice that they are there. Here's a quick test. I'll bet that when you pop bread into your toaster, you always do so with the "bottom" of the bread down. Why? There is no real bottom of the bread. It doesn't make any difference which edge of the bread is up or down when you toast it, but it just seems natural to put the bottom edge down. Why not toast your slice sideways? It might be easier to take out of the toaster when it's done.

There are dozens of similar examples in your life. Why do you do things the way you do? What would happen if you decided to change? What new perspectives might you get? Here's an easy place to start: If you live with one or more other people, check out the seats you take when having a meal. You probably sit in the same seats each time. Switch. You'll be surprised at the different perspective you get. Chances are that you'll talk more and about different things. The more people you live with, the more opportunities for switching there are. See what happens when you sit in your child's seat. See what happens when your son or daughter sits in yours.

So far I've described only the most basic form of reproductive thinking, a mode of thought below the horizon of consciousness that causes us to respond to stimuli with predictable reactions. These fossilized ideas can save us time and energy, but they can also cause us to repeat patterns that aren't particularly useful or are no longer valid.

In the second level of reproductive thinking, we *consciously* reproduce learned thoughts and actions to achieve predictable results. Accountants have well-developed procedures for recording and analyzing financial numbers. Marketers go through checklists of activities to be sure they understand and address their markets effectively. Doctors ask their patients diagnostic questions with almost programmatic precision to get to the heart of the matter. Seasoned homemakers write aisle-by-aisle shopping lists to save time in the supermarket. We often consciously repeat patterns because it makes good sense to do so. It makes us more efficient, more *proficient*, and less likely to omit crucial steps. This higher level of reproductive thinking is a wonderful asset. It marshals proven methodologies and approaches to design processes that are fast, efficient, and defect-free.

One of the more common human ailments is the abdominal hernia, which is caused by a weakening of the muscles that line the abdominal wall. When this happens, the abdomen can bulge through the muscle wall. If left untreated, the condition can cause complications and even death.[6] But hernias are relatively easy to diagnose, and effective surgical hernia repair techniques have been available since the late nineteenth century. Typically, fixing a hernia involves pushing the bulge back in and either patching the abdominal wall or stitching it closed. The operation takes about 90 minutes, requires a general anesthetic, and costs around $5,000. The average failure rate in hospitals across North America is 10 to 15 percent within five years, requiring that the procedure be repeated.

There is a small hospital in Canada just north of Toronto that specializes in hernia procedures. It's called Shouldice Hernia Centre. Its founder, Edward Shouldice, developed a unique surgical approach for correcting the condition during World War II, and since then hernias have been the Shouldice Centre's business. Exclusively. Its 10 full-time surgeons perform over 7,500 hemiorrhaphies each year. I imagine that if you arrived at their doors wanting a Band-Aid for a cut finger, they'd send you somewhere else. At Shouldice a hernia procedure takes not 90 minutes but 45. The patient is under a local anesthetic (you can actually talk to your surgeons while they perform the operation). The average cost is about half that of general hospitals, and fewer than 1 percent of Shouldice patients have a recurrence after the repair. Each Shouldice surgeon performs 600 to 800 procedures a year, more than most general surgeons do in a career. When it comes to hemiorrhaphies, these people are reproductive thinking geniuses. They can anticipate and correct anomalies and complications on the fly, they can pinch hit for each other at a moment's notice, and it's a fair bet some of them could even continue an operation in the dark. Shouldice Hernia Centre represents this second level of reproductive thinking, deliberately following proven patterns, at its finest.[7,8,9]

The third level of reproductive thinking is *kaizen* thinking: consciously following well-established, proven patterns while looking for ways to improve them. *Kaizen* comes from the Japanese. It literally means "good change" (*kai* = "change," *zen* = "good"). *Kaizen* has been the foundation and rallying cry of a variety of related productivity and quality movements in the United States and other modern industrial countries: continuous quality improvement (CQI), total quality management (TQM), quality circles, and Six Sigma, among others. Toyota and General Electric are famous for their use of it. Ironically, *kaizen* is both the most useful form of reproductive thinking in that it focuses on continually monitoring and refining processes, products, and procedures and the most dangerous in that it provides the illusion of innovation under the guise of incremental change.

Reproductive thinking can fashion the perfect buggy whip. Only productive thinking can imagine a car.

Kaizen is characterized by the principle of incremental change. It holds that each day a process can be made a little bit better than it was the day before. *Kaizen* has provided substantial benefits. It has been used to make production lines more reliable, reduce medical errors, and speed up emergency response times. But *kaizen* has its limits. No amount of incremental change will turn an adding machine into a spreadsheet.

Here's one way to visualize the kind of incremental change—and its limitations—represented by *kaizen* thinking. Imagine taking an excellent print of Leonardo da Vinci's *Mona Lisa*, placing it on a high-end color copier, and pushing the button. Out will come a pretty good but slightly inferior version of the original. Now copy the copy, copy that copy, and so on. Each copy will be a slightly less faithful version of the last. Let's say you do this a hundred times, so your final version is still recognizable, but its colors are wrong, it's blurry, it's lost its magic.

Now take your hundred sheets and examine them in reverse order. As you flip through the pages, you see that each one is an improvement over the last; each image is incrementally better than the one before it. Finally, you have an image almost indistinguishable from Leonardo's painting: near perfection. But as beautiful as it is, it will never be anything other than the *Mona Lisa*. No matter how many pages there are in your sequence, it will never become a Picasso.

Each level of reproductive thinking—rote repetition, conscious systematization, and continuous improvement—can be a powerful asset. Many organizations that have focused on it, particularly on *kaizen*, have prospered. But reproductive thinking alone can't do the whole job. It may be great for producing zero defects, but it will never produce breakthrough change. As Nicholas Negoponte, the founder of the Massachusetts Institute of Technology's Media Lab, has written, "Incrementalism is innovation's worst enemy."

Productive Thinking

Productive thinking is radically different. Reproductive thinking can fashion the perfect buggy whip, but only productive thinking can imagine a car.

Productive thinking is the kind of thinking that leads to new ideas and breakthrough change. In Wertheimer's words, it is insightful thinking rather than historical thinking. Productive thinking is important for meeting the challenges of changing environments and marketplaces, for differentiating products or services, for envisioning and developing new insights and processes, and for achieving growth. Earlier in this chapter I described reproductive thinking at its best as *kaizen* thinking. In my work with clients, I extend the Japanese metaphor and describe productive thinking as *tenkaizen* thinking, a neologism of my own creation, with apologies to Japanese linguists. *Tenkaizen* is a composite word deriving from *ten*, meaning "law" or "tradition," *kai*, meaning "change," and *zen*, meaning "good." In other words, you can interpret *tenkaizen* as "good revolution."[9] *Tenkaizen* turns things upside down. Rather than reproducing the old, it produces the new.[10]

Productive, or *tenkaizen*, thinking changes not only what we do but how we see the world. It is a way of both coping with change and creating change.

In 1997, Reed Hastings founded Netflix on the basis of the simple notion that he could provide a DVD rental service through the Internet, get people to order their movies at the Netflix Web site, and deliver them by mail. Netflix's original business model was virtually identical to the prevailing retail model pioneered by mom-and-pop shops since the earliest days of the video rental business except that he didn't have any physical stores. Hastings charged his clients $4 per rental plus $2 postage and applied late fees when DVDs were overdue. The only substantial difference between the online Netflix and the in-mall Blockbuster was the delivery channel.

Then, in 1999, Hastings had a *tenkaizen* idea. What if instead of renting movies he rented the *capacity to view movies*? Customers would no longer rent individual disks but instead would subscribe to varying levels of service, allowing them to keep movies for as long as they liked. As soon as a subscriber returned a disk, Netflix would ship another DVD from a list of titles the customer had pre-selected. There would be no individual rental fees, no postage fees, no late fees. This was not an incremental change but a whole new way to view a relationship with customers. Within three years Netflix was in the black, mailing nearly 200,000 DVDs per day to nearly a million subscribers. By 2007 Netflix had become one of the most successful dot-com companies, shipping 1.5 million titles a day to over 6.5 million subscribers. Its success has spawned dozens of imitators around the world and changed the way competitors such as Blockbuster and Hollywood Video do business.[11]

Here is another example of the power of *tenkaizen* thinking, this one from the world of science.

In September 2005 a group of European and American social scientists launched an unusual new publication. They called it the *Journal of Spurious Correlations, JSpurC* for short. Its mission was to provide a forum for unpublishable results, in other words, for studies and experiments that had proved nothing. Why publish the results of failed experiments? First, publishing negative results can help identify methodological errors and improve the quality of future studies. Second, it can serve as a warning, allowing researchers in a given field of study to analyze what has not worked so they can avoid repeating those procedures. Most of us recognize the value of learning from our own failures; why not give scientists the opportunity to learn from the failures of their colleagues? Third, the current system of journal publication promotes a phenomenon known as publication bias, which can dramatically skew our perceptions of what is true and what is not. If, for example, a single study by reputable researchers finds a positive correlation between homosexuality and suicide, that study stands a good chance of being published. There may be a dozen other studies by equally reputable researchers that fail to show such a correlation, but because their results are negative, they tend not to get published. As a result, despite a preponderance of contradictory evidence, the findings of the published study may become the accepted truth.[12] According to David Lehrer, one of the founders of *JSpurC*, "Everything we think we know may be wrong. The correct results could be sitting in people's file drawers because they can't get them published."[13]

These two stories do not illustrate mere incremental extensions of current thinking. Both *JSpurC* and Netflix turn traditional ideas upside down. They are examples of *tenkaizen*: "good revolution."

The Elements of Productive Thinking

Productive thinking consists of two distinct thinking skills: creative thinking and critical thinking. The overarching principle of productive thinking is this: Creative thinking and critical thinking have to be separate. Our normal approach is not to separate these two skills; instead, we tend to overlap them. Recall the last time you tried to solve a problem or come up with a new approach. Your thought train probably went something like this: *Hmm, I know. I'll. . . . No, too expensive. Okay, what if I tried. . . . Nah, I'd never get it done in time. Well, how about. . . . Nope, too risky. I could always. . . . Forget it. The guys would punch a hole in that in two seconds. Oh, well, maybe there really isn't a better way.*

The overarching principle of productive thinking is this: Creative thinking and critical thinking have to be separate.

By trying simultaneously to think creatively to generate ideas and think critically to judge ideas, you end up sabotaging any chance of success. It's like trying to drive with one foot on the gas and one foot on the brake: You won't get anywhere, and you'll probably burn something out in the process.

Creative thinking has three essential characteristics. First, it's generative; in other words, its primary function is to make something out of nothing. For different people, idea generation takes different forms: daydreaming, blue-skying, what-iffing, making unusual connections, or just wondering. Regardless of how you go about generating them, new ideas are wispy at best. They are only partially formed, ephemeral. It takes only a moment to forget you even had them. Think about the last time you were in the shower and came up with the world's greatest idea, only to have it disappear moments later.

These fragile new ideas come into being because of the second characteristic of the creative thinking mode: It's nonjudgmental. You cannot generate and judge at the same time. Your half-formed notions can't survive the onslaught of your intellect. How often have you judged your ideas out of existence?

The third characteristic of creative thinking springs directly from the first two: It's expansive. By generating ideas and letting them live by deferring judgment, you tend to get more ideas. Creative thinking, then, is generative, nonjudgmental, and expansive. In effect, when you're thinking creatively, you're making lists. Long lists.

Critical thinking is the *yang* to creative thinking's *yin*. Like creative thinking, critical thinking has three essential characteristics, each one a counterpoint. First, critical thinking is analytic: It probes, questions, and tests. When you think critically, you look at things deeply, penetrate below the surface, and unwrap nuance. You seek to understand, look for order, and discover meaning. Second, critical thinking is judgmental. Its job is to help you determine whether ideas meet or do not meet criteria for success or even further consideration. Critical thinking allows you to compare ideas with predetermined standards. Third, critical thinking is selective. It narrows down the long lists of ideas generated by creative thinking, sifting and filtering them to produce a more manageable few. You use critical thinking to identify the best ideas for further development, to converge on those with the greatest potential for success. Critical thinking, then, is analytic, judgmental, and selective. In effect, when you are thinking critically, you are making choices.

Productive thinking separates creative thinking and critical thinking. It is a process of suspending judgment to generate long lists of ideas and then returning to those lists to make choices by judging the ideas against preestablished success criteria: making lists and making choices. As you will see, beginning in Chapter 6, "Productive Thinking by Design," the full productive thinking process involves six discrete phases, from exploring the need for new thinking to developing a plan for action. Each of these phases involves creative and critical thinking steps.

The productive thinking dynamic is the ongoing alternation between creative thinking and critical thinking. Imagine a kayak paddle.

One side stands for creative thinking, the other for critical thinking. If you always used the creative paddle, you'd go around in circles. If you always used the critical paddle, you'd go around in circles the other way. The key is to alternate between the two: creative, critical, creative, critical. That way you develop enormous forward momentum. That way you can achieve *tenkaizen*.

The Monster under the Bed

So far I've described the observable differences between reproductive thinking and productive thinking. Reproductive thinking essentially repeats old patterns and at its best tries to improve on them incrementally. Productive thinking tries to break new ground and employs the separation of creative and critical thinking to do so. There is, however, another crucial difference between these two thinking modes.

Reproductive thinking is extremely valuable when the consequences of failure are high. You don't want your airline pilot, coming in for a landing, to muse, "Hmm, I wonder what would happen if I tried it this way." You want her to do what she was taught to do: calculate and respond to every contingency as though she's done it thousands of times before. In fact, the more times she's done it before, the happier you will be that she's your captain.

Productive thinking is different. It is most useful when the consequences of failure are low. Ideas are cheap. Failed ideas don't cost much. Even in prototype phases, risk is relatively low. That's why we prototype in the first place: to confine risk. In fact, in the productive thinking mode, it's often useful to *try* to fail, to find out what won't work, at a time when the consequences of failure are minimal. That's what experimentation is all about. The more you fail, the more you learn. As Edison once said, "I have not failed. I have merely found ten thousand ways that won't work."

As creatures of pattern, most of us spend more time doing reproductive thinking than doing productive thinking. As a result, we tend to view the world through the lens of the reproductive thinking experience: We see failure as undesirable. We avoid risky thinking because risky thinking can be calamitous. When you're coming in for a landing, you *want* your airline pilot to exercise every bit of reproductive thinking savvy she's developed—accounting for weather, visibility, and load conditions—to land that plane like a feather. Experiments are for simulators, not runways. Mistakes in reproductive thinking can result in patients dying, airplanes crashing, production lines going down, supply chains failing, and huge financial losses.

Here's the monster under the bed: We avoid risk in the productive thinking environment as though we were operating in the reproductive thinking environment. We are conditioned to avoid risk precisely because most of our training has been geared toward honing our reproductive thinking skills. We *want* boring cockpits and operating rooms. Our relationship to new ideas is often colored by a low tolerance for risk. We tend to shy away from the very risk-taking orientation that can make productive thinking so fruitful. And it's hard to change. In Chapter 11, "Masamune's *Katana*," you'll see how part of productive thinking model is designed to "fight for failure" to increase the chances of success.

When you come to a fork in the road, take it. *Yogi Berra*

Occasionally our clients ask us, "I get this good revolution stuff, but is revolution always necessary? Aren't there companies and industries that can do just fine, maybe even better, focusing on *kaizen* rather than *tenkaizen*? After all, revolution can be pretty dangerous."

If your environment is one of constant change, it makes sense to develop a tenkaizen *or "good revolution" attitude.*

No question about it. There's always a choice. Organizations and individuals can continue to do things as they have always been done—and perhaps do them very well, making incremental improvements along the way—or they can discover new and better approaches to serving their customers and themselves. For over 3,000 years, economies, technologies, and social structures changed very little in ancient Egypt. Proclaiming yourself to be a champion of "good revolution" in that kind of environment could well have gotten you killed. In contrast, if the environment in which you're working is one of constant and significant change, it may make sense to devote at least some effort toward developing a *tenkaizen* attitude and mastering productive thinking skills. Figure 3.1 is a simple representation of this relationship. The more change you face or wish to create, the more appropriate productive thinking becomes.

The more change you face, the more you need Productive Thinking.

Even in the most stable environments, turning things upside down can sometimes produce remarkable results. One of my clients is a very large mutual insurance company. Most insurance companies I've dealt with either as a client or as a consultant are not by nature particularly *tenkaizen*. Above all, the insurance industry values stability. A few years ago this client—I'll call it Fundamental Life—presented the following challenge. By law, mutual insurance companies are required to send periodic statements to policy holders outlining the nature of their investments, rates of return, risk factors, and so on. A typical quarterly statement would consist of 24 pages in tiny print. Because Fundamental has many millions of customers, the production and mailing of these statements is a significant business expense, costing hundreds of millions of dollars a year. Current regulations require that these statements be paper and individually delivered to policy owners: Web-based or e-mail solutions were not an option. To add to the company's frustration, customer surveys had revealed that most policy owners did not read the reports.

Fundamental's senior management wanted to find a way to reduce the costs of this reporting requirement while satisfying its legal obligations. A cross-functional team representing management, customer service, legal, and other disciplines had been working on the problem for two years but had produced no substantial results; the problem remained intractable.

When my think^x colleagues and I were brought in, we convened a small subsection of the cross-functional team and ran its members through a high-speed version of the productive thinking model, using an approach we call *Galeforce*. (page 235)

We asked the team to turn the problem on its head. What kinds of questions could they ask that would lead to the *opposite* of solving the problem? Responses ranged from "How might we close our eyes to the problem?" to "How might we make the problem worse?" to "How might we break the law?" to "How might we abandon our customers?" This last question led to the idea of getting customers to fend for themselves, which in turn led to the idea of allowing customers to design their own statements. By law, statements couldn't be *delivered* online, but nothing prevented customers from choosing which information they wanted to receive, using an online tool. If customers were sent only the specific information they had selected, the average mailing might be reduced from 24 pages to 6, a huge potential saving compared with the one-size-fits-all approach.

The Galeforce session had produced a potential solution in less than half a day. Several more days were required to work out how such an approach might be implemented, what regulatory requirements had to be accommodated, and how to fund a pilot project. To test the concept, a scaled pilot was run in a single geographic region. Customer feedback was positive, and regulatory hurdles were passed. Pilot results suggested that the company would save up to $12 million per mailing. This simple solution to a complex problem may not seem revolutionary at first, but Fundamental's initiative was launched two years before the 2007 Davos World Economic Forum, where the concept of customer-designed solutions was flagged as a future trend in innovation. For Fundamental, getting customers to design their own communication statements was unquestionably *tenkaizen*. It paid off in cost savings, increased customer satisfaction, and gave them a new marketing edge. If customers decide not to use the Internet, They automatically still get the full report.

Productive thinking doesn't have to take years to generate ideas worth exploring. Some of them may be just around the corner.

Productive thinking—that fine alternating balance of creative thinking and critical thinking—can change the world. It has. Imagine a thaumatrope. One face is painted like the sun: yellow, bright, creative; the other is like the sea: blue, deep, thoughtful. Sun and sea remain separate, one on each side of the disk. But when you spin the disk, you create something completely new, neither sun nor sea, neither yellow nor blue but green.

Stay in the Question

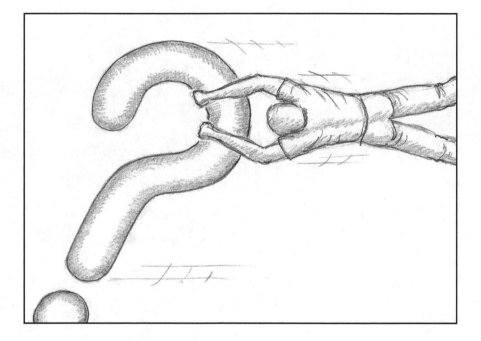

Computers are useless!
They only give you answers.

Pablo Picasso

Productive thinking requires us not to rush to answers but to hang back, to keep asking new questions even when the answers to the old ones seem so clear, so obvious, so right. One of the characteristics of productive thinkers is their ability to resist the urge to answer, the urge to know. They understand that settling *on* an answer may be the same as settling *for* an answer.

Staying in the question means being okay with the ambiguous. Being okay with ambiguity means being open to the possible.

My mother hated winter. Every year on her birthday, January 7, she would number the calendar, working backward from March 21, and then announce, "Only 73 days till spring!" Each morning she would cross off another day and announce the current countdown with increasing happiness. For my mother, the arrival of spring represented the melting of winter, new growth, and pleasant weather. The only problem with mother's expectation was that we lived in New York City, and as anyone who has lived in the northeastern United States knows, March 21 is no guarantee of good weather. Some of our best blizzards have been in March. But that didn't faze my mother. For her, the answer to the question "When will the weather get better?" was March 21. That answer took a little of the ambiguity out of her life.

All of us have the habit of assuming that the labels we give things are the same as the things themselves. Even though we know the weather won't magically change just because the calendar flips from winter to spring, the *concept* of spring, the category we've created for it in our minds, is very powerful. We associate it with warmer weather, budding flowers, and fresh smells. Conversely, the fact that it's not yet spring is a way of explaining lousy weather and slushy streets.

Explanations are important to us. Regardless of how hot or cold it is outside, being able to attribute the temperature to a cause makes us feel more comfortable inside. Ironically, it often doesn't matter to us whether the cause we ascribe is particularly accurate. What's important is that we maintain our illusion of the world as concrete, rational, and predictable. If there's anything that makes us more uncomfortable than a wind-chill factor of 10 below, it's uncertainty.

Human beings are constantly looking for answers that take the ambiguity out of our lives. For some of us "She's a Virgo" is the answer to the question "Why is Val such a compulsive organizer?" For others "Bad things always come in threes" is the answer to the question "Why did Rob smash his car after losing his job and breaking up with his girlfriend?" For still others "The international Jewish conspiracy" is the answer to the question "Why is my life less than I want it to be?" (For this last one you can substitute an almost limitless array of alternative answers, including Muslim extremists, communists, capitalists, Colombian drug lords, landlords, fundamentalists, hip-hop artists, gays, whites, blacks, immigrants, neocons, anarchists, Americans, or the Pope, depending on your preferences.)

> *Staying in the question means being okay with the ambiguous. Being okay with ambiguity means being open to the possible.*

The problem is not that all these answers are simplistic, though they are. Or that they don't explain anything adequately, though they don't. Or even that they encourage false beliefs, though they do. The real problem is that they stop us from thinking.

Ironically, the urge to know may be one of the most challenging obstacles to productive thinking. People who "know" can tell you all the things that can't be done and why. People who "know" don't need to learn because they already have the answers. People who "know" are complete—or perhaps just finished. More often than not, people who "know" are also people who "no." But knowingness is not the same as knowledge. Knowingness is sealed; nothing can get in. Knowledge is open. Knowingness sees challenge as threat. Knowledge sees challenge as opportunity. Knowingness is a portcullis that helps us feel secure. Knowledge is a road to new horizons.[1]

Productive thinking requires that we not rush to answers but to hang back, to keep questioning even when the answers seem obvious. George Bernard Shaw observed, "No question is so difficult to answer as that to which the answer is obvious." Staying with the ambiguity of being answerless forces one to think about alternative possibilities. The brilliant British physicist David Bohm echoed Shaw when he said, "Staying with ambivalence gives a creator access to . . . nuances usually obscured by our polarized patterns of thought."[2]

Resisting the urge to know means staying in the question. That's hard to do for two reasons. First, our brains are hardwired to categorize the sensory inputs from the world around us: to shoehorn what we see, hear, smell, touch, and taste into recognizable patterns of sight, sound, scent, feel, and flavor. Second, both our educational and occupational systems tend to reward answers more than they do thinking. Both biologically and socially, we are conditioned to jump to conclusions.

In English, neologisms are often introduced when no existing word adequately conveys a concept. One of my favorites is the word *mondegreen*. It was coined by Sylvia Wright in a 1954 *Harper's Magazine* article.[3] As a child, Wright had listened to the Scottish folk ballad, "The Bonny Earl of Murray," which included the following lines:

> *Ye Highlands and Ye Lowlands, Oh where hae you been?*
> *They hae slain the Earl of Murray, and Lady Mondegreen.*

Or so she thought. Only years later did Wright come to realize that the final line was not about a hapless lady who died for her liege but rather about how the assassins disposed of the earl's corpse: They "laid him on the green." Wright defined mondegreens as those common slips of the ear we all make when we're not quite certain about a word or phrase and interpret it in a way that makes sense to us. For one little girl, "And Lady Mondegreen" was the answer to the question, "How do I make sense of this song?"

All of us have our personal mondegreens, often associated with muffled song lyrics. Gavin Edwards has collected a whole book of them titled '*Scuse Me While I Kiss This Guy, and Other Misheard Lyrics*.[4] The title is a mondegreen of a Jimi Hendrix line from the song "Purple Haze": "'Scuse me while I kiss the sky." Some of the classics include "Sweet dreams are made of cheese" (the Eurythmics' "Sweet dreams are made of these"), "The girl with colitis goes by" (the Beatles' "The girl with kaleidoscope eyes"), and my favorite, "The ants are my friends, and they're blowin' in the wind" (Bob Dylan's "The answer, my friends, is blowin' in the wind"). A good friend of mine who grew up in Toronto remembers her father and older brothers rooting for a hockey team called the Make-Believes.

We don't interpret these lines incorrectly to be cute. We actually *need* to give them meaning—even incorrect meaning—because our minds are so uncomfortable with the unresolved. We're programmed to try to make sense of the world.

First answers are persistent. Once we assign a meaning, we're almost inevitably locked in to it. No matter how many times Sylvia Wright heard that lyric after learning the correct line, the image of Lady Mondegreen crowded out the image of poor old Murray's corpse on the commons.

Our minds hate not interpreting, not closing in on answers. When we do close in on one answer or interpretation, we effectively block out any others. For a simple illustration of this, look at the figure below, which shows a Necker cube, which was discovered in 1832 by a Swiss crystallographer, Louis Albert Necker.

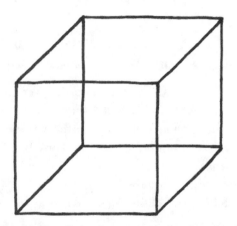

You can see this Necker Cube two ways, but only one way at a time.

While drawing crystal shapes for a paper he was writing, Necker discovered that when there are no definitive clues about perspective such as shadows, solidity, or foreshortening, the perspective of the cube appears to flip in space. The mind resolves the ambiguity in the drawing by alternating its interpretation of the cube. You can see one perspective (the cube from above) or the other (the cube from below), you can flip back and forth between the two, but no matter how hard you try, you probably can't see both simultaneously.

The answer to the question "Where am I in relation to the cube?" is that you are above the cube or below the cube but not both.

You might say these examples, which show only reflexive responses to visual and auditory ambiguities, are trivial. They just illustrate the brain's hardwired antipathy toward certain types of simple ambiguities. Optical and aural illusions are simply tricks of the subconscious mind. They don't have much to do with meaningful, deliberate thought processes. But the drive to simplify, to settle on single answers, extends into every area of our thinking.

Building on the philosophical frameworks of Immanuel Kant and Ludwig Wittgenstein, the psychologist Walter Mischel has demonstrated that we tend to classify people according to certain fundamental character traits, or cognitive prototypes, rather than seeing them as complex personalities with highly variable behaviors that depend on the situations they are in, their moods, their states of health, and so on. Mischel describes this tendency to simplify as a kind of "reducing valve" that allows us to make sense of the world and impose a false but comforting consistency on the personalities of the people with whom we interact.[5]

Think of almost anyone you know fairly well. Now think of how you might describe that person to someone else. Chances are that you'll describe Jan as a nice person, Pat as hard, or Adrian as fun. But what happens when Jan gets into a frustrating situation and yells at the kids, or Pat plays with a puppy and talks like Betty Boop, or Adrian wakes up at five in the morning to do the housework before catching the train to work? Are they still nice, or hard, or fun? We don't tend to classify Jan as a person who can be nice sometimes and quite unpleasant at other times. We assume that one trait dominates, that Jan really is nice but occasionally gets frustrated. In fact, each of us is far more complex than we're ever described. Most people are funny and angry and hostile and generous and warm and harsh at some time or other. Our natures depend very much on the circumstances we encounter. It's hard to be funny while you're doing your tax return, but it's easy to be funny the next day at dinner while describing your frustration at doing your tax return to your friends.

Despite the incalculable complexity and inconsistency of every human being we'll ever meet, as Mischel observes, our reducing valve compels us to think about our friends and acquaintances in more simplistic terms. Our lives are much easier when we do that because rather than having to evaluate every person we know in every situation in which we see them, we think of them in a particular way and respond accordingly. We don't have to requalify them all the time. We call a person a liar rather than someone who lies on certain occasions. Of course, it may be true that for the most part Jan is very nice and only occasionally snappy, but the reason for that is probably that Jan is very good at controlling his environment and operating in a comfort zone that allows him to be the person he's most amenable to being. Jan doesn't particularly like himself when he's yelling, so he tends to avoid situations that provoke his anger. Therefore, for most of his friends, "A nice guy" is the answer to the question "Who is Jan?" (By the way, until these last two sentences, was "A woman" your answer to the question "Who is Jan?" And what genders did you fix on for Pat and Adrian?)

Productive thinking requires us not to rush to answers but to hang back, to keep questioning even when the answers seem obvious.

When it comes to describing groups, our reducing valve can really get us into trouble. How depressingly easy it is for most of us, especially if we're stressed, to complete the following: the poor are . . . , the rich are . . . , management is . . . , labor is . . . , the old are . . . , the young are . . ., women are . . . , men are . . . , gays are . . . , straights are . . . , the sick are . . . , the healthy are. . . .

Even when we think about ourselves, we use the reducing valve to limit ambiguity. We land on self-descriptions that fail to take into account our own complexity or how much our natures may vary from one context to another. The old advice that the only person you can depend on is yourself is true only if the self is consistent, and the only way it can be consistent is by being unambiguous and simple. In his book *The Society of Mind*, Marvin Minsky, cofounder of the Artificial Intelligence Laboratory at the Massachusetts Institute of Technology, writes, "One function of the self is to keep us from changing too rapidly."[6] According to Minsky, our notion of the self is a way of keeping us constant so that we can rely on ourselves. If we changed our minds too rapidly, we might never know what we wanted next and we'd never be able to get anything done. If your energetic morning self, to give a simplistic example, makes plans to go to the supermarket after work to stock up for the week, you don't want your late afternoon tired and lethargic self to say, "Oh, what the heck, I'll do it tomorrow." If you want to have food in the house, your after-work self has to remind you of the plans your morning self wanted you to carry out. The way it does that is to assume a consistency between the two yous despite the fact that they are quite different. Given our dis-taste for ambiguity, the self's assertion of "I am" also becomes the answer to the question "Who's in control here?"

With our nearly obsessive reliance on labels to tell us who we are, it's no surprise that so many people have taken at least one psychological or typing test. By one estimate, profiling is a $3 billion industry in North America.[7] You can take a profile at school, at work, as part of a training program, in self-help books, in popular magazines, and even at social gatherings as conversation fodder. No matter how professionally these instruments are constructed, invariably you come up against questions you can't answer accurately. You're asked, for example, to check "yes" or "no" to statements such as "I enjoy being alone," "I enjoy taking time with tasks," or "I get along well with other people." And you say to your-self, "Well, sometimes yes and sometimes no: It depends on how I feel, whether I have a deadline, who those 'other' people are, what I had for breakfast, and a million other things!" But you answer them anyway because there are no intermediate choices. When you get your evaluation back, it says your primary type is **H**ighly **R**ational **S**ensate and your sub-type is **A**daptive **S**ocial **S**triver. Suddenly you forget you were ambivalent about the answers to many of the questions, that on a different day you might have given different responses. Most of us are so averse to ambigu-ity that we're even willing to label ourselves as "A HRS/ASS" (read Horse's Ass) as the answer to the question "Who am I?"

Ambiguity is so uncomfortable for most of us that it can even turn good news into bad. You go to your doctor with a nagging abdomi-nal pain. Though you're not a hypochondriac, in the back of your mind a little voice says, "It's cancer." Your doctor can't figure out what it is, so she sends you to the lab for tests. A week later you're called back to hear the results. In the waiting room that little voice is still whispering in your ear. When you finally get into her office, your doctor smiles and tells you the tests were all negative. And what happens? Your immediate relief ("Hey, no cancer!") may be replaced by a weird sense of discomfort. You still don't know what the funny pain was! There's got to be an explana-tion somewhere. Maybe it *is* cancer and they've just missed it. Maybe it's worse. Surely they should be able to find a cause. You feel frustrated by the lack of a definitive answer.

Uncertainty is pain. Astonishingly, in some cases even more painful than death. On February 7, 2002, police in British Columbia got a break in one of the most grisly cases of mass murder in North America when human remains were discovered on a pig farm near the town of Port Coquitlam. As many as 50 street workers from nearby Vancouver had disappeared over the years, and the fear was, of course, that they had been abducted and murdered. For four years the mystery had gone unsolved while families and friends relentlessly scoured Vancouver's Eastside tenderloin district for news of loved ones. On being called by the police and told of the discovery on the pig farm, Lynn Frey, the mother of one of the missing women, said, "My heart went to my stomach. I hope this doesn't sound callous. I don't know how else to say it, but I'm hoping . . . they will find bodies. Over the years you get your hopes up high to find her, only to have them drop like a falling elevator. I need closure now to carry on with my life. How many times can a mother do this?" For Lynne Frey and countless other parents whose pain is assuaged somewhat by the closure of certainty, even "Dead" may be preferable to "I don't know" as the answer to the question "Where is my child?"[8]

It seems clear that consciously or not, human beings will do almost anything to avoid the ambiguity of not knowing. And that's a problem. Because it's a tendency that stops productive thinking cold.

Not too long ago I attended a meeting at the office of one of my clients. The ostensible purpose of the meeting was to plan the agenda for an upcoming strategic retreat I was going to facilitate. Attending were the chief executive officer, several of his direct reports, the project manager from the company, and the two-person think[x] facilitation team. It was my first meeting with the CEO, who had a reputation for being friendly, clear-thinking, and decisive, and I had been looking forward to it.

The project manager began the discussion by introducing everyone, laying out the objectives of the upcoming strategic retreat, and setting out the agenda for our planning meeting. She then said that the first thing she wanted to do was to brainstorm about the agenda for the strategic retreat. At that point, the CEO chimed in, saying, "Not to worry. I've thought of everything already," and then proceeded to outline the retreat agenda as he saw it. This man wasn't consciously attempting to shut down the discussion. In fact, he clearly thought he was being helpful. But he was absolutely convinced that he had gone through all the possible alternatives and there was nothing further to think about. The company culture was such that no one else in the room questioned his assumption, except of course the outsiders from think[x]. After a little delicate tap dancing, we did eventually have a discussion about the agenda, but the tone had been set. Instead of a good productive thinking session with people offering useful, challenging ideas that might have moved the strategic planning retreat from the same-old, same-old format it had followed for years, the meeting turned into the popular corporate game of "guess what the boss is thinking." (We eventually did help in transforming both the shape and outcome of the strategic planning retreat, but it took several private meetings with the CEO before we were able to get there.)

Uncertainty is pain. Astonishingly, in some cases even more painful than death.

Because the CEO was uncomfortable with staying in the question, both he and his reports continually fell into the thinking trap of "satisficing." The concept of satisficing was first proposed in the 1950s by the brilliant polymath Herbert Simon, whose innovative thinking spanned the fields of economics, cognitive psychology, philosophy, information sciences, and decision making. Satisficing describes the condition of being so uncomfortable with an unresolved or problem state—in other words with the state of not knowing—that we jump to the first answer that puts us out of our misery. Once we land on that answer, we tend to stick with it.

Not only do we have a natural tendency to satisfice, the social advantages of satisficing are drilled into us and reinforced almost from the moment we begin to socialize. Satisficing helps us "fit in." In school we are taught that there is only one right answer. Two plus two must always equal four, though one of your first grade school jokes was probably to say, "No, it's twenty-two!"

At some point during your school years, you probably had to take a Miller Analogies Test. Here's a typical example:

WALK is to LEGS as

a. BLINK is to EYES

b. CHEW is to MOUTH

c. COVER is to BOOK

d. DRESS is to HEM

e. TALK is to NOSE

Which is correct? I can find pros and cons for at least three. BLINK:EYES might be a good choice. We have two eyes, and each of them blinks. But maybe not. Eyes blink in unison, whereas legs walk first one, then the other. How about CHEW:MOUTH? Mouths certainly chew and connect at hinged jaw joints, more or less the way legs do at hip joints. Then again, chewing doesn't get you anywhere. My favorite answer is TALK:NOSE. Talk and walk are both verbs. Legs and nose are both body parts. Both words have the same number of letters (as each other and as WALK and LEGS). If I'm looking for the orthographically correct answer, this would be a good choice. Unfortunately, I'd probably get marked down for choosing it. The more creative you are, the more you struggle with these kinds of tests. I find it sad that so many of our "intelligence" testing conventions actually punish students who are creative and courageous enough to come up with more than one "right" answer.

It seems clear that consciously or not, human beings will do almost anything to avoid the ambiguity of not knowing.

We're also patted on the head for coming up with that one right answer quickly: The faster you can answer, the smarter you are. This drive for singularity and speed continues in our adult lives. In business, the successful manager is the one who is decisive and always has the right answer. No wonder the CEO is uncomfortable with staying in the question. All his life he's been trained to believe that doing so is a sign of weakness.

And yet staying in the question, being okay with the ambiguous, being okay with *not* knowing, is one of the most powerful thinking skills we can develop. The more we question and the more we stay in the question, asking it over and over again, the more useful our ultimate answers will be. Herbert Simon was fond of saying that early ideas usually aren't ideas at all: They are little more than regurgitations of the patterns we already have. The reason they arise is simply that they lie so close to the surface of our consciousness. They have little to do with productive thought. They are merely recalled.

So ask your questions. Stay in them as long as you can. Ask why things are the way they are. Ask how might things be different. Then ask why and why again. And again. Live in your question until you can see the vast panorama of possible answers. Your mind is a treasure box of ideas and inspirations and insights ricocheting and resounding through your hundred billion neural connections. Sometimes you just have to wait for them to come into view.

The Miracle of the Third Third

The best way to have good ideas is to have lots of ideas —and then throw away the bad ones.

Linus Pauling

If you've ever worn a parka, shell, or ski jacket from L.L. Bean, Bass Pro, or North Face . . . If you've ever hiked in boots from Mephisto or Wolverine . . . If you've ever played in shoes from Nike, Adidas, Reebok, or Puma . . . If you've ever warmed your hands in gloves from Mountain or Mitts from Burton . . . If you've ever kept yourself dry in a rain slicker from Lands' End . . . You've worn Gore-Tex.

Gore-Tex is a miracle fabric that's windproof and waterproof on the outside but breathes and wicks away moisture on the inside. It's made by W. L. Gore & Associates, one of the most innovative companies in the world, consistently ranked as one of the best companies to work for in the many countries in which it operates. Founded by Bill and Vieve Gore in 1958 in their basement in Newark, Delaware, W. L. Gore now manufactures over a thousand products. You may know about W. L. Gore's innovative medical products such as heart patches and synthetic blood vessels. You may have heard about its revolutionary Elixir guitar strings. You may know that the company's products have been to the moon and landed on Mars. But you probably don't know one of W. L. Gore's most startling and game-changing innovations of all.

W. L. Gore's corporate culture is characterized by a relentless focus on the long term. In an interview for *Wired* magazine in 2004, Bob Doak, the manager of W. L. Gore's Dundee, Scotland, operations, said, "Gore has immense patience about the time it takes to get it right and get it to market. If there's a glimmer of hope, you're encouraged to keep a project going and see if it could become a big thing."

The basic Gore-Tex technology was discovered by Bill Gore's son, Bob Gore, in 1969. The first Gore-Tex fiber was manufactured in 1972. It didn't get its first commercial order until 1976. Despite excellent reviews, a batch of technology awards, and expanded applications in medicine and aerospace, sales of Gore-Tex fabrics grew only modestly until 1989. That was when W. L. Gore introduced its remarkable breakthrough, and it didn't have anything to do with technology.

One of the most significant sales barriers W. L. Gore faced was that Gore-Tex is a component product. You don't buy Gore-Tex windbreakers; you buy windbreakers by Boathouse. You don't buy Gore-Tex boots; you buy boots by Merrell. As a manufacturer of a component product, you don't sell to consumers; you sell to other businesses. And to do that you have to persuade a wide range of change-averse people in the supply chain—manufacturers, distributors, and retailers—that paying a premium to use your product makes economic sense. In 1989, W. L. Gore figured out how to do that. It would persuade its buyers by persuading *their* buyers. W. L. Gore took the unusual step of marketing the benefits of its fabric directly to end users by creating the "Guaranteed to keep you dry" warranty and label. Almost overnight, retailers began reporting that customers were pulling Gore-Tex products off their racks. Brands that didn't have the guarantee saw a slump in demand. For some manufacturers, jumping onto the Gore-Tex bandwagon became a matter of survival. Today Gore-Tex is worn worldwide and is a staple of the company's success. In Doak's words, it became "a big thing."[1]

Though known primarily for its technological innovation, W. L. Gore has also had a major influence on marketing. The company's pioneering concept of talking directly to consumers and thus creating "pull marketing" for its products has been adopted by hundreds of other component product manufacturers, including Intel, THX, Dolby, and McNeil Nutritionals for its sweetener Splenda.

The "Guaranteed to keep you dry" campaign is a great example of third third thinking.

Brainstorming and Cholesterol

Brainstorming is like cholesterol. There's good and bad, and most people have experienced only the bad.

Bad brainstorming goes something like this:

We could reengineer the line. . . . No way! Too expensive. Besides, we'd don't have the time.

Part-time workers? . . . No, the union would cream us.

We could put half the shift on overtime. . . . Who's gonna pay them, you? Forget it.

How about just negotiating a delay with the buyer? . . . In your dreams.

We could take over line two and make up the slack later. . . . Yeah, that might do it. Get back to me with the specs as soon as you can. Okay, meeting over. We've got work to do.

Sound familiar? I could write a whole chapter about what's wrong with the above, but here's the short version:

- There's no separation of the different kinds of thinking going on. Creative, idea-generating thinking is being stopped cold by critical, judgmental thinking. Ideas are being killed before they're fully articulated.

- This session isn't about new ideas at all. It's actually a version of a sad little business game called "Guess what the boss is thinking." Everybody in the room knows it, and so as soon as someone says the boss's secret word, the duck comes down and the meeting is over.

- Perhaps deadliest of all, the people participating in this braindrizzle stop as soon as they come up with "the first right answer." They satisfice on the first reasonable idea they think will solve their problem and put them out of their misery.

Brainstorming is like cholesterol—
there's good and bad, and most people have
only experienced the bad.

All too many brainstorming sessions end like this one—with first, and often weak, "right" answers.

Good brainstorming is different. It relies on the overarching principle of separating creative thinking and critical thinking to generate long lists of possibilities. Alex Osborn, the advertising genius who "invented" the concept of brainstorming in 1941,[2] developed a list of four essential rules for an effective brainstorming session:

- *Criticism is ruled out.* Adverse judgment of ideas must be withheld until later.

- *Freewheeling is welcomed.* The wilder the idea, the better; it is easier to tame down than to think up.

- *Quantity is wanted.* The greater the number of ideas, the more the likelihood of useful ideas.

- *Combination and improvement are sought.* In addition to contributing ideas of their own, participants should suggest how the ideas of others can be turned into better ideas or how two or more ideas can be joined into still another idea.[3]

Studies have shown that in Osborn's kind of good brainstorming, the first third of the session tends to produce mundane, every-one-has-thought-of-them-before ideas. These are the early thoughts that lie very close to the surface of our consciousness. They tend not to be new ideas at all but recollections of old ideas we've heard elsewhere. They are essentially reproductive thoughts.

Generally, the second third of a good brainstorming session produces ideas that begin to stretch boundaries. These are the ideas that are often still constrained by what we know but are more than simple regurgitations of what we've heard or thought before.

The third third is where the diamonds lie. These are the potential breakthrough ideas that often lead to innovative solutions. These are the unexpected connections. Whereas bad brainstorming tends to stop at the first reasonable idea and judge all other ideas out of existence, good brainstorming encourages the generation of long lists of ideas by separating creative thinking and critical thinking. Bad brainstorming is binary; ideas are either good or bad. Good brainstorming is full of maybes. In bad brainstorming, we never get to the third third. In good brainstorming, getting to the third third is the point.[4]

When the people at W. L. Gore were trying to solve the conundrum of the component manufacturer, it's unlikely that the idea of talking directly to end consumers came up in the first third of their thinking. The facts that presented themselves were these: We have a new product. It's better than anything on the market, but it's so revolutionary that there isn't a clear demand for it. The businesses we need to sell to have existing relationships with fabric suppliers. They also already have their production lines set up. Changing them will take time and cost money. Clothing is not a tech-driven business; it's a fashion-driven business.

Here are the kinds of ideas that might have surfaced in W. L. Gore's first-third thinking:

Maybe we could incent the corporate buyers by giving them deep discounts.

We could develop our processes and guarantee better delivery times than other fabric suppliers.

We could do a bang-up sales presentation.

We could make a promotional film or video showing how great our fabric is.

We could try to impress buyers with the fact that we supply NASA.

It's highly unlikely that the notion of communicating with end users would come up during this phase of W. L. Gore's thinking. Why? Because component manufacturers don't do that. After all, in 1989 who ever heard of Pratt & Whitney advertising its jet engines to the flying public? Why on earth would Magna International, one of the world's leading automobile component manufacturers, promote its door handles or wheelhouse assemblies to the car-buying public? Who cared about the company that makes the ink for Bic pens?

The second third of W. L. Gore's thinking might have been a bit more interesting, producing ideas like these:

Maybe we should look for manufacturers who are in trouble and need something fresh. Could we design our own clothing lines as a demonstration of what's possible?

What about forgetting the retail market altogether and focusing on technical clothing for industry? Maybe we could focus on a specialty area, like skiing.

These ideas are more interesting. They break away from the natural tendency to look at costs and supply chain efficiencies. And indeed some of them might be worth exploring.

However, good brainstorming sessions don't end with the second third. They go further, extending beyond the point at which the session participants start thinking, "Okay, we're dry. That's all there is." It's precisely at the "we're dry" stage that the magic happens, because by then the old ideas have been flushed out. It's the very frustration of running out of ideas that gives third third ideas a chance to develop.

One of the ways my think[x] colleagues and I encourage groups to get to the third third is to use the word *else*. How *else* might we solve the problem? Who *else* might be involved? Where *else* might a solution come from? What *else* haven't we thought of yet? *Else* is one of the most powerful words in the productive thinking vocabulary. I'll elaborate on the productive power of *"else"* in Chapter 11.

Once all their "reasonable" ideas had been exhausted, W. L. Gore's third third, or how *else*, thinking might have produced ideas like this:

> We could sponsor an Arctic expedition.
>
> We could get into the retail business and sell only our own fabrics.
>
> Maybe we could guarantee to make up any losses the manufacturers might sustain.
>
> Maybe we could go back in time and get a picture of an astronaut training underwater wearing a Gore-Tex label.
>
> Maybe we could get the textile workers' union to include Gore-Tex in their union-made labels.

Bad brainstorming is binary; ideas are either good or bad. Good brainstorming is full of maybes.

You can imagine what might be happening here. Suddenly ideas that are a little out of the ordinary begin to stimulate other ideas that are even stranger. Connections start being made. And it probably isn't very long before someone combines the idea of union labels with manufacturers' guarantees with W. L. Gore becoming its own retailer and comes up with an in-store Gore-Tex guarantee.

> After all, if unions can communicate with the buying public, why can't we?
>
> After all, if we can guarantee delivery performance to our direct buyers, why can't we guarantee clothing performance to the public?
>
> After all, if we can imagine ourselves with a vested interest in retail, why not imagine retailers with a vested interest in us?

Of course, there is no guarantee that third third ideas will be great ideas or even good ideas. In fact, it's likely that the vast majority of them will be lousy. But it's also true that you will have a greater chance of coming up with that one brilliant idea if you get all the way to the third third than if you stop at the first "right" idea.

Imagine that you are hiring someone to be your personal assistant. You've posted ads, gone to job Web sites, and contracted a placement agency. Over the several weeks of your search you collect about a hundred résumés. As you leaf through them, you see that résumé number 6 looks pretty good: right qualifications, relevant experience, impressive references, well written. Just because you've found what looks like a good candidate, would you stop at number 6? Would you throw away the 94 unread résumés without checking them out? Of course not. There could be 10 other résumés just as good or better lurking in that pile. You'd be crazy to close your eyes to them. Yet isn't that exactly what happens in bad brainstorming sessions? No, no, no, no, no, yes, meeting over. That first "right" idea may turn out to be the most dangerous idea you've ever had if it prevents you from generating the second right idea, the third right idea, the tenth right idea, and the hundredth right idea. It seems to me there's a remarkable degree of hubris in assuming that there's no better idea than the one that first pops into your head.

Generating long lists of ideas flushes those early ideas out of your head so that you can make room for new ones. Dee Hock, the founder of VISA and one of the great modern business pioneers, once wrote, "The problem is never how to get new, innovative thoughts into your mind, but how to get old ones out. Every mind is a building filled with archaic furniture. Clean out a corner of your mind and creativity will instantly fill it."

The notion of emptying oneself is hardly new. It plays a central role in many religions. The Greeks have a word for it: *kenosis*, which literally means "self-emptying." The wisdom of freedom through *kenosis* is woven into the stories of many cultures, as in the Zen tale of the sensei filling and then overfilling a teacup for his student and explaining that the student's mind is like the cup: Unless it is emptied, there will be no room for new learning. The concept of *kenosis* speaks to one of the most basic human truths: You must empty yourself before you can fill yourself again. A voice teacher of mine, Jan Simons, loved to point out that you never have to try to breathe in, you must only breathe out. Only by breathing out can you breathe in. We are literally inspired upon breathing in, but we must expire before we can do so.

As I discussed in Chapter 2, one of the most significant barriers to productive thinking is the brain's tendency to create and recall patterns. These patterned thoughts box us in and hold us back from being as creative as we could be. Sometimes they manifest themselves as "knowledge," sometimes as conceptual models, and sometimes as conscious beliefs. Patterns are most debilitating, however, when we don't even see them at all, when they influence our thinking without imposing on our consciousness. Here's a little experiment you can perform that might illustrate the power of these unconscious patterns.

Capturing Aliens

Close your eyes for a moment and imagine you've constructed a transportation machine that can beam you into a different universe. On your first journey, you encounter an alien creature. Imagine what that creature might look like. Be as creative as you can. Now take a sheet of paper and sketch a rough approximation of your alien acquaintance. Your drawing skills are irrelevant. All you want to do is capture the creature's essential features. If drawing holds you back, get a picture of the alien in your mind and write a few sentences describing what you see. Take a moment to do this. Don't read further until you've done a quick sketch.

Does your creature have eyes? Ears? A mouth? Does it have a head? Does it have legs? Some other form of locomotion? Does it have a body? A brain?

Despite the instructions to imagine a different universe, not a just a different planet or a different galaxy, and to be as creative as they can, most people will draw creatures that recapitulate the patterns they've lived with all their lives: creatures with many of the conventional body parts and attributes of creatures on earth. Yet there's nothing to prevent you from imagining an energy creature, a vapor creature, a bodiless creature, a multibodied creature, a creature that exists in multiple dimensions, and so on. Try this experiment with your workmates or with your family at home. You may be surprised how conventional most people are.

Overcoming patterns we can't even see is difficult. It can be like trying to fight a worry. There's nothing there to swat, yet it has a powerful influence on the way we think and act. Although it's almost impossible to escape from our patterns, there are ways to think beyond them. One of the best ones, as Hock suggests, is to think through them, to strive for quantity, to get to the third third: If we can empty ourselves of our old ideas, we automatically make room for new ones.

You'll have a greater chance of coming up with that one brilliant idea if you get all the way to the third third than you will if you stop at the first 'right' idea.

Some years ago, before cell phones had become ubiquitous, a regional telephone company encountered the following problem. It was losing money and getting customer flak as a result of its long-standing telephone booth policy. For years the company had provided free local calls from its booths. Originally, the policy didn't cost much, won the company praise for offering a public service, and encouraged new customers to sign up. As the system matured, however, and the subscriber base grew, the telephone booth policy started causing problems. Revenues from booth-originated long-distance, or trunk, calls were virtually nonexistent because the booths were in almost constant use by people making lengthy free local calls. Fights had broken out between people wanting to make calls and those already in the booths. Even worse from a public relations perspective, there had been a number of incidents in which customers needing to make emergency calls were unable to do so. Politicians and regulators threatened to require the company to build more booths to ensure capacity.

You can imagine how the company's problem-solving sessions unfolded. The first third ideas probably sounded like this:

We'll have to start charging for local calls.

Or maybe we can just put time limits on local calls.

We could build dedicated trunk-call-only booths.

Or build dedicated emergency calling stations.

Or maybe just install more booths generally.

There's nothing intrinsically wrong with these ideas, but they're not particularly good either. Although they might solve the problem as presented, they might also create other problems along the way. Charging for calls would probably be seen as a take-away by customers used to free local calls. Time limits might be seen in a similar light. Building more or specialized booths might be expensive.

The company's second third ideas might have included somewhat more interesting possibilities:

Perhaps we could still offer free calls for the first five minutes and charge after that.

Maybe the calls are free to the booth but charged to the recipient.

Maybe there's just a polite recording after a few minutes reminding people to be aware of the time they're spending on their calls.

We could make a sliding rate, free at the beginning, so much per minute after three minutes, with higher rates the longer people talk.

These second third ideas are more innovative, and some of them might be worth exploring. But none of them are breakthrough ideas; they're still Band-Aids.

So the meeting facilitators pushed further. As often happens in idea-generating sessions, frustrations began to rise. Participants complained that they'd thought of everything already. There were no more possibilities. They were tapped out. Still, the facilitators asked for more. At one point a participant said, "Why don't we just make it uncomfortable for people to stay in the booths?"[5] Others in the group thought that idea was worth exploring.

How might we make it uncomfortable to stay in the booth for too long?

Several other ideas were offered:

Make the booths smaller.

Plug up the air vents.

Introduce offensive odors.

Eventually someone came up with the brilliant idea of making the handsets heavier! And that is just what the company did. After preliminary testing to make sure the concept would work, they replaced the handsets in the booths with ones that were several times heavier. Call durations decreased, effective capacity increased, the cost was low, and there was no negative PR. The magic is in the third third.

Brainstorming Alone

So far, I've been referring to third third thinking as it applies to group work. But the value of getting to the third third also applies to thinking by yourself.

Over the years I've been exploring the world of creative and productive thinking, I've had the good fortune to meet a number of extraordinary people. One of them is a man by the name of Win Wenger. Win has spent his life studying how to help people think better, deeper, and more productively. Much of his work is based on what he calls the Venturi effect of the mind. Win's theory is straightforward: The more ideas you have, the more ideas you get. The principle works much like a carburetor in an automobile engine. Just as air flowing through a Venturi tube in a carburetor creates a vaccum that pulls fuel into the combustion chamber of the engine, so too does the flow of ideas create a vacuum that is filled with other ideas. In other words, the very process of articulating ideas creates the condition in which more ideas are generated.

Generating long lists of ideas flushes those early ideas out of your head so that you can make room for new ones.

Win uses a variety of tools to demonstrate the power of this theory. My favorite is a variation on one he calls Wind Tunnel. It's an extremely effective way to help people get to the third third. The technique is disarmingly simple.

I urge you to try the Wind Tunnel exercise either on your own or with a trusted partner. It's not easy. Like the folks from the telephone company story, you'll find that you get frustrated as you run out of things to say or write. You'll be tempted to stop before hitting your target. But if you can keep at it, you'll find it an astonishingly effective thinking technique. You'll be amazed at how many ideas you actually have and how creative you can be.

Wind Tunnel: Blowing Your Mind with Ideas

You will need either a voice recorder of some kind or a pencil and paper. Start with a question related to a problem you want to resolve or an issue you need to deal with. It's a good idea to write the question down so that you can keep looking at it throughout the exercise.

Once you have a question in mind, set a target either for the number of ideas you will generate or for the length of time you'll take. The first time you try this, I suggest going for 50 ideas or setting a five minute time limit. With a little experience you can set more ambitious targets.

Now with your question visible in front of you, write or talk as quickly as possible about everything and anything that comes to mind in relation to the question (if you're writing, use the number of ideas target; if you're talking, use the time target). You'll find that by generating a rapid flow of ideas, you will soon run out of obvious things to say or write. But the key is to keep going, to fill the vacuum you've created. Even if what's coming out of your head seems like absolute nonsense, keep generating.

As you dig for more and more things to say or write, you will discover that to keep going you will necessarily drop your judgmental censor. Without judgment, the ideas you generate will move farther and farther from the conventional, "acceptable" thinking characterized by the first third. It's in the digging for more that your thinking becomes truly creative and novel. The longer you talk or write, the more likely it is that you will experience the thrill of coming up with a brilliant third third idea. Some people find it easier to do Wind Tunnel with a partner whose role is not to contribute to the idea flow but simply to audit and write down the ideas that are generated.

The ability to break through to the third third is synonymous with the ability to produce breakthrough thinking. The more you push beyond the conventional, the more startling the ideas you will generate. As Win Wenger says, "The more ideas you have, the more ideas you get." Painful though it can be to work through those first and second third ideas, once you experience the miracle of the third third in your business, professional, or personal life, you'll be eager to take the time and spend the extra effort to ask how *else*, to push beyond. As a client of mine who works for the British government once said, "Forget about the third third; I'm going for the fourth quarter!"

Regardless of the domain in which you work, you will find that your later ideas tend to be better than the earlier ones. Imagine your idea stream like water from a tap. To get to the cooler, clearer water, you need to run the tap for a while to get rid of the sediment that forms in the pipes. The creative act is first the kenotic act, the courage to empty ourselves before we can fill ourselves with the new.

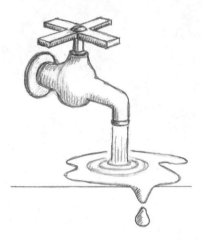

PART 3

PRODUCTIVE THINKING IN
THEORY

Productive Thinking by Design

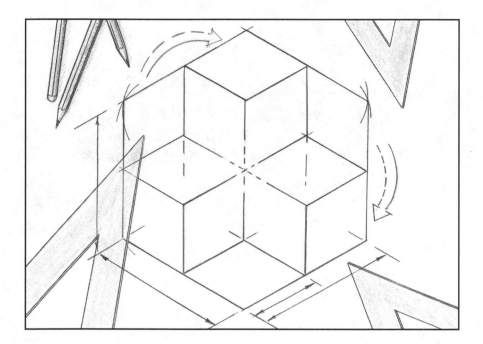

*Creativity is not an escape from
disciplined thinking.
It is an escape with disciplined thinking.*

Jerry Hirschberg

I magine the following scenario: You've been discussing the possibility of moving to a very attractive position at a new firm. You've met a number of the people you would be working with; the conversation has progressed beyond the preliminaries, and things are starting to get serious. Your potential boss and several of his direct reports—your future colleagues—would like you to join them for an informal dinner so they can get to know you better. In the language of the hunt, they're sighting you in.

The executive team has arranged a table at their favorite restaurant for entertaining clients. They've asked you to dress casually, and you've chosen a white silk crewneck under a sport jacket. The restaurant is intimate, expensive and impeccable, serving a leisurely Italian multi-course meal accompanied by several wines and ending with coffee. The small talk is going well, and as the waiter circles the table to take orders, you follow the boss's lead, selecting the spaghetti alla puttanesca. So far, so good.

By the time the spaghetti is served, you've all had a little wine and the conversation has warmed up nicely. You know you're still the show dog in the group, but things have relaxed enough for you to drop your guard. You curl a modest forkful of spaghetti, and as you suck the trailing bit of pasta into your mouth, it whips and flicks and lets fly a small globule of red puttanesca sauce. You can almost see it in slow motion as it arcs through the air and lands smack dab in the middle of your white silk crewneck.

I'd be surprised if anyone reading this book would need more than a fraction of a second to complete the following phrase: "Oil and water. . . ."

Anyone who's ever splashed a salad dressing, butter stained a shirt cuff, or dripped an ice cream cone knows that oil and water don't mix. The echoes of "oil and water do not mix" reverberate in just about all of us. You learned it at home, you learned it again in chemistry class, and you relearned it every time you smudged your clothing after holding a French fry. You *know* oil and water don't mix.

Or at least you think you do. I'll bet that even after all that learning and reinforcement, at least once in your life, when encountering a freshly deposited spaghetti sauce stain on your clothing, you did what just about everyone else has done: You took the corner of your napkin, dipped it into your glass of water, and dabbed the spot. I'll even bet that as your hand was about halfway between your glass and the spot, you knew beyond a doubt that it wasn't going to work, yet your hand kept going. The water transferred beautifully from the napkin to your shirt, but the only effect it had on the spot was to spread it out. Instead of removing the stain, you made it larger.

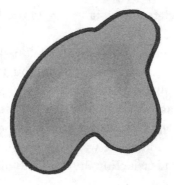

What's the problem here?

All of us have had the experience of coming up with a "solution" to a problem that hasn't done anything to solve the problem or that's made the problem even worse. Sometimes it's a big, complex problem such as how to reconfigure a marketing program, sometimes a comparatively insignificant problem such as a spot on a shirt. That's because whether responding to big problems or small, all human beings, across cultures, genders, ages, and races, take essentially the same imperfect approach to problem solving:

- Perceive a problem
- Pick a solution
- Do something

That's it. Three steps: Perceive a problem. Pick a solution. Do something. Simple but often not very effective. The problem with our problem-solving approach is that we usually don't address any of these steps particularly skillfully. We don't give ourselves the time or the tools to do any of the steps well.

Think back to the last spaghetti stain incident you encountered. Chances are that your perceptions of the problem were pretty limited. If

Our Natural Problem Solving Process.

you're like most of us, you probably jumped straight to the conclusion that the problem was a spot on an item of clothing. But that might not have been the real problem at all. What if the real problem was your relationship with the other person? Or the other person's perception of how resourceful you are? Or the need for you to stay focused on the conversation? If you took the time to see the problem more clearly, it's very likely that you would begin to think of different approaches to resolving it. Maybe there's no point in reaching for your napkin at all.

Not only did you operate from a limited perception of the problem, it's also a good bet you didn't pick your solution from a very wide range of alternatives. You probably just did the first thing that occurred to you: putting water on a napkin. But with a clearer perception of the real problem, you might have generated a wide range of possible solutions. If the problem was your relationship with the other person, maybe the best solution would have been to make a joke of it. If the problem was demonstrating how resourceful you could be, a simple shift of your scarf or tie would have done the trick. And even if you decided the problem was the spot on your crewneck, asking the waiter for help or advice would probably have been a lot more effective than water on a napkin since many restaurants have a ready supply of stain removers for just such a situation.

Even if you were convinced that your analysis of the problem and its solution was correct, your implementation left something to be desired. The immediate effect of dabbing your crewneck with a wet napkin is that the water soaks the silk fabric, making it transparent. Now, not only do you have a spot, your bra is showing. Well done! If your dinner mates didn't notice the spot, they'll surely see this.

Instead of reacting in a knee-jerk fashion, you'd be much better off using a disciplined process that taps both creative thinking and critical thinking strategies. By training yourself to think in a more productive, creative way, you might have been able to respond by making a joke, shifting your scarf, or asking the waiter for advice or a stain remover.

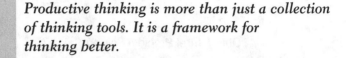

Productive thinking is more than just a collection of thinking tools. It is a framework for thinking better.

The good news is that the Productive Thinking Model builds on our natural three-step problem-solving process—perceive a problem, pick a solution, do something—and transforms it into a comprehensive, repeatable six-step framework for thinking better. Simply put, productive thinking is a way to come up with better answers. It allows you to sidestep the knee-jerk reaction and come up with creative, useful, and effective solutions. With productive thinking, you can train yourself to generate more options, better options, more of the time in almost any situation, from dealing with a spaghetti spots to creating full-blown business strategies. Productive thinking provides you with more time and more tools to perceive the problem accurately, pick the best solution from a broad range of possibilities, and do something in a way that offers the greatest chance of achieving success.

Productive thinking is more than just a collection of thinking tools. It is a framework for thinking better. I often use the analogy of a coat rack to describe the model. A coat rack provides capacity, structure, and stability; you provide the coats. In the same way, the Productive Thinking Model provides a disciplined framework for addressing problems that combines, balances, and orchestrates creative thinking and critical thinking. The model can be used with a wide variety of tools, such as DRIVE, a powerful way to develop criteria for success, and C^5, a technique for extracting the real gold from the long lists of ideas you generate (see pages 136–137 and 155 for more on these two tools). In the next several chapters I'll introduce you to some tools that may amaze you with their simplicity and power. Feel free to use them all.

You'll find that productive thinking is a practical, easy-to-learn process that will help you understand more clearly, think more creatively, and plan more effectively. It builds on over 50 years of research and experimentation on effective problem-solving methodologies.

In this chapter and the following chapters, you will notice that the Productive Thinking Model has its own vocabulary. There are three reasons for this.

1. In many cases the meanings of familiar words have become unclear in modern usage. The productive thinking vocabulary is precise and clear. When you use it in group work, your colleagues will know exactly what you mean. Better communication means better thinking.

2. Sometimes no existing term adequately describes a productive thinking concept or tool. For example, there is no existing term for the productive thinking concept of Catalytic Questions, which are the strategic questions you need to answer to achieve your goal, or for Powered-Up Solutions, the stress-tested, bullet-proofed ideas you will be generating.

3. Language is a powerful facilitator of cultural change. If you want to change the way people think about something, it's useful to provide them with new ways of talking about it. When people begin to refer to their Itches, which I define as the irritants that drive the desire for change, or Imagined Futures, which I define as visions of a future so compelling that they motivate action, they actually begin to think differently about the issues they face.

Productive Thinking in a Nutshell

The Productive Thinking Model consists of six interlocking steps that are described in detail in Chapters 7 through 12. Each step includes a variety of tools and techniques.

The Productive Thinking Model.

This chapter provides a quick overview of the six steps, using a simple example. Let's suppose you're an executive with JetWays Airlines. In this hypothetical situation, JetWays is a very successful regional carrier that focuses on business travelers. The airline has decided to expand nationally and is looking for ways to differentiate itself from the competition. One of the proposals is to improve the experience of sitting in the middle seats on JetWays planes. You and your team have been charged with coming up with innovative options for doing that. I've inserted *in italics* the kinds of answers you might give as you work your way through the various steps of the process.

Step 1: What's Going On?

What's Going On? is a series of five questions designed to help you explore an issue fully. It is usually one of the most time-consuming parts of the process. The five questions are as follows:

> 1. **What's the Itch?** List exactly what needs fixing or improving, the irritants that are driving you to action. In this case you would ask: "What's wrong with the middle seat?" to generate a long list of all the possible

Itches. You would then select the ones that express the issue most clearly: *Middle seats are uncomfortable. Middle seats are claustrophobic. Middle seats get spilled on. Middle seats have low status.*

2. **What's the Impact?** Explore how the issue affects people and the airline. Why is it a matter of concern? Why is it important? Again, you would first generate long lists and then select the most important items. For the passenger: *I often need to work in the plane, and that's difficult in the middle seat. I don't feel fresh when I land.* For the airline: *Middle seat passengers can be grumpy. If we had better middle seats than the competition, we might get more business.*

3. **What's the Information?** Examine the information you have about the issue and the information you need to acquire to understand it thoroughly. For example, you would want to know what the causes of the issue might be, what other effects it might be having, what hidden assumptions there might be, among other things. Once again, you would generate lists and make choices: *Traditionally, airlines have tried to maximize profit by maximizing seats. Airlines need to achieve certain load factors to be profitable. The weight of a seat influences fuel consumption.*

4. **Who's Involved?** This question looks at who the stakeholders are and what might be at stake for each of them. Who is affected by the Itch? Who might be contributing to it? Who benefits if things stay the same? Who might benefit if things changed? List all the potential stakeholders and then choose the most important ones: *The airline itself, a stakeholder in terms of profit; passengers, stakeholders in terms of comfort or the ability to work; cabin crews, stakeholders in terms of dealing with irritable passengers; travel agents, stakeholders in terms of their relationships with their own customers; regulators, stakeholders in terms of safety.*

5. **What's the Vision?** Here you switch focus from what is to what might be. This question asks you to set your sights on a powerful Target Future. In the productive thinking vocabulary a Target Future is the goal you want to achieve. To arrive at this statement you make long lists of possible Target Futures and then choose the most compelling one. For John F. Kennedy in 1962, the Target Future was to land a man safely on the moon by the end of the 1960s. For JetWays it might be: *Blow the competition away with a middle seat so great that passengers actually ask to sit there.*

The outcome of What's Going On? is a comprehensive understanding of the issue and an articulation of a compelling Target Future. This simple statement of the Target Future is the seed for the next step, in which you refine your vision and establish concrete criteria for success.

Step 2: What's Success?

What's Success? begins with the simple Target Future statement you developed in Step 1 and expands it into a robust image of a future in which the issue is resolved. It then lays out a series of concrete criteria against which to test the ideas you will later generate for achieving the Target Future. What's Success? consists of two substeps.

1. First, you imagine how it might be to live in your Target Future. How would it be different? In the case of JetWays, how would it feel to fly in a JetWays plane, what might passengers think about JetWays, how might it feel to work for such a company, and how might the competition respond? *JetWays is the number one airline. Our middle seats are so popular that passengers always ask for JetWays first. Wearing a JetWays uniform sets you apart as an elite member of the industry. The competition is always trying to imitate us, but we're always one step ahead.*

2. Second, using a powerful tool called DRIVE, you define specific, observable success criteria. Once you develop your ideas for a solution (in Step 4: Generate Answers), you will measure them against these crite-

ria. Will the solution resolve the issue? Will it get you to the Target Future? What must be accomplished? What must be avoided? What constraints will you have to work within? What are the metrics you will use? To arrive at the most important success criteria, you generate a long list of possible criteria and then select the most significant ones: *Our solution has to differentiate us from the competition. It has to generate more business. It has to make us the airline of choice. It must not be easily copied. It must not cause safety regulation issues. It must maintain our load factors. It must achieve a 15 percent return on investment.*

The outcome of What's Success? is a clear set of Success Criteria and a vision of a future so compelling that it drives you to want to get there.

You can increase your chances of having creative, effective ideas in virtually any situation, from the inconsequential to the critical.

Step 3: What's the Question?

What's the Question? is a pivotal step in the productive thinking process. Its purpose is to define the essential questions that must be answered to achieve the Target Future. We call these Catalytic Questions because they are catalysts for change. Although this part of the process is analogous to the problem definition phases of some other problem-solving models, What's the Question? takes a unique approach: It requires that each problem be phrased as a question. This is because problem statements are usually inert. Problem questions, on the other hand, invite answers. Problem statements have no energy; they just sit there. For example, the statement "We don't have enough budget" is little more than an opinion about a condition. It doesn't drive you anywhere. By contrast, the question "How might we increase our budget?" automatically invites a search for answers.

In the case of JetWays, you would start by generating a long list of possible problem questions, such as *How might we link JetWays middle seats with the needs of our customers? How might we get people to think differently about JetWays middle seats? How might we eliminate middle seats entirely?*

After generating a long list of possible questions, you would narrow the focus to one or more to use as your Catalytic Questions, the key strategic questions that, if answered well, have the potential to resolve your issue and lead to the Target Future you defined in Step 1. For example, you could ask: *How might we change people's perceptions about JetWays middle seats?*

Step 4: Generate Answers

Generate Answers is the idea generation phase of the Productive Thinking Model. Here you make long lists of possible answers to the Catalytic Questions, the key strategic questions you articulated in Step 3. You then select the most promising answers for further exploration and development. These are in effect embryonic ideas for a solution, though none of them are actually solutions yet. The outcome of Generate Answers is a small number of the most promising or intriguing ideas that, once fully developed, may result in useful ways to resolve your issue and achieve your Target Future.

Here are some examples: *Put the middle seat on rails so that it can slide back and forth to make more room. Turn the middle seat around. Make the middle seat cheaper. Call it a throne. Give the middle seat control of the entertainment console. Define the middle seat as a flying office.*

Step 5: Forge the Solution

Forge the Solution is where you take the most promising embryonic ideas from the previous step and develop them into robust, stress-tested solutions. Forge the Solution consists of two substeps:

1. First, evaluate the potential of the most promising ideas you selected in Step 4: Generate Answers by comparing them with the Success Criteria you developed in Step 2: *Low-priced middle seats might increase sales but could be copied by the competition. Turning middle seats around might increase comfort but could pose a safety concern. The flying office concept is unique and might appeal to business travelers.*

2. Second, once you have chosen the idea that best meets your Success Criteria, you stress-test, improve, and refine that idea to create a robust solution: *We will create the JetWays Flying Office. It will have custom seats equipped with special lighting and privacy barriers. To make room for this, we will remove every other middle seat. We will enhance the offering by launching a Flying Office Club. We will partner with a well-known office furniture company. We will use this partnership to create a unique brand to help us stay ahead of the competition.*

Step 6: Align Resources

Align Resources identifies the actions and resources required to implement the solutions defined in Step 5. It also assigns each action step to someone who will be accountable for its completion. Because it gets into considerable detail, Align Resources is one of the more time-consuming modules. It consists of six substeps.

1. List the action steps required to complete the solutions: *Survey market to test for interest in the Flying Office concept. Design prototype. Test prototype. Research safety regulations.*

2. Identify the people who may help you and those who may be obstacles. Find ways to create strong alliances with potential assisters and defuse the concerns of resistors: *Contact major furniture designer to propose joint venture. Write business case for development budget. Research safety or other regulatory concerns and develop point-by-point document.*

3. Ensure that each action step has someone accountable for its completion: *Liaise with furniture suppliers (Carlos). Business case (Rae). Regulatory case (Terri).*

4. Put the steps in order: *Recruit pilot team. Hire research firm. Conduct cost feasibility.*

5. Identify additional action steps needed to acquire the resources for each step and assign accountabilities as appropriate: *Schedule and liaise with cabin test facili-*

*ties (Bob). Research, select, manage designers (Alison).
Legal needs to craft ironclad nondisclosure agreements
(Stan).*

6. Identify and record observable outcomes for each
   step: *We'll know initial market testing is complete when
   we receive the report. Go–no-go if 70 percent initial
   acceptance. Business case complete when approved by
   JR. ROI hurdle 15 percent.*

The outcome of Align Resources is a realistic action plan, including people committed to and accountable for carrying out each step, that is designed to implement the solution, resolve the original issue, and achieve the Target Future.

Puttanesca Take Two

Suddenly you find yourself in the middle of an important business dinner with a glob of spaghetti sauce right in the middle of your silk crewneck. In take one, you saw the problem as *Aaargh! There's a spaghetti stain on my expensive crewneck! It'll be ruined! They'll think I'm a pig. I've got to get it off!*

In take two, using the Productive Thinking Model, you see the problem differently. It's not about your clothing at all. It's about how well you handle the situation. Instead of focusing on your crewneck, you focus on what's important. You come up with a solution that really works.

The puttanesca story is not fiction. It actually happened to a friend of mine. Her productive thinking solution? First she quipped, "Time sure flies when you're having fun. It looks like spaghetti sauce does too! Excuse me for a sec; I'm going see if I can't perform some quick magic." She went to the washroom, removed her jacket, took off the crewneck, put it on again with the spot at the back, and put on her jacket. She was back at the table in less than two minutes and said, "Success! I hope I don't do that again, though. They say a magician should never repeat a trick." She got the job.

Of course this is a trivial story. You might decide the spot isn't such a disaster after all, or you might simply ask the waiter if the restaurant has some spot remover. There are countless ways to approach this situation. What's important here is that you can increase your chances of having creative, effective ideas in virtually any situation, from the inconsequential to the critical. You can train yourself to think more productively, more creatively, and more successfully.

In the following chapters, you'll find detailed explanations of each step of the Productive Thinking Model, including case studies illustrating how the step works. Each chapter concludes with a summary guide: an outline of the procedure for that step and its appropriate outcomes.

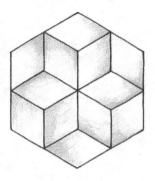

Step One:
What's Going On?

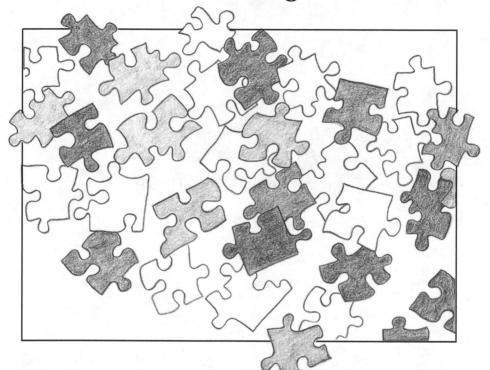

Step 1: What's Going On?

Step 2: What's Success?

Step 3: What's the Question?

Step 4: Generate Answers

Step 5: Forge the Solution

Step 6: Align Resources

Discontent is the first step in the progress of a man or a nation.

Oscar Wilde (1854-1900)

Step One: What's Going On?

Puzzles, Probes, and Possibilities

The exact date isn't recorded, but I imagine it must have been a crisp January day. The light was perfect for taking photographs. A successful 34-year-old physicist inventor had decided to take his family to New Mexico for a short vacation. He needed time to think. While working for the National Defense Research Committee, his company had developed a variety of technologies for the Allied forces fighting in Europe, including night vision goggles and a stereoscopic optical device that could reveal camouflaged enemy positions in aerial photography. The company had done well, but the war would end eventually. Then what? He needed to figure out what his 1,250 employees would do after their defense work ran out. The fresh air of the Sangre de Cristo foothills might be just the thing to stimulate fresh ideas.

The inventor and his family had spent the day sightseeing. He had been taking photographs of the scenery, his wife Helen, and their three-year old daughter Jennifer. When they got back to their hotel, Jennifer asked to see the photographs, particularly the ones of her. He told her he would have to send the film to the lab for developing, that it would be a few days before any pictures would be ready. In his later telling of the story, the inventor didn't go into the details of that conversation, but anyone who has had a relationship with a three-year-old knows what probably happened next.

"But Daddy, I wanna see the pictures."

"I know, sweetie, but they're just not ready yet."

"I wanna see the pictures!"

"Jennifer, as soon as we can get them to the drugstore. . . ."

"I wanna see the pictures *now!*"

After trying several times to explain why that was impossible, most fathers might have recognized the futility of reasoning with a three-year-old and tried to drop the subject. But not Edwin Land. Photographs you could show to your children instantly—there might be something in that. Perhaps he would noodle the idea back at his lab in Massachusetts.

And noodle he did. Just over three years later, on February 21, 1947, Land astonished an audience at the Optical Society of America by demonstrating a one-step process for producing finished photographs in 60 seconds. By Thanksgiving 1948, Land's company, the Polaroid

Corporation, had manufactured its first 60 Land Cameras and sold them out in a single day at the Jordan Marsh department store in Boston. By 1950 Polaroid was manufacturing 1 million packs of film a year and selling cameras and accessories through over 4,000 dealers across the United States. At $89.95 (that's over $800 in 2007 dollars) the camera that took you "from snap to print in 60 seconds" was flying off the shelves.

D escribing the process he used to create his newfangled camera and film, Land wrote, "You always start with a fantasy. Part of the fantasy technique is to visualize something as perfect. Then with the experiments you work back from the fantasy to reality, hacking away at the components."

Even before the fantasy, however, there's always the Itch: the irritation that needs to be soothed, the landscape that's out of balance, the discontent that calls for action. On that winter evening in Santa Fe, Land had two Itches: He needed to find a way for his company to prosper in a peacetime economy, and his daughter wanted to see instant pictures. Those two Itches came together to produce a revolution.

The Problem with Problems

One of the problems with problems is that they usually begin with a mess. Most people, especially businesspeople, don't like messes. But if things weren't messy or getting messy, there would be no discontent, and there wouldn't be a need for productive thinking in the first place. The mess comes when we begin to realize that things might be better than they are: faster, cheaper, more profitable, or just plain different.

A problem is a puzzle of sorts. Think about the last time you tried to put a jigsaw puzzle together. After unwrapping it, what was the first thing you did to get going?

Many people say they begin by finding all the edges and then separating out the four corners. Others claim that the most useful strategy is to start sorting by color groups. I have one friend whose first move is to count all the pieces. After all, she reasons, if there's a piece missing, why start the puzzle at all?

But if you observe puzzlers, you'll find that regardless of what people *say* they do, the first thing most people *actually* do after opening the box is dump out all the pieces and turn them face up. In other words, most puzzlers try to get a good look at the mess as a first step before beginning to sort into edges, corners, color groups, and so on.

That's exactly what the first step of the Productive Thinking Model is designed to do. What's Going On? is a series of questions designed to arrive at a comprehensive understanding of the issue, its impact, what we know and need to know about its dynamics and causes, who influences it and who it may affect, and what the future might be like if the issue were resolved.

If things weren't messy or getting messy,
there would be no discontent, and there wouldn't be
a need for productive thinking in the first place.

What's Going On? consists of five substeps, each in the form of a question:

1. **What's the Itch?** What is the discontent, the irritant that compels us to want to change?

2. **What's the Impact?** What effect does the Itch have? Why is it important?

3. **What's the Information?** What do we know about the Itch, about its causes? What else might we need to know?

4. **Who's Involved?** Who are the stakeholders, those who might also be affected by the Itch and those who might influence it?

5. **What's the Vision?** What is your vision of a future in which the issue is resolved?

The outcome of What's Going On? is a comprehensive context for further thinking.

Substep 1: What's the Itch?

Itches are powerful. They cause us to feel uncomfortable, to seek relief. Often we don't know what the problem is. Sometimes we don't even know that there is a problem. But we know things don't feel right. We know they could feel better. We've got an Itch.

Dictionaries define the word *itch* as a peculiar tingling or irritation that causes a desire to scratch. An Itch can also be a desire to do or get something, an uneasy restless longing. Our lives are full of Itches. They make us want to scratch, to relegate the Itch to the past.

Throughout history human beings have done amazing things in response to Itches. The European migration to the Americas is a history of Itches being scratched, from Columbus's encounter with Arawak natives on the island he called San Salvador to the separatist Puritan colony at Plymouth, Massachusetts, to the waves of Irish, German, Jewish, and Russian immigrants that followed. All were scratching Itches: Itches for trade, Itches for freedom, Itches for a better life.

The first substep of What's Going On? is What's the Itch? Here we investigate the need for the new idea in the first place. What's wrong, what could be better, what's out of balance, what needs improvement?

Sometimes Itches are obvious, like Edwin Land's concern about the future of his company. Nevertheless, there's always a danger of leaping to the first Itch that occurs to you. You can't begin solving your puzzle by picking out a single piece. You have to dump out all the pieces so you can see what's there. It's easy to assume that you know what the problem is simply because your thought patterns lead you toward some "obvious" (and possibly incorrect) conclusion. By listing a wide range of possible Itches, you give yourself a better chance to understand the real issue you need to address rather than something that doesn't get to the heart of the matter.

● ● ●

Even when working with clients who are certain they know their Itch, I encourage them to think divergently here, in other words, to make long lists of their possible itches. Like the doctor who wants to be sure she prescribes the right treatment, we need to understand not only the presenting symptoms but the underlying condition.

Begin exploring your issue by making a long list of possible Itches. None of them have to be justified. None have to be clearly defined. None even have to be particularly important. You're looking for nothing more than a broad list of possibilities.

Don't analyze. Don't discuss. Just list. At this early stage, trying to go deeper than that is like trying to write a final draft of a book or a business plan on the first go. The task becomes so daunting that you have a hard time even starting, let alone getting it right.

●　　●　　●

One of the major barriers to productive thinking is the almost compulsive drive in most business organizations to be right. We're often so concerned with getting the "right" answer, defining the "right" problem, or finding the "right" cause that we clam up like an actor with stage fright. I've attended countless so-called problem-solving meetings in which no one offers any ideas for fear they may suggest something that's wrong.

We can also be so focused on finding the "big" problem, the "root" cause, or the "seminal" concern that we overlook all the seemingly mundane issues that, if we addressed them, might reduce the Itch in the first place.

At this stage, take off your judge's robe, put down your gavel, and give yourself permission to be in total contempt of court. Just vent. It's productive, it gets the idea balls rolling, and it's fun.

Ask questions that begin to elicit possible Itches, such as the following: What's bugging you? What's out of balance? What needs to be resolved? What could be improved? What would you like to change? What would you like to see different? What challenges are you facing? What do you wish worked better? If your Itch were a T-shirt slogan, what would it say?

Look for Itches that are implicit as well as explicit. Does one Itch imply another? Is there an overarching Itch that may contain a number of the other Itches in your list? Are there any hidden Itches, Itches that you haven't named because they are too painful, too embarrassing, too politically incorrect?

In listing your Itches, your purpose is not to be organized or smart or even clear. What you're doing is dumping as many possible Itches on the table as you can, just like those jigsaw puzzle pieces, so you can begin to look at them. Once you've done that, you can begin to sense which ones resonate with you, which ones feel most important, which ones you really want to address.

Edwin Land's long list of Itches might have looked like this:

- There's no way to support 1,250 employees at our prewar production levels.
- We're so focused on the defense effort that we've let other research and development efforts suffer.
- We can't translate our defense products into things that will be useful for consumers.
- We haven't thought about consumer products in years.
- The company has expanded beyond what we can sustain with our prewar business.
- The products we do have may be out of date.
- We've lost the ability to develop consumer products.
- We don't have a rational approach to downsizing.
- We don't have a plan for pursuing postwar government contracts.
- We need to start thinking about new product opportunities now.
- We need to start looking at other opportunities for government contracts.
- We need to get back to the business of inventing.
- I don't feel challenged anymore.
- We've always been about inventing things; we're not inventing things anymore.
- We need to figure out how to reconnect with what people really want.

Once you have listed all your possible Itches, the next step is to narrow them down, to converge on the ones that seem most important. With long lists of Itches, one of the best ways to do this is to start by grouping or clustering the items on the list. In much the same way you would do with a jigsaw puzzle, sort your Itches into thematic groups. That way, you can begin to see the constellation of Itches that are driving you.

Edwin Land might have grouped his 15 Itch statements into the following clusters:

Itches relating to new business conditions

- There's no way to support 1,250 employees at our prewar production levels.
- The company has expanded beyond what we can sustain with our prewar business.
- The products we do have may be out of date.
- We don't have a rational approach to downsizing.

Itches relating to a government client

- We can't translate our defense products into things that will be useful for consumers.
- We don't have a plan for pursuing postwar government contracts.
- We need to start looking at other opportunities for government contracts.

Itches relating to how we've changed

- We're so focused on the defense effort that we've let other research and development efforts suffer.
- We haven't thought about consumer products in years.
- We've lost the ability to develop consumer products.
- We've always been about inventing things; we're not inventing things anymore.

Itches relating to the company's roots

- We need to figure out how to reconnect with what people really want.
- I don't feel challenged anymore.
- We need to get back to the business of inventing.
- We need to start thinking about new product opportunities now.

By clustering your list of Itches, you can gain a clearer perspective on the issue as a whole. If you first list and then organize various ways of expressing the Itch, the many different and sometimes even conflicting thoughts begin to make sense. Rather than being single points in an uncharted sky, the Itches begin to form constellations, some bright and prominent, others more dim and peripheral. After only a few minutes of thought, what began as "How can the company sustain itself after the defense contracts expire?" becomes a much richer expression of what's really going on. Clustering your list of Itches is like climbing a hill to get your bearings before moving on in any direction. From the height, you can see much more than you saw on the ground.

> *This process of diverging to make lists and converging to make choices is the heart of the Productive Thinking Model.*

Now you are in a position to make some meaningful choices. Which specific Itch or cluster of Itches do you feel most strongly about? Which resonates most for you? Which floats to the top? Which do you think would be most satisfying to resolve? How might you feel if it is *not* resolved?

If Land had made clusters like these, he might have identified his real issue as *I'm not connected with the joy of inventing for customers anymore.* That was the real Itch. If he could resolve that, everything else would likely fall into place.

In this first substep of What's Going On? I hope you can see the value of beginning with divergent, creative thinking—in other words, making lists—followed by convergent, critical thinking—in other words, making choices. This process of diverging to make lists and converging to make choices is the heart of the Productive Thinking Model.

Substep 2: What's the Impact?

The next step in figuring out what's going on is to focus on the impact of the Itch. To do that, you need to ask a series of simple questions. Again, the process centers on making long lists and then making choices. The key is to generate as many ideas as possible. To understand the impact of your Itches, ask questions such as the following: What concerns you about this situation? Is it a priority? If so, why? What's your gut feeling? Why did you choose the Itch or cluster of Itches that you did? What makes your Itches important to you? How do they affect you? How else do they affect you?

Land might have stated his impacts this way: *I no longer have the satisfaction of doing what I love to do. Being disconnected from customers is also an economic threat. It's important because inventing has always been the lifeblood of Polaroid. Unless I can find a way to reconnect Polaroid to its roots, the company may lose its reason for being.*

Look for the obvious. Then look beyond the obvious. When you think about your Itches, how do you feel about them? How do you feel about yourself? What emotions can you name? What other issues make you feel the same way? Might there be a relationship between those issues? If so, what is it?

Once you have generated a long list of impacts, choose the ones that are most significant to you, the ones you feel most strongly about. The final short list of impacts should give you a good sense of why your Itch is important to you. The more clearly you see the impacts and ramifications of your Itch, the more likely you are to develop the energy and passion you will need to resolve it.

Substep 3: What's the Information?

Now that you have selected an Itch and understand its importance to you, the next step is to articulate what you know about it already and what you need to find out. To help you do that, I'd like to introduce you to a powerful thinking tool called KnoWonder. KnoWonder lets you quickly and easily generate useful perspectives on any issue you want to explore.

KnoWonder is deceptively simple. Take a large sheet of paper, the bigger the better. Flip chart paper is ideal. Draw a vertical line down the center, dividing the sheet in half. At the top, label the left half "Know" and the right half "Wonder."

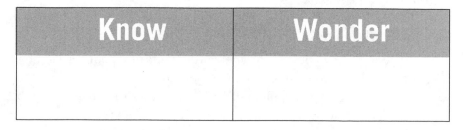

Know	Wonder

Start with the left half, and using divergent, creative thinking, list all the things you know about your Itch. If you run out of ideas, cue yourself by asking specific questions: What resources are involved: money, time, energy, material? What might be causing the situation? Why does it exist? What might be perpetuating it? Do other people or organizations experience similar Itches? Who? Why? How have they responded to it? Are there people or organizations that don't experience similar Itches? Why might that be? Have you attempted to resolve the Itch before? What have you tried? What have others tried? What happened? What worked? What didn't? What obstacles got in the way?

When you run out of steam listing what you know, move to the Wonder side of the sheet. What do you wonder about the Itch and the situation surrounding it? List all the things you don't know but would like to know. Write down anything that comes to mind. It's easy to convince yourself that a wonder isn't worth recording just because you think it would be difficult or even impossible to find the answer. But answers aren't as important as questions at this point. What do you wonder about your Itch? Be as exhaustive as you can.

Now look at your list and use convergent, critical thinking to select those items—ones that you know and ones you need to find out—that are most important to a comprehensive understanding of your Itch.

By the time you've finished even a brief KnoWonder exercise, you should have a robust list of the things you understand about your Itch and the things you don't understand. You have constructed a useful information platform on which to build.

One of the most powerful aspects of the Productive Thinking Model and its tools is that it makes your thinking visible. Not only can you see your output, you can compare it with the thinking and perspectives of others. In our work with clients, we often use KnoWonder to see where people in work teams agree and where they differ on the "facts" surrounding an issue.

Substep 4: Who's Involved?

How we see things depends on where we stand: our point of view. A machine may be a productivity enhancement tool to a businessperson, a way of manifesting code to a programmer, collateral to a banker, or a job threat to a labor leader. It all depends on your point of view.

So far you've looked at your Itch from where you stand. Now you need to change perspective. It's unlikely that you will be the only person affected by the Itch or the only person who influences it. Who else is involved in or affected by your Itch? In other words, who are your stakeholders and what's at stake for each of them?

Again, you start by generating long lists. List all the people or groups with influence over the issue. List all the people or groups affected by the issue. List what is or may be at stake for each one. How are they affected by the Itch? What's in it for them if things stay the same? What's in it for them if things change? How would they describe the Itch? How would they see it? The same way you do? A little differently? Completely at odds with your view? Then ask yourself who *else* might be affected by the Itch. What might be at stake for them?

Edwin Land's long list of stakeholders and what was at stake for them might have looked something like this:

- *Polaroid's employees*. For many, their livelihoods might be at stake; unless new markets can be found, they may lose their jobs.

- *Company shareholders, financiers, and lenders*. They would want healthy investments; most probably they would favor a conservative approach, perhaps trying to extend existing contracts.

- *Polaroid's suppliers with a financial stake*. They would almost certainly favor finding a way to continue the status quo.

- *His family*. Financial security would be an issue, but so would be recapturing the sense of adventure that had infused the company in the early years.

- *Customers*. Ah, there is a big unknown. More and more, customers were wanting something new, something different, but what?

- *Potential customers*. If he could create a new category, as he had with his specialized sunglasses, he might be able to create a whole new market. Surely there would be pent-up consumer demand in a postwar economy.

- *Polaroid's existing defense client*. Might there be any restrictions on what he could or could not do now that his company had become privy to classified information?

- *Possible technical partners*. Developing new products would undoubtedly involve relationships with outside suppliers. Perhaps there were ways of sharing the investment risks inherent in any new venture.

- *Potential competitors*. Any new development would almost certainly involve market disruption, as had his sunglasses. The company would need to understand and deal with competitive pressures and responses.

As in each of the previous substeps of What's Going On? the next part of the process is to look at the long list and select the items that seem most significant.

Land's short list of stakeholders might have looked like this:

- Polaroid's employees
- Company shareholders
- His family
- Customers
- Potential customers

Moving from the Present to the Future

So far all your work in this step of the productive thinking process has been an attempt to describe What's Going On? in the present. Now you need to picture a future in which your issue is resolved.

Suppose, for example, you are responsible for a team of people who are having difficulty communicating effectively. After thinking about the various aspects of what's going on, you converge on a description something like this: *The environment is unproductive. Performance is slipping. It looks like no one is enjoying being at work. People often come in late, leave early, and take long lunch breaks. A lack of trust has crept into the team, and it's self-perpetuating. People are becoming increasingly protective about information they hold. Their reluctance to share it only exacerbates the situation. If things don't change soon, the group is heading for a death spiral. I'm worried about how this situation might affect my career.*

These are all statements about a present condition. They describe things as they are, at least from your point of view. But as important as it is to see what's going on, it's unlikely that merely understanding the situation will do much to improve it. If you're interested in change, you need to develop a sense of *possibility*. One of the most useful ways to do that is to generate a range of desirable futures in which the Itch doesn't exist anymore.

Substep 5: What's the Vision?

The final substep in What's Going On? is to establish a vision for the future. In the Productive Thinking Model we call this vision the Target Future. The Target Future is the place you want to get to. It doesn't tell you how you'll get there; in other words, it is not a solution. Rather, it is a brief description of a future in which your issue is resolved and your Itch no longer irritates you.

It would be great if there was a smile on everyone's face when they came to work!

Here's how to search for a Target Future. Using all the thinking you've done about your issue, you employ divergent, creative thinking to list as many itchless futures as you can. It's not important that these futures be realistic or even make sense. What's important is to capture the dream. When I work with client groups, I often suggest that they use a series of stem, or starter, phrases to get their creative thinking going. The phrases I've found to be most useful are "It would be great if. . . ," "I wish . . . ," and "If only. . . ."

The "It would be great if . . ." stem is designed to stimulate musings or daydreams about possible Target Futures: the places you want to get to. A musing about the dysfunctional team described above might be "It would be great if there was a smile on everyone's face when they came to work!" or "It would be great if work was so enjoyable that we were constantly surprised how quickly the day seemed to end!" or "It would be great if I felt that my contributions really made a difference!"

The "I wish . . ." stem is designed to stimulate more tangible Target Futures. Examples might be "I wish we were as effective as the people in account management seem to be!" or "I wish our processes weren't so redundant!" or "I wish I didn't get everyone's voice mail every time I tried to call them!"

The "If only . . ." stem is designed to elicit Target Futures in terms of overcoming frustrations. In the dysfunctional team example, this stem might generate statements such as "If only people recognized the contribution I make around here!" or "If only we didn't have to redo things six times before we got them right!" or "If only management had some sense of how complex this job is!"

Using these three stems, generate as many Target Futures as possible. The source for these statements is the depth and breadth of thinking you've already done. Target Future statements can be stimulated by your initial list of Itches, by your descriptions of how the Itches affect you, by your KnoWonder lists, and even by the kinds of futures your key stakeholders might want. Additional useful statement starters are phrases such as the following: "What I'd really like to see is . . . ," "What this place really needs is . . . ," and "It would really make my day if . . . ," among others. There are as many statement starters as there are ways of dreaming about a better tomorrow. The key, as always, is to generate as many ideas as you can. The longer your list is, the more likely you are to find a Target Future worth aiming for.

Note that some of the statements in this list contradict one another ("It would be great if we could reengage with our roots" and "If only we could get contracts with other government agencies"). Others aren't realistic ("If only the bankers would just go away"). Still others are only fleeting thoughts that probably don't reflect Land's core values ("I wish I could sell the company"). Consistency, realism, and even core values are unimportant when it comes to generating lists like this. Remember, to generate long lists, you have to defer judgment. You can always eliminate the inappropriate later, when you return to your list to think about it critically. What's important here is the freewheeling generation of future states in the hope that one of them may be the Target Future you'd like to aim for.

Land's Target Future

Here's an excerpt of what Land's Target Future list might have looked like:

- I wish we could get back to the business of inventing!
- If only we could avoid laying people off after the war!
- It would be great if everyone would buy 16 pair of sunglasses!
- It would be great if I could feel the same sense of challenge I used to feel!
- If only we could roll our government contracts over into peacetime pursuits!
- It would be great if we could reengage with our roots!
- I wish I could sell the company!
- It would be great if the automobile industry would demand polarized windshields!
- If only the bankers would just go away!
- I wish we could reengage with consumers!
- If only I could find a product as innovative and compelling as our polarized lenses!
- I wish I could demonstrate a smooth transition plan to our financial backers!
- If only the government came up with postwar financing for its contractors to make the transition!
- It would be great if we could embark on something now so that we'll be ready when the war ends!
- If only we could get contracts with other government agencies!

Converging on a Vision: Sighting your Target

Once you've generated a long list of potential Target Futures, the next step is to select one or two that you have the energy to work on now. The most effective tool I know of to do this is I^3.[1] I^3 allows you to determine which items on your list will be useful to work on .I^3 stands for the three criteria you use to evaluate the items in your list: *Influence, Importance,* and *Imagination.* Here's how it works.

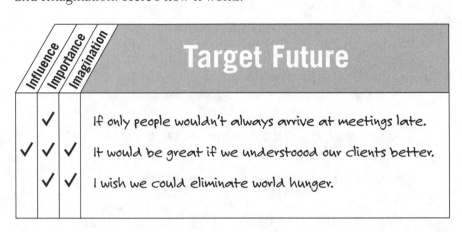

After generating a long list of potential Target Futures, draw three narrow columns to the left of the list. The first is for Influence. Place a check mark next to each item in the list over which you have influence. If the Target Future is completely out of your control, you may not want to spend time or energy on it. Be careful here, though, because you may have more influence than you think. In some cases you may not have complete control over an Itch but may have a degree of influence. At this early stage, it's better to err on the side of optimism. If you have some influence but not complete control, note that.

The second column is for Importance. Place a check mark next to each item in the list that is important to you. Do you care enough to put in the work it will take to get there? If your Target Future addresses an Itch that's only a minor or occasional irritation, you may not want to devote a lot of energy to resolving it. Be sure that you are really motivated to get to your Target Future and that you'll have the energy to carry through with your solution. In the words of the great nineteenth-century architect and city planner Daniel H. Burnham, "Make no little plans; they have no magic to stir men's blood." Your blood needs to be stirred a bit. As with Influence, you will often discover that there are degrees of Importance. Don't overthink these distinctions at this point. Trust your gut. Is this important? If so, check it. If not, let it go for the time being.

The third column is for Imagination. Place a check mark next to each Target Future that might require some imagination to achieve. If it will be served by new thinking or an imaginative solution, it deserves a check. But if you think there may be an off-the-shelf solution available, you may be better off simply going to that shelf. Many business problems are amenable to so-called best practices. Again, be cautious. Just because an off-the-shelf solution is available, that doesn't mean it's the *best* solution available. Ask yourself whether you might want a solution that worked better, faster, or more cheaply than a ready-made solution. If you think so, check the third "I".

Your Target Future is the platform for all the rest of your thinking as you move through the productive thinking process.

If one or more of your Target Futures has check marks in all three columns—if you've answered yes to all three I questions—there's a good chance you will benefit from applying the Productive Thinking Model. If your answer to any of these questions is no, you may want to think about redefining your Target Future in a way that does meet the I^3 criteria or working on a different challenge.

Your final step is to choose the Target Future you'd like to work on now. Review all the statements that you have influence over, that are genuinely important to you, and that might benefit from imaginative, novel thinking. If more than one Target Future meets all three criteria, choose the one you have the most energy to work on now.

Don't be concerned about the Target Futures you leave behind. They haven't disappeared. You can always come back to work on them later. Many of my clients keep running lists of Target Futures. You can too. In reviewing them over time, you may find that a Target Future you initially felt was unimportant has become more relevant to your life or business or that a Target Future over which you had little or no influence is now one over which you have a great deal of influence.

Once you've selected a Target Future to work on, rewrite it in a way that will motivate you to get there. The way you phrase your selected Target Future is significant. Your Target Future is the platform for all the rest of your thinking as you move through the productive thinking process. As I mentioned in Chapter 2, thinking is the hardest work there is. It can be exhausting, and it can be frustrating. Thinking an issue through requires both emotional and physical stamina. If you phrase your Target Future in a way that doesn't pull you forward, you may not be able to sustain the energy you need to achieve success. Target Futures stated as "to get fit" or "to increase profit" or "to find the perfect job" are not particularly galvanizing. You'll find it's far more engaging, motivating, and productive to use the whole Target Future statement, including the stems you used to generate it and a little punctuation as well. "It would be great if I loved going to work every day!" Note the exclamation point. Give it the energy of an exclamation. "What this company needs is to make more money!" Build motivation into your language. After all, you do want to reach that Target Future, don't you? "If only I could find that perfect job!"

What's important is the freewheeling generation of future states in the hope that one of them may be the Target Future you'd like to aim for.

So how might Edwin Land have expressed his Target Future? It might have sounded something like this: *It would be great if I could invent something that really got my passion going again, something that had the potential to hit a home run with the public!* A Target Future like that would really be worth aiming for. Achieving it would certainly take care of those Itches.

●   ●   ●

For me, one of the great things about Land's story is how his Itch and his daughter's Itch intersected. Little Jennifer Land, who wanted to see her pictures now instead of later, gave her father the perfect vehicle to drive toward his Target Future. Now *there* was an Itch to scratch: instant pictures! *It would be great if a camera could produce instant pictures!* It didn't take long for Land to realize that he could probably make one.

In doing so, he transformed both his company and the way millions of people around the world experienced the special moments in their lives.

In recalling the shower of ideas pouring through his mind that day, Land said, "It was as if all that we had done in learning to make polarizers . . . had been a school and a preparation for the first day in which I suddenly knew how to make a one step dry photographic process."

No doubt it was a great moment, but it was only one of many possible moments. I find it fascinating that once Land had formulated his Target Future for Polaroid, instant photography was only one of many possible ways to get there. The idea of resolving Jennifer's Itch was exciting, but hers wasn't the only Itch. After all, Polaroid had been in the business of bending light for years. What if Land had been struck by the sun's reflection off his hotel window melting a patch of snow on an adjoining roof? He might have thought, "Wouldn't it be something if we could concentrate light so effectively that it could melt steel!" He might have gone on to create a laser more than 10 years before it was first demonstrated at Hughes Research Laboratories. What if the sparkling snow had reminded him of semaphore signal lamps and caused him to think of the ability of light to carry information? He might have thought, "If only we could use concentrated light to carry information faster and better than telephone cables!" He might have gone on to develop optical fibers over 20 years before they were produced by Corning Glass Works. Or might he have imagined something else completely, something that hasn't even been invented yet.

SUMMARY

What's Going On? consists of five substeps, each phrased as a key question and each with a list-making phase and a choice-making phase.

> **What's the Itch?** What needs changing?
>
> - List as many ways of expressing the Itch or Itches as time allows.
> - Cluster to reveal themes and relationships among the various statements of the Itch.
> - Choose the most compelling Itch or cluster of Itches to work on.

What's the Impact? Why is it important?

- List why and how the Itch affects you.
- Choose the most important impacts.

What's the Information? What do you need to know?

- List (using KnoWonder) all the things you know and all the things you wonder about the Itch.
- Choose the most important items.

Who's Involved? Who are the stakeholders?

- List all the stakeholders and potential stakeholders for the Itch and what is at stake for each one.
- Choose the most important stakeholders.

What's the Vision? What is your Target Future?

- List as many potential Target Futures as time allows.
- Review all your potential Target Futures and select all that meet the I^3 (Influence, Importance, Imagination) criteria.
- Select three to five potential Target Futures that are the most important or compelling.
- Select the one Target Future (or combination of Target Futures) to work on now.
- Restate the selected Target Future in a powerful, energizing way that motivates you to achieve it.

What's Going On? seeds the rest of the productive thinking process. The desired outcomes of this step are a comprehensive context for further thinking and an articulation of a compelling Target Future.

T.T.T

What's Going On? is one of the longer steps in the productive thinking process. Whenever I'm tempted to rush through it instead of carefully examining all those puzzle pieces, I remind myself of a poem by the great Danish scientist, mathematician, inventor, author, and poet Piet Hein. Hein dispensed his wisdom in delightful little word packets. This is one of my favorites.

Put up in a place
where it's easy to see
the cryptic admonishment
T.T.T.
When you feel how depressingly
slowly you climb,
it's well to remember that
Things Take Time.[2]

Finding out what's going on, discovering the real Itch, setting the context for thinking, and establishing a compelling Target Future—all these things take time. Don't shortchange this step. You may find yourself champing at the bit to get to solutions. But the purpose here is to start slow and steady in order to finish fast and strong.

What's Going On? provides the foundation on which you will build your entire thinking structure. Thus, it's important to immerse yourself in it. In some cases, a robust What's Going On? session, followed by a period of mental incubation (going for a walk, "sleeping on it," or simply turning your attention to other things for a while), may be all you need to solve your problem or come up with a brilliant new idea.[3] In most cases, though, you'll want to use the insights you've gained to continue to work through the process. Once you have articulated a compelling Target Future, you're ready to move to the next productive thinking step, What's Success?, which establishes the success criteria against which you will measure the solutions you eventually design.

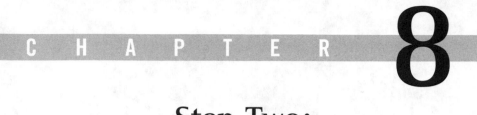

Step Two:
What's Success?

We can see the past but not influence it.
We can influence the future but not see it.

Stewart Brand (1938–)

Step Two: What's Success?

The Future Pull Principle

He wasn't a big man physically, only five feet, six and a half inches tall. But on August 28, 1963, when the 34-year-old preacher from Atlanta stood on the steps of the Lincoln Memorial in Washington DC, and addressed the 200,000 people who had gathered there, he set in motion a chain of events that would change his nation forever. The words he spoke that day have come to be known as the "I Have a Dream" speech, ranked by many scholars as the most important American speech of the twentieth century.[1]

Martin Luther King, Jr., knew the power of dreams. In eight years of marches, protests, and other forms of activism after Rosa Parks had been arrested for refusing to give up her seat on a Montgomery, Alabama, city bus, King and his fellow civil rights leaders had made some progress in promoting their vision—their Target Future—that black people in the United States would have the same rights and freedoms as whites. But in the 15 minutes he spoke to the crowd, King transformed that Target Future into a robust dream. He imagined for his audience not just a future defined by the abstract terms *rights* and *freedoms* but a future they could see, hear, smell, taste, and feel. According to U.S. Representative John Lewis, "By speaking the way he did, he educated, he inspired, he informed not just the people there, but people throughout America and unborn generations."[2]

Within 18 months of Dr. King's speech, the U.S. Congress passed both the Civil Rights Act, which outlawed discrimination on the basis of race, and the National Voting Rights Act, which enfranchised millions of Americans who had been denied the right to vote.

King knew the power of dreams. With his speech he created not simply a goal but what I think of as *Future Pull*, a vision of the future so powerful, so compelling, and so real that it literally pulls us toward it.

In a sense, Step 2 of the Productive Thinking Model is like King's speech. Its purpose is to create Future Pull.

Once you know what you want your Target Future to be, you need to figure out how you'll know when you've gotten there. That's the purpose of the second step in the productive thinking process. What's Success? takes your embryonic idea of what the Target Future should be and enhances it in two ways: by painting a compelling picture of what that future might be and by establishing criteria that will help you determine whether the solution you've chosen will help you get there.

I don't know what the statistics are, but I do know that almost everyone who's worked in an organization that has gone through a change program will be able to relate to some version of the following scenario. After much studying and reporting, much to-ing and fro-ing, and much Sturm und Drang—sometimes by specially convened internal cross-functional teams, sometimes by external big box consulting gurus, and sometimes by the boss's spouse—the (drum roll please) *New Horizons* (or similarly named) change document appears. Sometimes it's a manifesto, sometimes a new strategic plan, sometimes a sheaf of inserts for the policy and procedures manual, sometimes an executive directive, and sometimes just an e-mail. It's often accompanied by pithy slogans, revamped nomenclature, PowerPoint presentations, change management manuals, carefully calculated metrics, revised accountabilities, and of course meetings—lots of meetings.

After the initial wave of chills moves through the organization, people look at the proposed changes and generally settle on one of five positions:

- Things were fine before. I don't see what good any of this is going to do.

- Anything would be better than the way things are now.

- Not as good as I'd hoped but not as bad as I'd feared. In fact, some of these ideas are okay.

- This is the (you fill in the ordinal number) (you fill in the expletive) change program we've had in the last (you fill in the cardinal number) years!

- There goes my workload again.

But regardless of which camp they are in, most people will also think the following:

- *It'll never stick.*

And most often, most people will be right.

Behaviors, whether individual or group, are like organisms in an ecosystem. They have an inexorable urge to survive. They cause us to do anything to thwart their extinction, from feigned compliance to overt resistance, from seduction to subversion, from passive aggression to hibernation. No matter how dysfunctional the present, no matter how sensible the reasons for change, most people and organizations would rather wring out the old than ring in the new. Old behaviors are hard to kill. As a result, even the most well-intentioned and well-conceived change initiatives simply don't stick.

No matter how dysfunctional the present, no matter how sensible the reasons for change, most people and organizations would rather wring out the old than ring in the new.

Earlier in this book I talked about the power of patterning. You can see how powerful these patterns are every day and in every area of your life. We are constantly drawn to repeat old ways of seeing, old ways of doing things. One way to characterize this is to think of it as the gravitational pull of the past. Anyone who has worked in an organization knows how inexorable that gravitational pull can be. It's as though the past had a Jupiter-strength gravitational field: Make a change, and before you know it, the past pulls you back.[3] Whether organizationally or individually, we human beings are very comfortable with our patterns. After all, we've spent a lifetime developing them. It's only natural that we have difficulty letting them go. So how can new ideas escape the gravitational pull of the past?

The answer is Future Pull. In describing the first step of the Productive Thinking Model, What's Going On?, in Chapter 7, I introduced the concept of a Target Future. One reason for using that term is that the meaning we ascribe to the word *objective* is so variable. Six people will have seven different senses of what "objective" means. But that's not the only reason. Objectives are cold. They're *objective*! They don't have much emotional pull. Unless a potential future incorporates a powerful emotional pull, it will have great difficulty overcoming the gravitational pull of the past. The simplest way to create emotional pull is to convert the objective into the subjective, and the easiest way to do that is to create a vision of a Target Future that is so real, so compelling, so desirable that people actually want to reach it.

The purpose of What's Success? is to create Future Pull: to make you care. Deeply. I like to think of this phase of the Productive Thinking Model as throwing a grappling hook into the future. You wind up and hurl that hook into the most compelling future you can imagine. It latches on firmly, and then you start to pull yourself into that future. That's creating Future Pull.

In practice, you create Future Pull in two ways: by imagining how it might feel if you actually achieved your Target Future and by establishing observable Success Criteria so that you can recognize your destination once you get there. The power of Future Pull lies in creating a compelling vision that literally pulls you toward solutions.

Imagining the Future

One of the most useful tools to establish Future Pull is the Imagined Future (IF) excursion. You can use IF excursions to generate what it would be like if you succeeded in resolving your Itch and reaching your Target Future. To conduct an IF exercise, you begin with divergent, creative thinking. You suspend judgment and try to generate a long list of ideas about what your Imagined Future might be like: how it might it look, sound, smell, taste, and feel. Once you've generated a long list, you use convergent, critical thinking to choose the ideas that are most meaningful to you.

Here's how IF works: Tell yourself a story about a day in the life of your Imagined Future. Be as vivid and sensory as possible. The more robust your description is, the more compelling it will be for you. Don't worry about what's realistic or not realistic. Just imagine the ideal future you would like to see. What would life feel like if you achieved your Target Future? How would your workplace feel? How might your relationships change: with your work, your colleagues, your family? What might your friends and family think of you? What might you think of yourself?

IF (Imagined Future)

Close your eyes and imagine actually being in the future you've targeted. Imagine waking up in the morning, arriving at your place of work, greeting the people you meet. Imagine how it feels to be at your workstation. What is in your in box? What implications does that have for your day?

Imagine the meetings you attend throughout the day. Are they any different from the meetings you attend now? Imagine your telephone and e-mail interactions. What are your customers or clients saying? What has changed for them?

Now imagine your workday winding down. How might you spend your evening? Who would you spend it with? What would you do? Finally, imagine ending your day, thinking about the kind of day it was. How do you feel about it?

Once you've gone through your imaginary excursion, open your eyes and begin writing. Describe your journey. Write down everything and anything that comes to you. Be as vivid as you can, describing how it might be to live in a world in which you've resolved your Itch and achieved your Target Future.

You may not feel comfortable playing with your thoughts this way. Nevertheless, I encourage you to try. One of the keys to breaking out of the patterns we are locked into is to stretch our imaginations. As Einstein said, "Imagination is more important than knowledge." Giving ourselves permission to imagine allows us to access a huge resource of cognitive capacity that we often ignore. Isn't it true that some of your best ideas are the ones you have in your shower or while you're driving? Those ideas occur to you because you've let go of your inhibitions. The ideas flow because your gatekeeper is taking a smoke break. Try giving your gatekeeper a whole day off. You might be surprised what you discover. The irony is that sometimes we think better by "thinking" less. Mark Twain captured this when he wrote, "You can't depend on your judgment when your imagination is out of focus." I highly recommend daydreaming!

Here are some other approaches to conducting an Imagined Future exercise:

- Project what your company's annual report might say once the Target Future has been achieved. What does

the message from the CEO say? What do the finan-
cials look like?

- Write a future press release announcing the launch of
  your new product, service, or initiative.

- Review the way you described your Itch and its
  impacts; then invert those statements to describe a
  future in which the Itch has been resolved. For example, in step 1 you might have said, "It really bugs
  me when I wade through an endless telephone tree
  for service and then, when I finally get to the department I want, hear, 'Due to an unexpected level of
  calls, all our service associates are currently busy.'" In
  your Imagined Future, you might write, "Whenever I
  call, I immediately get through to a human being
  who actually knows my name and seems ready to
  help me."

*Unless a potential future incorporates a powerful
emotional pull, it will have great difficulty
overcoming the gravitational inertia of the past.*

Whatever technique you use, your purpose is to generate a
description so powerful and compelling that you are motivated to do
whatever it takes to get to your Target Future. Your intent is to make it as
desirable as possible. It's just a short trip from imaging your compelling
future to developing the aspiration to achieve it. The word *aspire* literally
means to pant with desire. How many obstacles could you overcome if
you were literally panting with desire to achieve your future? How creative could you be in figuring out how to get there? How committed
would you be to trying? In a sense, Future Pull is using aspiration to create inspiration.

What if you're not there yet? What if despite conducting your
Imagined Future exercise, you haven't ignited the aspiration that can
lead to inspiration? If you haven't caught fire yet, there are several possible causes and several useful remedies:

- You may have been too conservative in choosing your Target Future in What's Going On? Maybe you haven't aimed high enough. Review both your Itches and your Target Futures to see if there's more of a stretch target for you to reach.

- You may have conducted your Imagined Future excursion into areas of your life that have little to do with your Itch and your Target Future. Your daydreams may have carried you far afield or been too confined. (One of the great things about daydreams is that there's no telling where they'll lead you). If your excursion was too far removed from your Itch, try again, making an effort to focus on things directly relating to the resolution of your Itch.

- You may not be comfortable imagining and writing down your thoughts. If so, try talking out your Imagined Future. Ask someone to prompt you, using the kinds of questions I listed above. Record the session so that you can review your thoughts later. Instruct your interviewer to ask lots of "why" questions, such as "Why do you say that?" and "Why is that important to you?" These questions can give you both the opportunity and permission to go a deeper, to the essence of how you think or feel about an issue.[4]

- You may be the wrong person. Achieving the Target Future may be more meaningful to others than it is to you. In Step 1, you probably identified several stakeholders. Find out how they might feel about it. Ask your coworkers or your spouse, your children, or your customers how they might imagine a future in which the Itch has been resolved.

In whatever way you've managed to generate a long list describing a future that's worth achieving, the final part of the Imagined Future exercise is to use convergent, critical thinking to highlight the most compelling words or phrases: the ones that resonate most strongly with you. Don't worry if those words seem difficult to calibrate. Remember, it's not only the practical, measurable criteria you'll want your eventual solution to meet but those softer ones as well. If your Target Future involves driving an economical, environmentally friendly, aesthetically appealing car, for example, only two of your three criteria may be measurable. The third, aesthetically appealing, criterion is purely subjective. Yet all three may be equally important to you. Intangibles are important. As Einstein said, "Not everything that counts can be counted, and not everything that can be counted counts."

The Peril of Logic

In a sense, your Imagined Future is your dream of how things might be. Like a dream, it shouldn't be constrained by reality. In establishing Future Pull, don't worry about what's rational, what's logical, or even what's possible. In lamenting a colleague's resistance to a theory he was postulating, the Nobel physicist Niels Bohr reportedly said, "No, no, you're not thinking, you're just being logical." Often the unreasonable is exactly what you need. In the JetWays example in Chapter 6, the airline was looking for ways to differentiate itself as it expanded its market. The least desirable seats on an airplane are the middle seats. If JetWays could somehow enhance the value of the middle seats on its planes, it might have a shot at attracting and retaining more passengers. The Imagined Future statement generated by the JetWays innovation team might have been something like this:

> *When people think of flying, they think of JetWays first. One of the reasons is that we offer the best middle seats in the world. Our passengers consider them to be the best seats on the plane. They are so good that customers actually compete for them. They signify prestige. When people choose to fly us, they always feel they've made the best choice. In fact, people often fly our planes just for the pleasure of it, even if they have nowhere to go. JetWays middle seats offer business and pleasure travelers an experience like no other.*

Although the whole statement offers a compelling vision for the company, the most important sentence in the Imagined Future is the one that's the least realistic: *In fact, people often fly our planes just for the pleasure of it, even if they have nowhere to go.* It's absurd to think that passengers will jump aboard JetWays' planes just to fly around in circles, and everyone involved in creating the IF statement knows it. But imagine how great an airline seat would have to be even to contemplate such an outcome! The Imagined Future doesn't have to be real or logical or achievable. All it has to do is pull you into the future. That's its purpose.

The concept of Future Pull reminds me of a game, popular throughout Europe, known as bocce or pétanque. The game is usually played with two teams standing outside a real or imaginary circle.[5] To begin each round, one of the team members throws a target ball or a jack somewhere in the circle. The object of the game is for each player to toss a playing ball as close to the target ball as possible. At the end of the round, the team whose ball is closest scores a point for each ball closer than the opponents' best ball.

Giving ourselves permission to imagine allows us to access a huge resource of cognitive capacity that we often ignore.

There's an odd thing about bocce. In most games, such as basketball, darts, or soccer, it's possible to achieve the goal of getting your missile through the hoop, into the bull's-eye, or through the net. In bocce, it is physically impossible for a playing ball to land smack dab on top of the target ball. It just can't happen. Either the playing ball will roll off, or it will push the target ball away. One thing it won't do is balance on top of it. Thus, in bocce it is impossible to hit the target, *yet without the target there is no game!* It's the same with the concept of Future Pull. It may not be possible to get exactly where you want to go, but without the target there is no game.

Driving for Success

In 1986 a young British commercial artist who specialized in drawing cartoon crowd scenes for clients had the idea of publishing his illustrations in book form. His idea was to depict humorous crowd scenes in various locations, including a beach, a train station, a sports stadium, a museum, a department store, and a county fair. To create a unifying theme for the many crowd scenes, he invented the character of a backpacking tourist who would appear in each location. In the original British editions of the book, the character's name was Wally. The artist, Martin Handford, went on to publish seven more *Where's Wally* books, create a television show, syndicate a comic strip, and license several video games. Even though the fad declined in the late 1990s, there is still occasional talk of a Wally movie. Wally is licensed in at least 17 countries, where he looks pretty much the same but often goes by different names. In the United States he's known as Waldo; in Norway, Willy; in Iceland, Valli; in Germany, Walter; in France, Charlie; in Israel, Effy; and in Italy, Ubaldo. In China he's 威利, or Wei Li. In Japan, you would ask for ウォーリー, or Wari. In Denmark he's Holger.

If you haven't explored a *Where's Wally* scene, you probably know dozens of people who have. I used to search for Wally among crowds of partygoers, rock bands, battling monks, and even other members of his fecund family. Despite his distinctive appearance, Wally can be pretty tough to find. Even after you've spotted him, he can be easy to lose again. To give you some consistent clues as you scan the crowd scenes, Handford never varies Waldo's striped shirt, toque cap, and Harry Potter specs. But imagine trying to locate Wally if you had no idea what he looked like. Chances are you couldn't.

The same thing is true in productive thinking. How will you know you've arrived at your destination if you don't know what it looks like? DRIVE, is a simple way to define the characteristics of a successful outcome, to allow you to recognize your goal once you've achieved it. The outcome of DRIVE is a set of observable Success Criteria. In a sense, DRIVE lets you know what Wally looks like so that you'll know him when you see him.

DRIVE is an acronym for *D*o, *R*estrictions, *I*nvestment, *V*alues, and *E*ssential Outcomes. DRIVE asks five basic questions designed to generate observable criteria for success:

- *Do*: What do you want your eventual solution to do? What must it achieve?

- *Restrictions*: What changes or impacts must you avoid?

- *Investment*: What resources are you willing to allocate? What are your "not-to-exceeds"?

- *Values*: What values must you live by in achieving your solution?

- *Essential Outcomes*: What are the nonnegotiable elements of success? What measurable targets must be met?

The easiest way to conduct a DRIVE exercise is to get a long sheet of paper, orient it horizontally, and divide it into five columns (see Figure 8.1). If you're working with a group, use a roll of butcher paper taped to a long wall. Label your five columns "Do," "Restrictions," "Investment," "Values," and "Essential Outcomes."

D	R	I	V	E
Do	Restrictions	Investment	Values	Essential Outcomes

The DRIVE tool for establishing success criteria.

In the first column, list all the things you want your solution to **Do**. Use divergent, creative thinking to come up with as long a list as possible. What outcome are you looking for? What must be accomplished? What do you want to happen? What might your stakeholders want to happen? Generate as many ideas as possible. Don't judge; just list. You can eliminate irrelevancies and redundancies later. If you are working in a group, you may find sticky notes a convenient way to add to your list of Dos. Your Dos might include statements such as the following: *increase profits, increase market share, improve employee morale*, or *get return customers*.

In the second column, **Restrictions**, using divergent, creative thinking, list all the things your solution must *not* do. What outcomes must you make sure do not occur? What must you *prevent* from happening? List as many outcomes you must avoid as possible. Examples of Restrictions might include the following: *don't create regulatory issues, don't cannibalize our other markets, don't increase workload*, or *don't alienate Bob*.

In the third column, **Investment**, list all the resources you are willing to invest to achieve your Target Future. These are your maximums, the "not-to-exceeds" beyond which you or your organization is unwilling to go. Be rigorous in this step. Be sure your limits are real. Typical Investment columns might include the following statements: *maximum one person-year, pilot project under $10,000,* or *proof-of-concept within three months.*

The fourth column is for Values. This is where you list all the values you or your organization have that cannot be compromised in working toward the solution. What are you willing to live with? What are you *not* willing to live with? As with investments, be realistic. Push back to ensure that the values really are values and not simply empty statements. Values statements might include the following: *work and family balance, uncompromising customer service,* or *green manufacturing.*

How will you know you've arrived at your destination if you don't know what it looks like?

Use the final column to record your Essential Outcomes. Here you list all the things that absolutely must happen for you to consider the solution a success. What specific targets must be met? What are the measurables? What are the nonnegotiable elements of success? In listing your Essential Outcomes, also review the items in your other columns. It's likely that you will find several that are both critical and measurable and should be transferred to the Essential Outcomes column. Examples of Essential Outcomes include the following: *generate 15 percent ROI, increase customer satisfaction ratings by 5 percent,* or *reduce CO_2 emissions by 30 percent within two years.*

Engineers often refer to Essential Outcomes as the functional specifications of a project. These are the metrics that can't be compromised if the project is to be considered a success. In London, the newest bridge across the Thames is a footbridge between Saint Paul's Cathedral and the Tate Modern. Built as a millennium project, it's a stunning piece of design: a suspension bridge in which the supporting cables are improbably set *below* the level of the deck. The tourist books refer to it as Millennium Bridge, but Londoners still call it Wobbly Bridge. Three days after the opening in June 2000, the authorities closed it down for extensive modifications because it had begun swaying from side to side as people walked on it. The Wobbly Bridge might have *looked* like a bridge, but it wasn't a bridge because it didn't meet the structural specification of remaining stable under its load of foot traffic. In productive thinking terms, it wasn't successful because it didn't achieve its Essential Outcomes. Almost two years and £5 million later, Millennium Bridge was reopened, and it has been functioning perfectly ever since. It makes for a lovely walk across the Thames. Really.

Be sure you list all your Essential outcomes in your DRIVE exercise. If you don't, you risk coming up with a solution that isn't a solution at all.

For an example of how a DRIVE exercise might look for JetWays, the airline that wants to enhance the value of its middle seats, refer to the Appendix.

Once you've filled out your DRIVE grid, you will probably find that there are some repetitions. As you can see in the Appendix, the airline group mentioned the issue of average load factor three times. I've seen DRIVE grids in which items such as not exceeding budget or improving customer service are repeated several times. There's no problem with that. In fact, it's a good thing. DRIVE is designed as a tool with built-in redundancy. You want as many opportunities as possible to ferret out relevant Success Criteria. You'd much rather list something more than once than miss it altogether. Moreover, if an item appears in more than one column, there's a good chance it's particularly meaningful.

After you've made a long list of all your potential Success Criteria, your next step is to converge to choose the ones that are most important. Often these will be the items in your final column, Essential Outcomes, but don't forget to review the other columns as well. Achieving a Do that represents a significant stakeholder perspective may be as important to success as a return on investment (ROI) measure is. Ensuring that your Values are maintained may be as important as hitting a production number. Remember what Einstein said about things that can and can't be counted.

There's no magic formula for determining how many final Success Criteria to select. That depends very much on the nature of the issue and the complexity of your tasks. Bear in mind, though, that the more criteria you choose, the more time-consuming the process of evaluating your potential solutions against your Success Criteria will be. I've found that if you select the most important (anywhere between three and nine) criteria, you can use them to filter your ideas for a solution, and if necessary, apply secondary or more detailed criteria at a later time.

SUMMARY

What's Success? consists of two substeps. The first is to robustly imagine an ideal future in which your issue is resolved: to create a powerful motivation to reach your Target Future. The second is to establish clear, observable Success Criteria that can be used in subsequent phases of the productive thinking process to evaluate potential solutions. Here are the two substeps:

- Conduct an Imagined Future (IF) excursion to project yourself into a future in which the issue is resolved. Review the IF exercise and highlight the items that seem most important or have the most emotional impact.

- Using DRIVE, list as many potential Success Criteria as possible in terms of what an eventual solution must do, what it must avoid, what you are prepared to invest, the values you must live by, and any essential outcomes. Review the DRIVE exercise and highlight the most important observable Success Criteria.

The outcome of this phase is Future Pull: a clear and compelling vision of a future in which the issue has been resolved, the Target Future has been achieved, and a set of observable Success Criteria have been stated that can be used to evaluate both potential solutions and outcomes.

The Power of Pull

Future Pull is a vital part of achieving any goal, whether it's the solution to a problem, the completion of a task, or getting a ball into a hoop. Future Pull is a way of making intentions tangible. Once you visualize your goal, ideas for achieving it appear virtually everywhere. It's like buying a new car. As soon as you've purchased that new Chevy, Toyota, or Volkswagen, the roads seem to be filled with Chevys,

Toyotas, or Volkswagens. They've always been there, of course, but you never noticed them. You weren't primed to see them. It's the same with Future Pull. As soon as you establish a concrete intention, you begin to notice all kinds of things in your world that relate to that intention. Ideas and opportunities seem to appear from nowhere, almost as if by magic. The power of Future Pull is that it stimulates the generation of relevant new ideas. It stimulates the unexpected connections that are the heart of productive and creative thinking.

Step Three:
What's the Question?

Step 1: What's Going On?
Step 2: What's Success?
Step 3: What's the Question?
Step 4: Generate Answers
Step 5: Forge the Solution
Step 6: Align Resources

*The most serious mistakes are not
being made as a result of wrong answers.
The truly dangerous thing is
asking the wrong question.*

Peter Drucker

Step Three: What's the Question?

Great Answer (Wrong Question)

The year 1889 was one of those years. It saw the opening of the Eiffel Tower, at that time the world's tallest structure, nearly doubling the height of its closest rival, the Washington Monument, which was opened to the public in 1888. It was the year of the Great Oklahoma Land Rush, which, starting at noon on April 22, opened wide stretches of the American West and created the most populous city ever founded in the shortest time: Oklahoma City had an official population of more than 10,000 by the end of the day. It was the year of the Johnstown Flood, when the collapse of the South Fork Dam drowned over 2,200 people in Pennsylvania. It was also a year of significant births. The seminal philosophers Ludwig Wittgenstein and Martin Heidegger were 1889 babies. So were Charlie Chaplin, who delighted the world by satirizing an inhuman dictator, and Adolf Hitler, who was one. That year also gave birth to several institutions that still affect the lives of millions of people today, including the *Wall Street Journal* and the Nintendo Company, which launched a card game called Hanafuda.

Perhaps the most influential birth of 1889, however, was the barely noticed founding of the American settlement movement by Jane Addams and Ellen Gates Starr in Chicago. In both the United Kingdom, where it began, and the United States, where it took root, the settlement movement changed forever the Victorian equation of gender, poverty, and despair that had become the norm in urban society. Settlement houses in large U.S. cities offered kindergartens, clubs for older children, night schools, open kitchens, music classes, libraries, job training, and emergency shelter to thousands of people. For many, settlement houses offered both the possibility of and the means to escape urban poverty.

Settlement houses still play a significant role in many American cities. New York has thirty-five of them. One of the oldest and largest is Hudson Guild, which operates in the Chelsea area of Manhattan. In addition to its traditional services, Hudson Guild offers English as a second language (ESL) courses, mental health services, job counseling, seniors services, and family assistance programs. Every year, through its 120 staff members and 250 volunteers, Hudson Guild touches over 10,000 lives.

But the guild had a problem: People were falling through the cracks. Few of its clients used more than a single service even though day care clients, for example, might benefit from ESL programs and job counseling clients might benefit from family counseling. Many people who might benefit from programs were missing out simply because they were unaware that the services existed. Hudson Guild's executive director believed that an advertising program might help promote the guild and inform the community about its many services.

My company, think^x, provides pro bono services through a separate organization called Facilitators without Borders (FWB). One of my colleagues, Paul Groncki, volunteers as a board member for Hudson Guild and offered to assemble an FWB team to address the issue. We arranged a two-day productive thinking lab with Hudson Guild's marketing director, its operations director, and fourteen representatives of various guild services.

During the first morning of the lab we explored the guild's issue and articulated a straightforward but compelling Target Future: "Wouldn't it be lovely if our clients could access the full range of Hudson Guild services whenever they needed to?" As we were working on Step 2: What's Success?, a side conversation developed about the variable quality of the guild's programs. Although the people around the table were proud of their own service offerings, they were uncertain about the quality of the services provided by their colleagues. For example, one of the day care managers said that she would not refer Spanish-speaking clients to the psychiatric program because its services were available only in English. The director of the mental health program responded that although that had been true some years earlier, his staff now served clients in several languages.

Sensing a critical issue, the FWB facilitators called a time-out to have an offline discussion with the guild's marketing director, Brian Saber, who had been mandated to develop the new marketing plan. We told him that we thought it was essential to explore the issue that had surfaced—different service areas might not have confidence in one another's offerings—and that such an exploration might lead down a very different strategic path. With considerable trepidation but even more courage, Brian agreed.

Further discussion revealed that each of the guild's services, having evolved separately to meet emerging community needs, was operating in a silo with little understanding of other guild offerings. Once that was revealed, the potential for a completely new solution emerged. The problem might not be that the community didn't know enough about Hudson Guild but rather that Hudson Guild didn't know enough about itself!

In my experience, one of the most common reasons that programs, products, and change initiatives don't work is that the wrong question has been asked.

To reach the Target Future, the question was not "How might we develop an advertising program to promote our service to the community?" but "How might we know ourselves better so that we can feel comfortable referring clients to one another?"

What a breakthrough! Over the next day and a half the room was vibrating with energy. In a few short hours the group developed a preliminary strategy consisting of a Hudson Guild "ambassador" program, job sharing, and ongoing interdepartmental education. Instead of spending hundreds of thousands of dollars on an external advertising campaign with questionable results, Hudson Guild began a comprehensive client referral program. The result was a better understanding of client needs, more effective service offerings, increased program use, and dramatically improved staff and volunteer morale. According to Brian (now Hudson Guild's executive director), "This has been an extraordinary program for us, literally transforming the organization."

The Right Question

How often have you come up with a great "solution" that, when applied, didn't really change anything? Great answer, wrong question! Too often, problem solvers ask the wrong questions. Step 3 of the Productive Thinking Model, What's the Question?, helps you find the *right* questions to get you to your Target Future.

In my experience, one of the most common reasons that programs, products, and change initiatives don't work is that the wrong question has been asked. Imagine analyzing your situation and coming to the conclusion that the reason sales are down is that your advertising is ineffective. You hire the best creative agency you can afford, conduct focus groups to test your messaging, and revitalize your packaging. You spend more money than ever before relaunching your product. At first it looks like your efforts are panning out, but within a few months reports show that sales are still sluggish. What if you're answering the wrong question? What if the problem is your product, your sales process, or the changing profiles of your customers? If so, all the advertising in the world won't help.

The reason we start the productive thinking process with What's Going On? is to give us a chance to hold back and not jump to assumptions about what the problem is. It's all too easy to start off with obvious and often incorrect problem statements: *We don't have enough money. Our sales force isn't motivated. Cost control is the central issue. We need more skills training programs.* If you start with the wrong problem, it's unlikely you'll ever arrive at an effective solution.

What's the Question? is probably the most crucial step in the productive thinking process. Its purpose is to find the right questions to ask. Throughout history, great thinkers have recognized that the single most important step a person can take in thinking productively is to find the right question. Francis Bacon said, "A prudent question is one-half of wisdom." The playwright Eugene Ionesco wrote, "It is not the answer that enlightens, but the question." Alfred North Whitehead observed, "The silly question is the first intimation of some totally new development."

You may be familiar with other problem-solving models. Many of them place great emphasis on constructing "problem statements." But problem statements are useless; they just sit there like great rocks in the road. A person who wants to get somewhere is often tempted to drive around them rather than through them, and with good reason. More often than not, problem statements are dead ends or black holes that will break your axle or suck you into a vortex of despair. "We don't have a big enough budget" is just a declaration of an opinion about a condition. It's static; it doesn't get you anywhere.

Productive thinking takes a different approach. It asks you to generate problem *questions* that actually invite answers, such as "How might we get a bigger budget?" I often describe What's the Question? as seeding the rain cloud. In Step 4: Generate Answers, you will be trying to come up with as many ideas as possible. You want a torrential downpour of ideas in the hope that one or two of those drops will be liquid gems. Here, in What's the Question?, is where you seed your brainstorm.

Once you have established your Itch, your Target Future, and your Success Criteria, you have the basic ingredients for beginning to ask useful problem questions. As in the other phases of the process, you start with divergent, creative thinking to list as many questions as possible. Then you revisit your list and use convergent, critical thinking to choose the questions that seem most interesting or useful. The outcome is one or more problem questions that are worth exploring.

I call this short list of problem questions your Catalytic Questions: the questions that have the potential to get you to your Target Future. Catalytic Questions have a special power. Even before they are answered, the process of discovering and articulating these perspective-changing questions can get things moving. As the group from Hudson Guild experienced, the right question starts generating energy. Things start shifting and shaking in new ways. The question that suddenly unblocks your thinking is exhilarating.

Anglers and parents of four-year-olds know the feeling. We've all had it. Your line or your child's shoelace gets into the most awful tangle, a snarly knot that seems impossible to undo. It's so dense, you can hardly see the individual strands. You pick and pick until eventually you find just the right strand that you can pull loose. That one seems to loosen up others, and those strands free up still more, and eventually the knot isn't a knot anymore. Before finding that one strand, you were hopelessly stuck. Once you find it, the way through becomes possible—not necessarily easy but possible. That strand is your Catalytic Question.

The Catalytic Question is the plumber's helper that unblocks your pipes. It's the Archimedes' fulcrum that enables you to move the world. It's the final crystal that turns a supersaturated solution into an explosion of crystalline forms. Finding the Catalytic Question changes everything. For the team from Hudson Guild, "How might we know ourselves better so that we can feel comfortable referring clients to one another?" got them to their Target Future and beyond.

Finding the Question

It's useful to phrase problem questions in a specific form that makes it easier to compare, contrast, and combine long lists of questions when you are ready to converge to your short list of Catalytic Questions. I've found that the most useful form for problem questions is to begin them with the phrases "How might I . . ." or "How might we. . . ." For convenience, we refer to these forms as HMI or HMW.

Using divergent, creative thinking, ask as many HMI or HMW questions as possible. The raw material for generating those questions comes from the work you've already done, and the most useful starting point is the Target Future you developed in Step 1: What's Going On?

> *Unless you figure out the right question—*
> *a truly Catalytic Question—it doesn't matter*
> *how good the rest of your work is.*

If your Target Future had been "If only I had a more flexible budget!" your first HMI might be "How might I have a more flexible budget?" But don't stop there. Remember, generating long lists is what produces the magic. You need to ask as many variations of that original question as you can. For example, you might distill the question down to its essence: "How might I have more money?" Then you might look at it from another perspective: "How might I need less money?" That might lead to "How might I budget better?" or "How might I spend less?" Those variations might lead to "How might I do things that cost less?" "How might I do things with no budget?" or "How might I negotiate a better deal between my spending self and my earning self?" By generating basic variations of the original question, you automatically expand the scope of your thinking.

Your original Itch statements from Step 1 are also seeds for problem questions. Perhaps one of your Itches was "At the end of the month, I don't have money to do what I want to do." That could transform into "How might I feel less frustrated when I don't have the money to do what I want to do?" or "How might I do more of the things I want earlier in the month?" "How might I pace my spending better?" or "How might I rethink the things I want to do?" All those questions derive from the same Itch, but each is subtly and importantly different.

Another excellent source for generating problem questions is the work you did on the impact of your Itch. In exploring your feeling about the Itch, you might have said, "Not having enough money makes me feel like a loser." That could transform into questions such as "How might I feel like less of a loser?" "How might I feel like a winner?" and "How might I feel more successful?"

The KnoWonder exercise, which helps you assess what you know and what you need to know about your issue, also provides rich material for problem questions. In the Know column, you might have written, "My monthly income is a function of how many sales I make." That could stimulate you to ask, "How might I make more sales?" In the Wonder column, you might have written, "How does Bob always seem to have money to spare?" That could stimulate problem questions such as "How might I manage my money like Bob?" and "How might I learn about how others manage their money?"

Problem questions can also reflect the perspectives of your stake-holders: "My wife says we really need to spend more family time together" could become "How might I might I travel less and work from home more?"

Another source for problem questions is the work you did in Step 2: What's Success? In your Imagined Future excursion, you might have said, "It would be so great to walk through a mall and not even have to think about whether I could afford that impulse purchase." From that statement you might derive problem questions such as "How might I have a slush fund for impulse purchases?" or "How might I get the satisfaction of impulse purchasing without actually having to buy something?" The Success Criteria you generated by using the DRIVE tool are also sources for problem questions. From a single Success Criterion such as "Have a more fulfilling career" you could create a broad range of problem questions, including "How might I have a more fulfilling career?" "How might I learn the skills I'll need for a more fulfilling career?" "How might I think of income in a way that has nothing to do with work?" and so on.

As you can see, your early thinking reveals many rich veins of material to mine for problem questions. But you're still only at the first third. The principle of striving for the third third applies in every phase of the Productive Thinking Model. Although you may discover powerful Catalytic Questions in the first third, it's far more likely that the more interesting and provocative questions will come up in the second or third third of your exploration. One way to dig deeper is to use a simple tool called AIM.

AIM stands for Advantages, Impediments, and Maybes.

First, list all the Advantages of achieving your Target Future. Why is this Target Future desirable? Why do you want to get there? What benefits might it produce? List as many as you can. If your Target Future is to increase organizational sales, the Advantages might include the following: *More sales will produce more black ink on the bottom line. More sales will result in better relationships with suppliers. More sales offer a chance to move to a new and more productive location.*

Second, list all the Impediments to achieving your Target Future. What are the barriers? Why isn't it a reality already? What's stopping you? Make a long list of the things that seem to be standing in the way. Possible Impediments to more sales might include the following: *We don't have*

A ADVANTAGES	*List the Advantages inherent in your Target Future. Ask questions such as:* • What are the Advantages of attaining your Target Future? • Why is the Target Future desirable? • Why do you want to get there? • Why might it be good for you or your organization? • Why might it be good for your stakeholders? • What benefits might it produce?
I IMPEDIMENTS	*List the Impediments to achieving your Target Future* • What are the barriers to achieving it? • Why isn't it a reality already? • Why aren't you or your organization already there? • What's stopping you?
M MAYBES	*List the things that might result from achieving your Target Future but may not be related to the original Itch.* • What else might happen if you achieve your Target Future? • What other outcomes might be possible?

enough salespeople. We have insufficient sales incentives. Shipping costs are hurting our ability to sell to distant markets.

Finally, list all the Maybes: the things that *might* result from achieving your Target Future. What else might happen if you achieve your Target Future? What other outcomes might be possible? Don't confine yourself to guaranteed outcomes. Daydream. List as many Maybes as you can. What *might* happen? *Increased sales might open up new markets. We might be able to develop new products or services. We might have to look for partners to address new geographic markets. Increased sales might mean improved employee health benefits.*

Once you've generated a robust AIM list, use it to generate more problem questions. Here are some possibilities that are based on the examples above: "How might we strengthen the sales–profitability equation?" "How might we explore new markets?" "How might we reduce shipping costs to distant markets?" "How might we establish partnerships in other geographic markets?" "How might we address employee benefit concerns?"

Taking AIM at the Target Future is a good way to extend your thinking into the second third. But there's more to do. To get to the *third* third you really have to stretch. When I work with individuals and groups, I try to help them explore the third third with probes designed to shift their perspectives. To get to your own third third, you'll find it useful to challenge yourself with probes such as "What questions would I ask if I knew I couldn't fail?" "What questions would I ask if money were no object?" "What questions might someone who knows nothing about my business ask?" "What questions might my competitors ask?" "What questions might a child ask?" "What questions might get me fired?" "What questions might lead to failure?" "What questions might bankrupt the company?" "What questions might land us all in court?" "What are the worst possible questions?" Shifting perspective is one of the most effective ways to get to the third third.

Caveat Cogitor

Before moving on to the convergent phase of this step, I want to mention one caveat about problem questions. What's the Question? is a pivotal step in the productive thinking process. Unless you figure out the right question—a truly Catalytic Question—it doesn't matter how good the rest of your work is.

Throughout the earlier chapters in this book, I described the tendency we have to jump to conclusions either because we are following the deeply ingrained patterns we've all developed or because we feel so uncomfortable with irresolution that we're eager to jump to any answer that gets us out of the misery of not knowing. As you work through this step of the Productive Thinking Model, you will notice how easy it is to dispense with the question entirely and attempt to jump to solutions. Of course, we are not quite that blatant about it. What we do most often is *disguise our answers in the form of questions,* as though the camouflage might somehow change the nature of what we're actually doing. Here's what such subversion might look like.

Let's say you were unhappy with your physical condition and generated the following Target Future: *If only I could look and feel like I did when I was 26!* You then went through What's Success?, imagining how great it would be if you were able to accomplish this transformation and defining Success Criteria such as fitness and weight loss targets. You have arrived in Step 3 and want to generate a wide range of problem questions. One of them is "How might I use the South Beach diet?" Stop! Using the South Beach diet isn't a bad idea, but it's a lousy question. Why? Because it's really an answer disguised as a question. There's nowhere to go with it other than starting the South Beach diet. It is far more useful to construct a question such as "How might I change my eating habits?" or, even better, "How might I balance my energy intake with my energy output?" Now you have questions with a range of possible answers. The broader and more open-ended your problem questions are, the more useful they will be. Keep in mind that the intent here is to create questions that will invite long lists of answers, not close down the conversation.

The tendency to jump to solutions is strong, particularly in the What's the Question? step. You'll find that you are champing at the bit to get to answers. Be vigilant in hunting down "How might I . . ." questions that are really ideas for solutions in disguise. Make sure they ask *how* you might achieve success, overcome barriers, or meet stakeholder needs rather than actually prescribing solutions. I'm not suggesting that you discard these potential ideas. They might be a great resource eventually, but at this stage there's a risk that they'll plug you up and close down your thinking. Record the questions that are really ideas for solution in a "parking lot" for later use. You haven't lost them. You can always unpark them for consideration in Step 4: Generate Answers.

Converging on the Question

Once you have a long list of problem questions, it's time to use convergent, critical thinking to narrow down the list. Your intent is to come up with a range of interesting questions that are focused enough to provoke useful areas of investigation but broad enough to invite a wide range of possible answers. My preferred tool for converging down to Catalytic Questions is C[5]: Cull, Cluster, Combine, Clarify, and Choose. C[5] usually works best if you or your group has been writing your questions down on sticky notes that can be moved around easily. Here's how it works.

C[5]: Cull, Cluster, Combine, Clarify, Choose

Cull

Review your list and separate out the questions that are really potential answers in disguise. Take each disguised answer and try to distill the general principle within it. In this way, "How might I use the South Beach diet?" becomes "How might I change my eating habits?" or "How might I balance my energy intake with my energy output?" Then take the original question, "How might I use the South Beach diet?" delete the HMI ("How might I . . ."), and place it in your idea parking lot for consideration in Step 4.

Cluster

Start grouping similar problem questions. Clusters should generally have no more than five questions. As you cluster, you will note duplications. If the questions are *exact* duplicates, discard one, but if there are differences, even subtle ones, it's best to keep them on the table at this point.

Combine

As your clusters begin to emerge, you will see the possibility of combining individual questions into more comprehensive single questions (this is where you'll begin to eliminate some of those near duplicates). After a while, you should arrive at a series of clusters each one of which is somehow thematically related. Again, try to keep clusters to five questions or fewer. The reason for this is that large clusters tend to dilute the meaning and richness of questions.

Clarify

Look at each cluster and name the theme it represents. For example, you might have clustered the following questions: "HMI ("How might I . . .") budget more effectively?" "HMI plan my spending?" "HMI anticipate my needs better?" "HMI live within my means?" and "HMI create an emergency slush fund?" You might label this cluster "HMI budget for both my regular and my unforeseen needs?" This restatement captures the essence of the items in the cluster but remains a question rather than a solution. You still don't know *how* you will do this, but it's a good question to explore.

Once you have clarified the theme of each cluster, review your work to see if any of the clusters overlap or if there are further possibilities for combining themes in a way that captures the essence of the individual questions while remaining open enough to invite a range of answers.

Choose

Look back at all the work you've done so far. Pay particular attention to the Itches you've described, the perspectives of your key stakeholders, your Target Future, and your Success Criteria. Ask yourself if any overarching themes have merged in your clusters. As you look at the clusters, do you see patterns or relationships between them? Have any new perspectives emerged? Have you changed your sense of what is relevant and what is not? Which of your questions or clusters really gets to the heart of the matter? Which looks most promising? Which makes you a little nervous? Which do you really want to work on now?

As you begin to narrow down your problem questions, ask yourself, If I answer this well, is there a chance I'll arrive at my Target Future? Look for the questions that are most exciting or interesting, that strike you as unusual or untried, that are perhaps even a little disquieting or frightening. Often it's the disturbing questions that produce the richest range of answers.

Depending on the complexity of your issue, you may end up with one Catalytic Question or several. In either case, you have now framed your puzzle. You have one or more questions that if answered well may lead to innovative solutions. In a sense, you've got all the corners and edges of the puzzle in place. You are ready to move on and fill in the empty spaces.

Recall the JetWays example from Chapter 6, in which the airline was looking for ways to enhance the value of its middle seats as a way to differentiate itself. After exploring the issue in Step 1 and establishing Success Criteria in Step 2, the JetWays team worked through Step 3 to converge on the following Catalytic Question: *How might we change people's perceptions about JetWays middle seats?* This new articulation of the challenge is subtly but importantly different from the original notion of enhancing the seats' value. You could enhance a middle seat's value by giving it more padding or upgrading the upholstery. Both of these possibilities call for manufacturing solutions, but changing people's *perceptions* calls for a *marketing* solution, which will take the innovation team in a very different direction. With the right question, you have, as Bacon says, "one-half of wisdom."

Note that at this point in the process you may have converged on more than one Catalytic Question. If that is the case, you will have to select the one that's most appropriate to work on in the current session. It may be the one you have the most energy for, a question on which other questions depend, or the one that's most urgent. However if you prioritize, you can work on only one Catalytic Question at a time. I'll discuss strategies for dealing with multiple Catalytic Questions in Chapter 13, "Productive Thinking Redux."

SUMMARY

What's the Question? is a pivotal step in the Productive Thinking Model. In it you diverge to generate as many problem questions as possible and then converge to focus on one or more Catalytic Questions that if answered will create the potential to get to your Target Future.

- Using divergent, creative thinking, list as many problem questions as possible in the form "How might I . . ." (HMI) or "How might we . . ." (HMW).

- Using convergent, critical thinking, select one or more Catalytic Questions that if answered will create the potential to get to your Target Future.

The outcome of this step is a clear articulation of the essential problems or opportunities in the form of one or more Catalytic Questions that invite ideas for solution.

Defying Gravity

Earlier I discussed the almost inexorable gravitational pull of the past. Particularly in organizations, there is a strong tendency in this step to go back to the tried and true, the safe, the questions that don't rock the boat too much, the questions that aren't too disturbing.

Here's why I think you should avoid this tendency.

First, you're probably using the productive thinking process because whatever you've tried so far hasn't worked. You started on this track because you thought you needed a new approach. Don't back out now.

Second, thinking back to your I^3 criteria, you chose a Target Future that called for an imaginative solution. Honor your first impulse. Imagination is what you're looking for, not safety.

Third, the risk in productive thinking is low. Thought experiments carry little or no penalty. If you head down a path that doesn't work out, you can always double back. Take the opportunity to stretch. Find a question that sends chills down your spine. There's a good chance it will lead to a solution that warms your heart.

Step Four:
Generate Answers

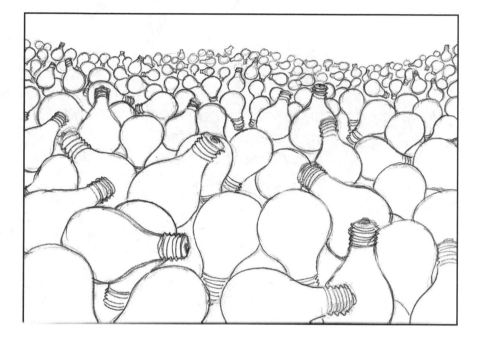

I make more mistakes than anyone else I know.
And, sooner or later,
I patent most of them.

Thomas Edison

Step 4: Generate Answers

Ten Thousand Failures

Pete Rose is probably the best baseball player never to be inducted into the Hall of Fame.[1] Rose played from 1963 to 1986, mostly for the Cincinnati Reds. He played in 17 all-star games and won three World Series rings, three batting titles, and two gold gloves. He played more games and had more at bats than any other baseball player in history. Among all his talents, however, none was more spectacular than his ability to get on base. Aptly nicknamed Charlie Hustle, Rose is the all-time major league leader in hits with 4,256, 67 ahead of Ty Cobb in second place and almost 500 ahead of Hank Aaron in third. To get those hits, he stood at the plate 14,053 times.[2] In other words, on his way to becoming baseball's all-time best hitter, *Rose failed to get a hit nearly 10,000 times.*

It's the same with ideas. No matter how good you are at getting them, you'll have a lot more duds than dazzlers. In fact, the *better* you are at getting them, like Pete Rose getting hits, the more failures you'll have. So it's important to remember that the consequences of failure in productive thinking are much less than they are in reproductive thinking. Failed ideas are just that: *ideas* that haven't made the cut. They're not money, they're not systems, they're not lives. They're just thoughts. The primary risks are spending a little time and a taking a little hit to your pride. If we didn't know how to risk those things, none of us would ever have learned to walk or ride a bike. We wouldn't be able to read or dance or succeed in our business lives. We'd certainly never have fallen in love. The irony is that by *not* risking, we risk not succeeding in anything at all.

I often refer to this step, Generate Answers, as the sales call step of productive thinking. Salespeople often talk about their hit rates: For some it's 1 success in 10 qualified leads, for others 1 in 20, and so on. For unqualified leads—cold calls—the ratio is much lower, perhaps 1 sale for every 200 calls. When you try to generate ideas, think of yourself as a salesperson knocking on a whole subdivision of doors. Some won't open at all, some will open a suspicious crack, and some will slam in your face. But the more doors you knock on, the greater your chances of being invited in.

Generate Answers is the step most people think of as brainstorming, the part where you come up with the ideas. If you have followed the model till now, you've done a lot of work on understanding your issue and where you want to go with it. In the process, you've probably been full of ideas waiting to pop and you've probably had a tough time not popping them. One of the great strengths of the productive thinking process is that it forces you to hold back from coming up with answers. Think of what you are doing as aiming an arrow. Coming up with answers too early is like drawing a bow just a few hand lengths before letting it go. Your arrow will fly, but only for a few feet or meters. But if you keep drawing back the bowstring tighter and tighter, your arrow will fly true and far.

"You write down the problem. You think very hard. Then you write down the answer."
— Richard Feynman

This chapter will help you tap the energy you've stored up in the first three steps of the process so that you can have a powerful brainstorm and not just a braindrizzle. The chapter has two parts: first, some guidance on how you can use divergent, creative thinking to generate as many ideas as possible and second how to use convergent, critical thinking to focus on those ideas that have real potential.

Think Very Hard

In *Genius*, his biography of the Nobel physicist Richard Feynman, James Gleick reports that a colleague once joked that he had figured out Feynman's approach to solving problems: "You write down the problem. You think very hard. Then you write down the answer."[3] According to Gleick, Feyman's IQ was measured at a respectable but by no means genius level of 125. Yet many scientists equate his contributions with those of Einstein. He is responsible for major advances in quantum electrodynamics, superfluidity, and particle theory, and his work is the basis for countless research projects in both theoretical and applied physics. The problem-solving methodology attributed to Feynman is almost exactly the same as the one we use in the Productive Thinking Model: You write down the problem, think very hard, and then write down the answer. But in productive thinking you don't write down just one answer; you write down as many answers as you can and then try to develop the best candidates for a solution.

In this step of the Productive Thinking Model, Generate Answers, your aim is to look for lots of ideas—practical ideas, whacky ideas, controversial ideas, impossible ideas, disrespectful ideas, unaffordable ideas, ideas born of dreams, ideas born of stress, ideas born of ignorance, ideas from other fields, ideas guaranteed to fail, ideas that open new doors, combinations of ideas, ideas that come from unexpected connections—so that you can test and select the best ones. The outcome of Generate Answers is one or more solution alternatives: embryonic ideas that, if developed, may lead to a robust solution.

In the previous step What's the Question? you seeded your idea rain clouds with one or more Catalytic Questions: questions that, if answered well might resolve your issue. Now it's time to let it rain. You want to generate a downpour of ideas, a torrent of possibilities, so you can have lots to choose from. Remember Linus Pauling's axiom, "The best way to have good ideas is to have lots of ideas, and then choose the best ones." To generate as many options as possible, this is a good time to review and apply the divergent (creative) thinking guidelines discussed in Chapter 5: Defer both negative and positive judgment, build on your ideas, go wild, and set stretch targets for quantity. In other words, let it rain.

Remember, *there is no risk in expressing a bad idea.* Ideas are nothing more than thoughts, mental constructs. They have no substance. They are as powerless to hurt anyone as they are to help anyone. They are both invaluable and worthless. They exist only as potential. That potential can be realized only if they are expressed. A hidden idea is not an idea at all. The only dumb idea is, quite literally, the one that is unspoken. An unarticulated idea is like an unlit flame. In the divergent, creative part of Generate Answers, your job—your *only* job—is to light your ideas so they may be seen.

There are hundreds of techniques for generating ideas.[4] You've already used several of them in previous phases of the model, and I'll show you more in the chapters to come. But the main intent of this book is not to supply a compendium of tools. Instead, the Productive Thinking Model provides a framework within which you can apply a wide variety of tools, some of which you may already know, some of which you will learn, and some of which you may even invent yourself. Tools and techniques can be helpful, but they are not the essence of the productive thinking process. In my productive thinking sessions with clients, I use tools only when just plain thinking runs a little dry. The key, as in all phases of the model, is to use divergent, creative thinking to make long lists and then to use convergent, critical thinking to make choices.

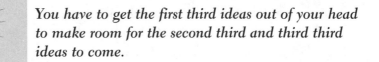

You have to get the first third ideas out of your head to make room for the second third and third third ideas to come.

Having Ideas

Once you've selected a Catalytic Question to work on, begin by listing possible answers for it. List whatever comes to mind. Your initial ideas will almost definitely be first third ideas, those normal, obvious, rational, everyday, everyone-has-already-thought-of-them ideas that you've probably had or heard dozens of times before. Don't worry. It's not a problem to start with those mundane ideas. In fact, it's necessary. You have to get the first third ideas out of your head to make room for the second third and third third ideas to come. In describing this phenomenon, Dee Hock, the founder of VISA, once said. "The problem is never how to get new, innovative thoughts into your mind, but how to get old ones out. Every mind is a building filled with archaic furniture. Clean out a corner of your mind and creativity will instantly fill it." So go ahead and empty your head. It's the first thing you need to do.

The First Third

Here's an experiment to demonstrate the concept of the third third: Get a pad and pencil. Think of all the things that are impossible for human beings to do but that it would be really great if we could. As quickly as you can, write a list of 10 things you think it would be great to be able to do.

Now, there's no possible way I could have read your mind, but on the next page I've listed my prediction of the 10 things I think you wrote down. Look at the box on the next page to see how I did.

- Fly
- Walk on or under water
- Live forever, come back from the dead
- Never be sick
- Communicate with other beings telepathically
- Be invisible or shape shift in some way
- Teleport, as in "Beam me up, Scotty."
- Travel through time
- Have X-ray vision
- Keep promises to yourself, such as losing weight

When I do this exercise with groups, I bat 70 percent or more. Is that because there are no original thinkers out there? Not at all. It's because these are all first third ideas. Remember what Herbert Simon said about early ideas: They are not so much a function of productive thought as they are of memory.

Flush that first third out and you begin to gain access to the many other connections your brain can make. You'll find that the farther they are from the surface of your consciousness, the more interesting they get. Go back to the exercise in the box. Think of 10 more items to add to your list of impossible things. Is your list starting to get a little more interesting and creative? Almost undoubtedly it is.

I'm not suggesting that people won't come up with any creative or unusual ideas in the first third, but it's more likely that you came up with ideas that played out the patterns you've learned throughout your life. And what happens in this little exercise is exactly what will happen when you begin generating answers to your Catalytic Question. The obvious ones will come out first.

Once you've listed the ideas that lie closest to the surface, the hard work begins. Many people stall here for a while, and one useful way to kick-start a new wave of thinking is to give yourself some simple provocations such as the following: *How might your customers answer the question? How might your boss answer it? How might your best friend answer it? Your worst enemy? How might your mentor answer it? A retired person? A child?*

One of the most powerful cues you can give yourself is to add the word *else* to your question. In our sessions with clients, I deliberately change the HMI ("How might I . . .") stem to HEMI, or "How *else* might I. . . ." How else might you answer the question? How else? How else? When you do this, the question is never really "answered" at all. Each answer is just a drop of rain. You want to gather as many drops as you can. "How *else* might I . . ." is a good way to keep that rain falling.

Somewhere during those "How else . . ." questions, you probably made a transition to second third answers: answers that are a little less obvious, a little more of a stretch, even a little strange. Inevitably, the longer you let it rain, the stranger some of those raindrops become. Some of them may not even look like drops at all. And that's a good thing. Alex Osborn, who coined the term *brainstorming*, once said that the wilder the ideas, the better, because "it's much easier to tame a wild idea than invigorate one that has no life in the first place." So go for the unusual, the unexpected. More often than not, that's where the potential lies.

Here are some more cues to help you get to the next third: *What might you do if you had only 10 minutes to solve your problem? What if you had unlimited time? What if you had unlimited funds? What might you do if you knew you couldn't fail?*

How might your favorite author answer your question? How about a favorite fictional character? A fictional hero? A fictional villain? How might Spiderman respond to your Catalytic Question? What ideas might each of the Fantastic Four have? Batman? Donald Duck? Humphrey Bogart?

What are the worst possible answers to your Catalytic Question: the answers guaranteed to fail, to get you fired, to land you in jail? Now reverse those "bad" answers. Turn them upside down and inside out to come up with potentially useful answers.

You can also force your mind to make connections. *How is your question like the chair you're sitting on? The pen you're writing with? The route you take to work each morning?* Generating answers that are based on analogies and forced connections between your question and other things in your life can open new perspectives. For example, in thinking about your daily commute, you might muse: *I used to drive the freeway to work, but the traffic made me crazy, so I started taking side streets. They were nicer and certainly more relaxing. The best part is I usually get to work faster. What if instead of aiming straight at my problem, I tried a more indi-*

rect route? What "side streets" might I look at in answering my Catalytic Question?

Prompts like these give you the opportunity to move beyond the conventional, the logical, the patterned. You start to move into that precious third third territory.

On September 5, 1995, a 48-year-old man by the name of Virgil Simons emerged from successful surgery for prostate cancer. His condition hadn't been diagnosed until it was nearly too late. Without a little bit of luck, he might have died. Simons researched the issue and found that prostate cancer is the second leading cause of cancer-related death among North American men. Over 40 percent of men over age 50 have not had the simple blood test for the elevated PSA (prostate-specific antigen) levels that can warn of the disease. One of the main reasons: African Americans and Latinos have significantly higher incidences of prostate cancer than the general male population, and those groups tend to be medically underserved. As with many forms of cancer, early detection dramatically changes the odds of survival, but if detected too late, prostate cancer is fatal. Simons asked himself a simple question, "How might these men be made more aware of the importance of PSA testing?" The obvious, first third answer was to use the media to urge men to have regular medical checkups. The message was simple, but how could it be delivered effectively? Advertising would be costly and might have only marginal credibility. What about language and cultural barriers?

Simons then asked himself "How *else* . . ." and started exploring beyond the conventional, first third answers. Why not fight prostate cancer by going for a haircut? In 2004 he signed up a small army of barbers to talk to their customers about the issue. Here's what Simons said in an interview with the Associated Press: "Not everybody goes to the doctor. But the barber is someone they've seen . . . since they were a kid. He's a pillar of the community, a business leader, a culturally credible communicator. When he's cutting hair, he can say, 'Hey, when was the last time you had your PSA checked?'" The results? Although, it is impossible to measure how many clinical visits the program has produced or how many lives it may have saved, Simons's Web site, Prostate Net (prostate online.com), has received nearly 4 million hits since it started and now averages over 80,000 per day.

So far I've focused on stimulating answers cognitively with verbal cues such as "How *else*" or by thinking from other perspectives, such as Batman's. But the cognitive is only one level of consciousness. There are millions of other answers that you can access from other levels. Ideas are often generated through logic, but they can also be ignited by observing the world around you.

Listen to music. What ideas does it spark for you? Look at paintings or photographs. How might they stimulate answers to your Catalytic Question? Experiment with tastes and smells. Do they tell you anything? When you feel the softness of a feather, are you reminded of something that might trigger an answer? When you feel the skin of an orange? When you imagine its citrus taste exploding on your tongue?

One simple way to generate dozens of additional answers is to take a short excursion. It might be around your house or office. Or down the street. Or, better yet, if you can arrange it, to a place with more exotic sights and sounds and smells, such as a museum, a factory, a football game, or a parade. Take a notebook and list the things you notice. Stretch. Note 20 different things that you see, 20 you hear, 20 you taste or smell, 20 you feel. What answers do those things stimulate as you relate them to your Catalytic Question? Philo T. Farnsworth watched his father plowing a field and thought of using straight lines to scan a picture. Researchers at IKEA walked into supermarkets and noticed that when shopping carts were placed only at entrances, customers passed up impulse buys. After walking his dog in a field, George de Mestral noticed burrs sticking to his pants and thought of the idea for Velcro.

If you let it, your mind will jump on new stimuli and automatically make dozens of unexpected connections. If you pay attention to them, you may discover the answer you've been looking for.

When you think you've exhausted yourself of ideas, don't give up. There's more third in that third third than you think. Here are two more things to do to generate even more ideas.

First, take a break. Focused attention can make the difference between success and failure, but it can also get in the way. Sometimes we can accomplish a lot more by not trying. When it comes to coming up with new ideas, it's often more productive to use the incubation technique than to try to generate new ideas by brute force. Those billions of synapses in your brain are an endless reservoir of possibility. Fostering a sense of possibility is often just a question of letting go and watching your mind do the work for you. It happens to us all the time when we dream, when we daydream, when our monkey minds take control. Sometimes getting the second, the fifth, or the tenth right answer may just be a matter of relaxing.

Often our minds work best in the background. A basic productive thinking principle is to steep yourself in your issue and then forget about it for a while.

How many times have you remembered the thing you were struggling to remember as soon as you forgot trying to remember it? How many times have you had a great idea in the shower or while driving? Often our minds work best in the background. A basic productive thinking principle is to steep yourself in your issue and then forget about it for a while. Relax. Daydream. Stroll in the sunshine. It's important to give your subconscious the time it needs to do its magic. So if at first you don't succeed, take a break.

Second, review the ideas you've already generated and see if there are any interesting combinations. Pick two of your ideas at random. What's the connection between them? If you don't see one, make one. What does that connection suggest? Swiss knives are combinations of several tools in a pocketknife. Radio alarm clocks are a combination of clocks and radios. When she was a graduate student at the Massachusetts Institute of Technology, Gauri Nanda combined two ideas to dream up a completely new kind of alarm clock. Like many of us, Nanda would hit the snooze button repeatedly, often oversleeping as a result. She combined the idea of an alarm with the old saying "time flies" and invented Clocky, a shockproof alarm clock with wheels that rolls off your nightstand and runs away after you hit the snooze button.[5] Combining two or more ideas is a great way to generate the new.

Panning for Gold

Once you've finished generating your long list of answers, you may have dozens, hundreds, or even thousands of ideas. That's both a blessing and a curse. It's a blessing because somewhere in all those ideas is some pure gold. It's a curse because that gold is necessarily buried in a big pile of mud.

This phase of Generate Answers always reminds me of the story of the twin brothers who presented a big worry to their parents. One brother was an inveterate optimist. No matter what he encountered, he immediately saw it as promising. The other was exactly the opposite, an inveterate pessimist. He saw the cloud around every silver lining. Concerned that neither child had an appropriate perspective on life, the parents consulted a psychiatrist, who offered the following advice: On the twins' next birthday, prepare two rooms full of gifts, one room for each boy. Fill the pessimist's room with all the toys and games and treats a child could ever want. Make it a wonderland. For the optimist, fill a room with nothing but manure.

The parents did as he suggested and placed their sons in front of the doors to the two rooms. The pessimist opened his door and immediately started to cry. The toys were all wrong: the wrong size, the wrong color. Even the ones that might be good would surely break eventually. The boy was inconsolable, and his parents were more distressed than ever.

The optimist opened his door and immediately dived into the pile of manure, laughing and digging joyfully. The parents were astonished. "What on earth are you doing?" they asked. The optimist popped his head out of the pile and said, "With all this horse shit around here, there's got to be a pony somewhere!"

You've got a pony somewhere in that idea pile of yours. You may even have a whole herd of ponies. The challenge is to find them.

Making lists and making choices is the overarching principle behind every step of the Productive Thinking Model. It's like panning for gold. You scoop up a mass of raw material and sift through it till you see a few glistening specks emerge. The more material you sift, the greater your chances of finding gold. The best way I've learned to sift through ideas is by using the C^5 tool. It's one of the most powerful tools for convergent, or selective, thinking in your toolbox.

C^5 usually works best if you or your group has been writing your ideas down on sticky notes that can easily be moved around. Remember, C^5 stands for Cull, Cluster, Combine, Clarify, and Choose. I recommended C^5 as a useful way to converge, or narrow down, problem questions in the previous step, What's The Question? I often use it in Generate Answers as well, with some important differences.

Cull

In Step 3: What's the Question?, you reviewed your list of questions to cull those that were potential answers on disguise. In *this step*, *Generate Answers*, you cull for a different purpose. You want to separate all those answers that are really wild, the ones you'll be tempted to dismiss without even looking at them further. Any answer you think may be too far out to ever make your final cut should go into a "What was I thinking?" category. Put those answers aside for the moment. We'll come back to them later.

Cluster

Just as you did in Step 3, review your long list and group similar ideas, placing no more than five ideas per cluster. If you find a cluster with more than five ideas in it, break it into two or more logical groups. As you cluster, note duplications. If they are exact duplicates, discard one, but if there are differences, even fine ones, it's best to keep them on the table at this point.

Combine

As your clusters begin to emerge, you will see the possibility of combining individual answers into more comprehensive single answers (this is where you'll begin to eliminate some of those near duplicates). For example, "a clock that runs away from you" and "a clock that jumps off the nightstand" could be combined as "a clock that runs away from you by jumping off the nightstand." Eventually, you should be able to converge on a series of clusters each of which has no more than four answers.

Clarify

Label each cluster with a descriptive statement that captures the essence of each of its ideas. For example, "clock stays out of reach by jumping off the nightstand, running away, or moving as soon as it senses an approaching hand." Having clarified each cluster, you have your raw material for further development.

Now let's come back to those wild and crazy answers you culled and placed in your "What was I thinking?" pile. Even though people are often able to *generate* wild and crazy ideas, when it comes time to *choose*, they almost invariably exhibit a strong tendency—especially in organizational environments—to stick with the familiar, the stable, the logical, in other words, the "possible." In practice, this means that some of the best ideas are often left on the table. The reason for culling these wild and crazy ideas is so you can treat them a little differently from the other ideas you've generated.

The UP stands for "underlying principle."
"What is the underlying principle behind this idea?
How can it be practically applied"?

If you work with groups, you will discover that some participants enjoy generating ideas, while others prefer to evaluate and discuss them. In this phase of Step 4, those who like evaluating are usually eager to begin clustering, combining, and clarifying. The idea generators, on the other hand, often hang back from these tasks. But they can play a crucial role in panning for the gold in the wild and crazy ideas in your "What was I thinking?" pile. To do that, I invite them to use a tool I call What's UP? The *UP* stands for "underlying principle." The method is very simple. It asks, "What is the underlying principle behind this idea? How can it be practically applied?"

Some years ago, one of my think[x] colleagues, Steve Fox, conducted a session for a small restaurant supply company in the Midwest. Among their key products were the plain tumblers used as water glasses by every lunch counter or roadside diner you've ever been to. The company had come up against a production bottleneck with an unusual cause. At the end of the production line, the tumblers were packed in partitioned cartons, 24 to a box, for shipment. To help prevent breakage, each glass was stuffed and wrapped with old newspaper. The newspapers were stacked beside each worker. As it turned out, the packing lines were slowing down because the workers couldn't help periodically glancing at and being distracted by reading the newspapers. Management wanted to solve this problem, but with two important constraints: Using unprinted newsprint would be too expensive, and using Styrofoam would be too environmentally unfriendly. The challenge was to solve the problem without changing any of the materials.

As you might expect, the first third of the answers generated in the management brainstorming meeting were the standard, everyone-has-thought-of-them-before answers: put video cameras on the shop floor to monitor the workers, threaten the workers, punish the workers, fire the workers, bonus the workers. Eventually the group moved to second third suggestions: rotate the workers, distract the workers, bribe the workers, acquire foreign-language newspapers. Finally the group got to the third third, stimulated in part by the frustration of being pushed for more and more answers. Eventually someone yelled, "Why don't we just poke their damn eyes out!" Up on the wall went that idea, along with all the others.

Normally, "poke their eyes out" wouldn't survive very long in a brainstorming session. Not only is it cruel, it could land you in jail. But by culling "poke your eyes out" along with numerous other third third ideas, the group was able to examine the ideas for their potential. By looking for its underlying principle, they transformed "poke their eyes out" into "How might the workers not see the newspapers?" Answers to that question ranged from making them work in the dark, to blindfolding them, to hiring people who couldn't see in the first place, in other words, hiring people who were blind!

This turned out to be the most promising answer of all. Not only did it solve the problem as presented—the new workers weren't distracted by the newspapers, resulting in a measurable increase in the speed of the packing line—but it produced three other benefits as well: First, because people who are visually impaired often have superior tactile senses, breakage was reduced; second, the company could offer jobs to people who have a difficult time finding employment; and third, the company received good PR within the community. Not bad for an idea that would probably never have made the first cut. What's UP? is a great way to mine the gold out of ideas that might otherwise never survive the cut.

Choose

The last step in C^5 is to select the ideas you want to develop further. You may have anywhere from six to several dozen idea clusters with detailed descriptions. Which ones do you want to explore further? Your gut is often your best guide at this stage. Thinking about your Itch and Target Future (from Step 1), keeping in mind your Success Criteria (from Step

2), and looking at your Catalytic Question (from Step 3), what feels right? What feels interesting? What feels different? What gets your pulse racing? What worries you? What intrigues you? What scares you? Don't limit yourself to the tried and true. Don't back off the ideas that make you nervous. After all, you haven't resolved your issue to date, and you did say you were looking for imaginative ideas. Don't crumble now.

Also, don't worry about the ideas you're leaving behind. They aren't going anywhere. If it turns out that you can't develop the ones you've chosen into useful solutions, you can always go back and look at some of your tamer ideas later. Right now you should be going for it. Generally, you'll want to come out of this phase with somewhere between three and six promising ideas. These aren't solutions yet. We call them preliminary solution alternatives, embryonic possibilities for solutions. You'll evaluate them and power them up in the next phase, Forge the Solution.

SUMMARY

Generate Answers is the step in the Productive Thinking Model that generates possible answers for the Catalytic Questions you identified in Step 3: What's the Question? These answers are not yet full-blown solutions. Rather, they are embryonic ideas that, if developed, may lead to solutions.

- List as many ideas for answering the Catalytic Question as possible.
- Converge on three to six ideas that, once fully developed, may result in useful solutions.

The desired outcome of this step is usually three to six promising or intriguing ideas that, once fully developed, may result in useful ways to resolve your issue and achieve your Target Future.

The North Star

Sometimes it's easy to lose focus on the purpose of the productive thinking exercise. Even though you might have started out saying you wanted imaginative, novel ideas, the tendency to drift back into the conventional is powerful. Keep reminding yourself of your goal so you can avoid three common pitfalls that can sabotage your work in this step.

First is satisficing: the insidious tendency to stop thinking once a "right" answer surfaces. Don't stop listing ideas simply because a good solution seems to have appeared. The more answers you generate, the greater your chances of finding brilliant ones.

Second is losing the "juice" in your individual ideas by creating clusters that are too broad. Limit your clusters to a maximum of five ideas.

Third is gravitating back to safety. Don't leave your wild third third ideas on the table just because they don't fit your notion of what's acceptable. Plumb them for their potential by asking, What's UP?

Remember why you started this quest. You were looking for fresh, innovative ideas. Keep that passion alive.

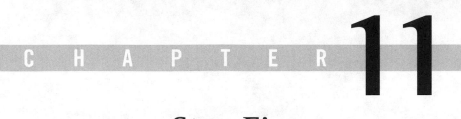
Step Five:
Forge the Solution

Ideas are not solutions;
they are the raw material of solutions.

Arthur VanGundy

Step 5: Forge the Solution

Masamune's Katana

Masamune was a blacksmith. He spent his days pounding and polishing steel, but not the high-quality steel of today. In the early 1300s, the relatively low temperatures achievable in Japanese steelmaking resulted in a product with substantial inconsistencies and impurities. Until he began working it, Masamune could never be sure of the carbon and glass content of his raw material. And yet in the 700 years since he crafted them, Masamune's katanas—the Japanese backswords most westerners think of as samurai longswords—have never been equaled.

Masamune is recognized as Japan's greatest swordsmith. His surviving katanas are national treasurers, the finest and most beautiful ever made. He was both a brilliant artist and an uncompromising technician. His swords are beautiful, light, and deadly: perfectly balanced not only in their weighting but also in their composition; hard enough to hold an edge yet supple enough not to shatter in combat.

Masamune was clearly a genius at his craft. His forge, his hammer, and his skill transformed the imperfect raw material with which he worked into an exquisite balance of the aesthetic and the practical. His blades are the standard by which all others are measured.[1]

So it is with this fifth step in the productive thinking process. Preliminary ideas are often weak and impure and have to be driven through a forge to become powerful, workable solutions. Forge the Solution is the step in which ideas are repeatedly heated and hammered and then honed. Their flaws are ferreted out and transformed into strengths. I often describe this part of the process as fighting for failure. We hunt for every flaw, every imperfection. We beat and sear and challenge our ideas so that they emerge from the forge as strong as possible. Then, like Masamune, we burnish them and give them the best edge possible. We imbue them with transformative power. We fight for success.

Selecting Ideas for Development

In Step 4: Generate Answers, you rained ideas. Then you applied convergent, critical thinking to your long list to choose the ideas you thought were the most promising. Those ideas are not solutions yet. They are embryonic notions for solution, what I call solution alternatives. They are the stuff from which you will build your solutions in the final two steps of the process. In this step, Forge the Solution, you will create a lot of heat. Your ideas will begin to boil and churn and build up steam. Then, in Step 6: Align Resources, you will harness that steam and translate it into action. As they enter Forge the Solution, your ideas are still only potential energy. By the time they exit Align Resources, they will be kinetic.

As a result of your work in Generate Answers, you now have three to six ideas that are worth exploring further. Ideally at least some of them are stretch ideas: ideas you wouldn't normally have thought of, ideas that may even be a little scary.

Just as Masamune had to select the steel he would burn and pound into his blades, you need to select the ideas you will be working on further. Your first task is to evaluate your short list of ideas against the key Success Criteria you established in Step 2: What's Success? There is no magic number of key Success Criteria. Simple challenges may have two or three. Very complex challenges may have dozens. At this stage, however, I recommend that you try to keep things simple and select no more than three to seven criteria for your initial evaluation. If necessary, you can add Success Criteria at a later stage, but for now you probably want to focus on your "deal makers," "deal breakers," and "near deal breakers."

One of the easiest ways to assess ideas against Success Criteria is to use an Evaluation Screen.[2] Create a grid with as many columns as you have key Success Criteria and as many rows as you have ideas. Add a title row at the top to hold the descriptions of your key Success Criteria. Add a title column at the left to hold short descriptions of your ideas.

Here is a simplified Evaluation Screen that the JetWays innovation team might have used (see page 181):

Each blank cell in the grid represents the relationship between an idea and a single Success Criterion.

Now evaluate each idea against each Success Criterion by placing a plus sign in the intersecting cell if that idea meets that criterion or a minus sign if it doesn't; if you feel it neither meets nor doesn't meet the

	Appeal to Business Travelers	Avoid Safety Regulation Concerns	Hard for Competition to Copy
Middle seats cheaper			
Middle seats face backward			
Middle seats as Flying Office			

criterion, leave the cell blank. Do this *criterion by criterion*. In other words, first fill the leftmost blank column so that each idea is evaluated against the first Success Criterion. Then move to the next column, evaluating each idea against your second Success Criterion. Continue filling out the grid column by column until you have worked through all the Success Criteria.

It is very important that you proceed through the Evaluation Screen criterion by criterion, completing one column at a time, rather than going through it by ideas. If you evaluate a single idea first (by each of your criteria before moving on to the next idea), you may inadvertently be setting up that idea as a benchmark against which all the other ideas will be measured. By evaluating criterion by criterion, you tend to minimize the common evaluation distortions that result from two well-known cognitive biases called the halo effect and the contrast effect.[3]

When you've finished working through your Evaluation Screen, you should have a matrix filled with pluses, minuses, and blank cells.

Here is how the JetWays Evaluation Screen might be filled in:

	Appeal to Business Travelers	Avoid Alienating Other Passengers	Hard for Competition to Copy
Middle seats cheaper	+	+	−
Middle controls entertainment		−	
Middle seats as Flying Office	+		+

Glancing at the grid as a whole may give you an instant sense of how the ideas stack up. Some will probably stand out as meeting many of your Success Criteria. Others may appear weaker. But even if you see one or two ideas that appear far superior to the others, you are not ready to make final decisions yet. You need to make a second pass through the screen.

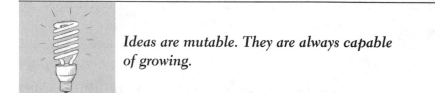

Ideas are mutable. They are always capable of growing.

The first time through, you looked at how each idea might or might not meet a given criterion. This time, once again going through the matrix criterion by criterion, you look at how you might *alter* each idea to give it a better chance of meeting a given criterion. Ask yourself how you might you change an idea to erase its minus against a particular criterion (or even to transform it into a plus), how you might change an idea from a neutral to a plus, and how you might change an idea from a plus to an even bigger plus. In the JetWays case, for example, "middle seat controls entertainment" might shift from a neutral for business travelers to a positive if the entertainment console contained a stock ticker and "middle seat as flying office" might be an even bigger plus for the business traveler if some sort of business club concept were attached to it.

One of the pitfalls of evaluating ideas is that we often tend to judge them in their static, prepubescent state. As soon as we write them down, we fossilize them. We think of them as frozen, just words on paper. But ideas are mutable. They are always capable of growing. Each time we look at them, we can see something new. We just need to give ourselves permission to do so. By reevaluating your ideas, you give them a second chance to live. I call this kind of assessment Generative Judgment: a philosophy of evaluation designed to improve the quality of the things we're examining rather than simply accepting or rejecting them. Generative Judgment contrasts with the traditional binary approach to judgment. Binary judgment is a zero sum process. It assesses things as either good or bad, acceptable or unacceptable, winners or losers. Generative Judgment asks instead, "How can I make this better?" By looking at your Evaluation Screen a second time and trying to rethink your ideas so that they perform better against your Success Criteria, you increase your chances of developing truly excellent ideas.

A second pitfall of traditional evaluation schemes is that many of them tend to fool us into thinking we are being more rational than we're actually capable of being. You might be saying to yourself, "This plus, minus, blank thing is far too crude a measure. Where are the numbers? Where are the probabilities? You can't possibly compare alternatives effectively using such a gross calibration!"

Many versions of decision matrices use finer calibrations, but those more complex systems generally fail on two counts.

First, our perceptions are usually not as fine as the calibrations that are proposed. Think about the last time you filled in an evaluation sheet with a 10-point scale. I'll bet you scratched you head more than once. Let's say you are rating three items against three criteria on an even simpler 7-point scale, with 21 points in total. You add up your rows and see that one idea scores 14, another 17, and another 18. What's the real difference between a 17 and an 18?

Second, even if you could make such fine distinctions, is the item that scores 18 better than the one that scores 17? Not necessarily. Decision analysis suggests that there will always be criteria that we don't include in our grids but that are emotionally present and deeply important to us. That's why in group sessions one often sees people become uncomfortable with choosing the alternative with the highest score. Often someone will suggest that the ideas be reevaluated. In the second round, the idea that scored 17 the first time now magically gets 19 and the idea that originally scored 18 is demoted to 15. People have transferred their hidden criteria to the visible categories on the grid to come up with the decision they wanted to make in the first place.

Human beings are just not very good at making decisions based on multivariate analysis. Cognitive research conducted by Daniel Kahneman, Paul Slovick, and Amos Tversky has demonstrated that far from aiding effective decision making, intense analysis can actually result in poorer decisions than relying on one's "gut."[4] The irony is that although we *want* to justify our decision making with finely calibrated metrics, in the end we often call a mulligan on the first decision and rejig it to suit our gut feelings. It's the "scientific" version of the coin-flipping technique we've all used. When we lose the flip, we say, "Okay, how about two out of three?"

The Danish mathematician and poet Piet Hein described the decision-making dilemma in one of his lovely little Grooks. It's called "A Psychological Tip":

> *Whenever you're called on to make up your mind,*
> *and you're hampered by not having any,*
> *the best way to solve the dilemma, you'll find,*
> *is simply by spinning a penny.*
> *No—not so that chance shall decide the affair*
> *while you're passively standing there moping;*
> *but the moment the penny is up in the air,*
> *you suddenly know what you're hoping.*[5]

Unless you're measuring something that is absolutely measurable (kilowatts per hour, rotations per minute, computations per second), don't bother going into the fine detail of mathematically comparing one alternative with another. It takes a lot of time, and in the end it's neither very useful nor very accurate. What's much more useful and much more human is to get a broad sense of how well your options meet your Success Criteria and choose the ones that seem to offer the most potential for further exploration.

Once you have worked through your Evaluation Screen a second time, upgrading as many ideas as you can from minuses to blanks, from blanks to pluses, and even from minuses to pluses, you are ready to move

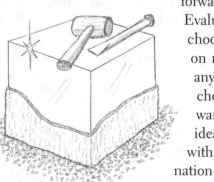

forward. Look at the big picture, the Evaluation Screen as a whole. Then choose the one idea you want to work on now. Remember, you haven't lost any of the ideas that haven't been chosen. You can and probably will want to go back and work on those ideas later. But for now, move forward with the one idea (or possibly a combination of ideas) that you have the most energy to develop.

Powering-Up the Solution

You're now ready for the next substep: Powering-Up your solution. Here again, you'll be using Generative Judgment.

One of my favorite tools in the productive thinking arsenal is called POWER. Just as wood and wind can transform the smallest spark into a raging forest fire, so too can POWER transform an embryonic idea into a robust solution. POWER can supercharge almost any idea.

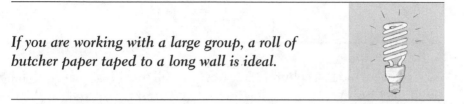

If you are working with a large group, a roll of butcher paper taped to a long wall is ideal.

POWER is an acronym for Positives, Objections, What else, Enhancements, and Remedies. POWER asks five basic questions:

- Positives: What's good about the idea? Why might it succeed?

- Objections: What are the idea's flaws? Why might it fail?

- What else?: What else might be in the idea that hasn't been articulated yet?

- Enhancements: How might the positives be made even stronger?

- Remedies: How might the objections be overcome?

Here's how it works.

The most useful way to conduct a POWER exercise is to work with a large sheet of paper and orient it horizontally. If you are working with a large group, a roll of butcher paper taped to a long wall is ideal. You can also use five sheets of flip chart paper arranged so that you can see them all at once. Write your selected idea at the top of the sheet. You can write the idea in a short form, but be sure you have a complete version of the idea to refer to, particularly if you've already modified it in the Evaluation Screen exercise. Next, divide the sheet into five equal columns, as shown here.

Make the Middle Seat a Flying Office

P	O	W	E	R
Positives	Objections	What else?	Enhancements	Remedies

Label the first column "Positives." List all the things that are good about the idea. What do you like about it? What might others like about it? Why is it practical? Why is it brilliant? Why is it sexy? Why is it guaranteed to succeed? Why will this idea get you were you want to go? Why are you a genius for thinking of it? List as many positives as you can. Praise your idea until its face turns red with embarrassment.

Here is an abbreviated example of what JetWays' Positives might look like:

Make the Middle Seat a Flying Office

P	O	W	E	R
Positives	Objections	What else?	Enhancements	Remedies
More middle seat demand				
Good differentiator				
Hard to copy first in				

Label the second column "Objections." List all the things that are wrong with the idea. Why won't it work? What are the chinks in its armor? What are its fatal flaws? Why will it get you fired? Arrested? Why will your friends think you've lost your mind? Why will your enemies rub their hands together in glee? Why does your idea suck? Be its worst critic. Grind it into the ground. Stomp on it. Tear it apart. Fight for failure.

Here is an abbreviated example of what JetWays' Objections might look like:

Make the Middle Seat a Flying Office

P	O	W	E	R
Positives	Objections	What else?	Enhancements	Remedies
Elevates status of middle seat	Could still be copied			
Good differentiator	Not enough room to fit it in			
Hard to copy first in	Privacy concerns while working			

Label the third column "What Else?" Having examined the pluses and minuses of your idea, you have undoubtedly developed new perspectives. List all the things that might be implied by the idea that didn't occur to you earlier. What does it remind you of? Is there something you can add to it? A hidden assumption you should articulate? What else might the idea allow you to accomplish? Are there any other ideas you generated in Step 4: Generate Answers that might dovetail nicely with this idea or extend its impact? Focus on the word *else*. What *else* is in the idea? How *else* might it be expressed? Who *else* might be involved? Where *else* might it work? When *else* might it be useful? List all the elses that occur to you about your idea.

Here is an abbreviated example of what JetWays' What elses? might look like:

Make the Middle Seat a Flying Office

P	O	W	E	R
Positives	Objections	What else?	Enhancements	Remedies
Elevates status of middle seat	Could still be copied	Test market for receptivity		
Good differentiator	Not enough room to fit it in	A flying office club?		
Hard to copy first in	Privacy concerns while working	Partnership opportunities?		

Label the fourth column "Enhancement." Review your list of Positives. Now list all the ways in which each one might be made better, made stronger, improved. How might you make your idea even stronger? How might you make it even more likely to succeed? How might you build on the positive attributes you identified? How might you emphasize them? How might you use your resources better? Is there something faster, bigger, better, smoother, longer, hotter, colder, or snappier that you might apply to your idea? How might it be more solid? More stable? More cost-effective? Longer-lasting?

Here is an abbreviated example of what JetWays' Enhancements might look like:

Make the Middle Seat a Flying Office

P	O	W	E	R
Positives	Objections	What else?	Enhancements	Remedies
Elevates status of middle seat	Could still be copied	Test market for receptivity	Partner with Herman Miller?	
Good differentiator	Not enough room to fit it in	A flying office club?	Brand the entire program	
Hard to copy first in	Privacy concerns while working	Partnership opportunities?	Offer tools, connectivity	

Label the fifth column "Remedies." Review your list of Objections. Now list all the ways in which each of them might be overcome. How might you remediate your idea's shortcomings? How might you fix its flaws? How might you counter other people's concerns about it? Don't satisfice on merely neutralizing the weak spots in your idea. Go further. Turn some of the objections into positives. How else might you reduce the downsides to the idea? How might you bulletproof it? When you were listing all the objections to the idea, you were fighting for failure. How might you now fight for success?

Here is an abbreviated example of what JetWays' Remedies might look like (see page 189):

Once you've filled out your POWER grid, you will have developed a new perspective on your idea. It may not seem like the same idea at all. POWER is a transformational tool.

Make the Middle Seat a Flying Office

P	O	W	E	R
Positives	Objections	What else?	Enhancements	Remedies
Elevates status of middle seat	Could still be copied	Test market for receptivity	Partner with Herman Miller?	Brand it, make it central to image
Good differentiator	Not enough room to fit it in	A flying office club?	Brand the entire program	Remove alternate seats
Hard to copy first in	Privacy concerns while working	Partnership opportunities?	Offer tools, connectivity	Create blinders, special lighting

Whether the idea has merely evolved or transformed entirely, the next step is to review your POWER grid. Highlight or circle items that seem particularly interesting or relevant. See if some of the thoughts you added to your grid stimulate yet other ideas. Take a few minutes to revisit your idea clusters from Step 4: Generate Answers. Are there any ideas you left behind that might be incorporated easily and naturally into your evolving solution?

You can also iterate your POWER exercise several times to keep evolving, strengthening, and refining the idea. Conducting successive POWER exercises is analogous to a technique used by traditional Japanese bladesmiths. To compensate for their imperfect raw materials, they used a method of repeatedly heating, folding, and beating the metal. That iterative process produced multiple benefits. It eliminated bubbles, which are potential weak spots that might have been lurking in the metal. It burned off many of the impurities and homogenized others, spreading them evenly throughout the finished product, also reducing weak spots. And it created layers of steel, enhancing both the strength and flexibility of the blade and giving each katana a unique and highly prized "grain." By iterating your POWER exercise, you are in effect folding, flattening, and refolding your solution, imbuing it with greater strength and flexibility.

As with any good thing, however, it's possible to go too far. Too much sugar in your coffee will ruin it. Too much exercise can destroy muscles. Too much sleep may sap your energy. Too many POWER iterations can result in *over*thinking your solution, second-guessing it, and draining it of its creative vitality. To produce blades with the optimum balance of strength and flexibility, 8 to 12 folds (resulting in 256 to 4096 layers) works best. Modern metallurgy reveals that more than 12 folds may actually weaken the blade. Although some katanas are known to have as many as 20 folds (resulting in over one million layers!), those made by Japan's greatest swordsmith are always within the range of 8 to 12 folds. So, by all means, iterate your POWER exercise, but remember the moderation of Masamune.

Your final task in this substep is to write your Powered-Up solution in detail. Look at all the work you've done so far and write two or more paragraphs completing the phrase "What I see myself doing is . . ." or "What I see us doing is. . . ." This is a detailed synopsis of your idea. It offers enough substance to allow anyone reading it to get a good sense of what the solution will actually look and feel like once it's been implemented. This expression of your solution contains a robust description of what your idea will accomplish, what its benefits are, what resources it will require, and how it will overcome the obstacles to success. Think of these several paragraphs as the executive summary of your idea. Through POWER, you've given yourself the opportunity to tell the story of your idea, transforming it from a vague headline into something that can spark the imagination of those who hear it.

The Hidden Power of POWER

The primary power of POWER is its ability to transform run-of-the-mill or even weak ideas into robust solutions. But in our work with organizations we've often observed other benefits from using POWER tool.

One of my colleagues, Scott Carlisle, does high-level coaching for a team of senior executives at a highly successful Hollywood entertainment company.[6] The company was conducting a strategic planning retreat, focusing on cultural change and management development as two of its main operating objectives for the next three to five years. These are sticky issues for many organizations, and this one was no different. Often the terms *cultural change* and *management development* are seen as code words for *reorganization and purge*. Nevertheless, the executive in charge was determined to push the strategy forward. He was convinced that unless the company was perceived to be acting aggressively, the leading-edge image it had worked so hard to cultivate would be undermined. In Hollywood, image is everything. So the issue was important.

The atmosphere in the strategy session was cool. According to Scott, "You could feel the tension just below the veneer of collegiality. People were reluctant to talk about the issues. But I knew that one way or another we had to come to terms with the moose on the table. We could either go to war over it. Or we could do it productively." Rather than try to tackle the brewing discomfort directly, Scott decided to kick off the conversation by using POWER not to evaluate ideas for a solution but to frame a discussion around the issues themselves. The team members were already familiar with the principle of creative and critical thinking, so he asked them to list their ideas and defer judgment. He then led them through a POWER exercise:

What was positive about addressing cultural change and management development at this time? Why might it be good for the company, for its employees, for its standing in the industry?

"You could feel the tension just below the veneer of collegiality. People were reluctant to talk about the issues."—Scott Carlisle

---

What were the objections to focusing on such a strategy now? How might it harm the company and its ability to compete?

What else might the senior team consider as it discussed those two issues? What other ideas for corporate revitalization might be worth exploring? What other models might there be to learn from? Who else might be involved? How else might the issue be framed?

How might the positives that had already been identified be enhanced? How might the company take advantage of its new focus? How might it promote itself both within and outside the industry?

How might the objections that had been raised be overcome? How might those who felt threatened see the benefits of change? How might the proposed change initiatives focus not only on enhancing the effectiveness of the company but also on improving the effectiveness of those who worked for it?

Through the POWER exercise the concerns of the group were aired and addressed. As a result, many of the group's fears and suspicious began to dissipate. The people at the retreat actually became energized by the potential benefits that had emerged. Each person wrote down the five ideas from the POWER exercise he or she thought were the most intriguing. They structured their points in a mindmap to understand how the ideas and concerns related to one another. By the end of the weekend, they had developed a coherent action plan. What had looked like an inevitable train wreck had been transformed into one of the most productive sessions the team had ever had.

Scott was happy. His direct clients were happy. And the company emerged from its strategic retreat with a course of action that the entire senior team was committed to.

POWER was designed specifically for use within the Productive Thinking Model, but if you begin to use it, I think you'll see it has many other applications as well, from defining the key issues in conflict situations to problem analysis to team building. Whenever Generative Judgment may help move issues and people forward, POWER can be a great way to get things going.

SUMMARY

Forge the Solution consists of two substeps, both of which employ the principle of Generative Judgment and both of which may be iterated several times depending on the complexity of the issues and the time available. The first substep is to use an Evaluation Screen to compare the three to five ideas you selected in Generate Answers with the key Success Criteria developed earlier in What's Success? Then you choose the most promising ones to develop further. The second substep is to use the POWER tool to analyze, improve, and refine an embryonic idea into a robust solution.

- Using the Evaluation Screen, compare the most promising ideas from Step 4: Generate Answers with the key Success Criteria identified in Step 2: What's Success? Review the first pass comparison, using the principle of Generative Judgment to improve each idea as measured against each Success Criterion. Select the most promising ideas for further development.

- Using the POWER tool, evaluate, stress-test, improve, and refine each selected idea to create robust, Powered-Up solutions. Rewrite each

> Powered-Up Solution in a way that clearly commu-
> nicates its essence and can form the basis of a pre-
> liminary action plan: an executive summary that
> tells the story of the idea

The desired outcome of Forge the Solution is a clear articulation of one or more Powered-Up solutions that meet Success Criteria,
are stress-tested to reveal potential weaknesses, create value for
stakeholders, and have a good chance of resolving the Itch and
achieving the Target Future.

Growing Ideas

Think of POWER as a way to grow your idea. In a sense, growing an
idea in POWER parallels the stages of human development. When you
were young, if you were lucky, your parents and the other adults
around you encouraged you. They named and praised all the positive
things about you. The people who loved you highlighted your positives,
praised you to the sky, and got you ready to explore the wonderful
youness of you. This stage of your personal development is analogous
to the Positives in POWER. It pats you on the back.

Eventually, you had to leave the protection of your home and
confront the outside world. That new, outside world wasn't nearly as
positive or supportive as the world you experienced at home. It can be
difficult to succeed in school. It can be painful to try to make friends.
It can be frustrating to be thwarted. Life is full of suffering and disap-
pointment. This stage of your personal development is analogous to
the Objections in POWER. It's a dose of reality that can hit you hard.

Eventually, as you travel through the outside world of school,
jobs, and friends, you are exposed to a wide range of stimuli that
didn't exist in your home, things you never dreamed of. There's a great
big world out there full of the new, the exciting, the frightening, the
exhilarating. These are the What elses? in POWER.

As you strive toward your goals in life, whether they are clearly
or vaguely defined, you tend to reinforce and enhance your strengths.
You build on your natural gifts. You practice, you sharpen, you make
yourself better. This stage of your development is analogous to the
Enhancements in POWER.

Finally, as you grow, you begin to acknowledge, understand,
and be dissatisfied with your weaknesses. You make efforts to address

them, patching the cracks, filling the holes, sometimes transforming your life with new revelations and new possibilities. This stage of your personal development is analogous to the Remedies in POWER.

Your ideas are not much different from you. And they deserve no less than you do. They are, after all, an expression of you. Like you, they need nurturing and encouragement, challenges and hurdles, to be the best they can be.

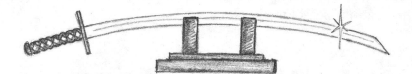

Step Six:
Align Resources

Step 1: What's Going On?

Step 2: What's Success?

Step 3: What's the Question?

Step 4: Generate Answers

Step 5: Forge the Solution

Step 6: Align Resources

In preparing for battle
I have always found that plans are useless,
but planning is indispensable.

Dwight D. Eisenhower

Step 6: Align Resources

Here Be Lions

On April 13, 1970, at almost exactly 9:08 PM U.S. Central Daylight Time, after a slight delay caused by traveling 321,860 kilometers, a radio signal crackled in a large room in Texas. Often misquoted, the voice on the radio said, "Okay, Houston, we've had a problem here." That initial report from *Apollo XIII* Command Module pilot Jack Swigert began an unprecedented 87-hour period during which just about everyone with access to a radio or television was focused on the lives of three men whose names, prior to that moment had meant nothing to most of them.

As a result of a series of minor mistakes, mechanical faults, and mistimings, each of which would almost certainly have been inconsequential in isolation, the number two tank on the *Apollo XIII* Service Module, which supplied both oxygen and power to the spacecraft, blew up. The explosion destroyed the tank, damaged the plumbing that supplied *Apollo*'s fuel cells, caused a leak in the remaining oxygen tank, and damaged the main engine of the ship. At that moment *Apollo* was 56 hours away from earth and rushing toward the moon at thousands of kilometers per hour.

O ver the next three and a half days, thousands of engineers at NASA's Manned Spacecraft Center in Houston, Grumman Aircraft Engineering in New York, and North American Aviation in California worked day and night to keep astronauts Lovell, Swigert, and Haise alive and bring them safely home. During those days they made hundreds of life-and-death decisions, including the following[1]:

- Continue traveling to the moon and take the so-called free return option, using the moon's gravity to slingshot the capsule back to earth, instead of trying to fire the main rocket to turn the ship around in midflight.

- Move the three astronauts into the Lunar Module and use it as a lifeboat for nearly four days even though it was designed only to keep two men alive for two days.

- Figure out how to use the batteries in the Lunar Module to boost the batteries in the Command

Module to power up the Lunar Module (something like trying to start your car with a battery designed for a flashlight in order to recharge the flashlight).

• Jury-rig a system to filter carbon dioxide from the air of the Lunar Module, using a plastic bag, tubing, a sock, the cover of a flight manual, and lots of duck tape.

Each of these and countless other decisions, along with the actions that stemmed from them, was executed perfectly even though the controllers on the ground and the astronauts in space were stressed, sleep-deprived, and, in the case of the astronauts, very, very cold. Even today those who saw it get emotional when they recall the television image of the *Apollo* capsule and its parachutes—three red and white canopies—appearing in the blue morning sky above the southern Pacific Ocean.

The Value of Planning

In Chapter 11, "Step 5: Forge the Solution," I described some of the ways we fool ourselves into thinking we make clear, dissectible, rational decisions. Daniel Kahneman and Amos Tversky, among others, have produced a body of evidence that strongly suggests we don't, that most of our decisions are based on partial information, and that the decisions we make from our gut are often as good as or better than the ones we ponder.

We often also fool ourselves about the value of our plans. Plans give us the illusion of control. We think that the more detailed and exhaustive our plans are, the more likely it is that the future will actually mirror our vision. But it rarely even comes close. As *Apollo XIII* and the war in Iraq and your last dinner party all make abundantly clear, we have very little control over events. One of history's greatest and most successful military strategists, Field Marshal Helmuth von Moltke, once observed, "No plan survives contact with the enemy." Or as Gilda Radner, playing Roseanna Roseannadanna, used to say on *Saturday Night Live*, "It's always something!"

A plan is a thing, an organized set of data marshaled around targets and timelines. In some sense, it's a snapshot of how people felt and thought at one instant in time. A plan is a noun. Often, we stick with our plans even though the world around us has changed. But the word *plan* can also be a verb, and therein lies its power. *To plan* is to prepare, to understand, to steep yourself in your material until you know its every nuance. That's what Eisenhower meant when he said that "plans are useless, but planning is indispensable." It is not the plan that is important but the plan*ning*. The plan for *Apollo XIII* failed: They never did land on the moon. The planning for *Apollo XIII* was a brilliant success. Without it, Lovell, Swigert, and Haise could never have made it home.

The value of planning is threefold:

- Planning gives you an opportunity to know your stuff. It is a way to learn what you'll need to know to succeed. The more you know about the territory you will be entering, the more capable you will be of making adjustments as you go.

- Planning is a way of gaining commitment. By involving other people in your planning, you give them a chance to buy in, to make the project their own. One of the most effective team-building strategies is to plan together.

- Planning is a powerful way to visualize success. Throughout the planning process you are constantly forced to reference the future you are imagining. The more you do that, the more deeply ingrained that vision becomes and the more likely you are to be motivated to make it real.

In short, the value of *planning* is that it makes you better at *doing*.

This final step in the productive thinking process, Align Resources, is not about having a plan. It's about planning. Planning is essential to productive thinking. In this chapter I will introduce you to several powerful tools to help you think through your project: brainslipping to define your action steps, Assistors and Resistors to analyze who will support you and who won't, the Great Wall of Time to create a timeline, and EFFECT to ensure that you identify all the resources you will need.

•   •   •

Early mapmakers used the phrase *hic abundant leones,* loosely translated as "there are lots of lions around here," to denote unexplored regions that might abound in wild animals or other dangers. It was an all-purpose warning not to trust the map completely, since some of it might be guesswork. Even today mapmakers know that no map, no plan, can be entirely accurate. Even the most modern satellite-generated map can fail us, as anyone who has encountered a roadblock or an unmarked one-way street while using a GPS navigation system can attest.

The same is true of plans. No plan is perfect. No plan can foresee all eventualities. But where plans fail, planning can see you through. That's why Step 6: Align Resources is so important. I recommend that all my clients work through this step even if their projects will eventually be supported by project management professionals with sophisticated critical path methodologies and resource allocation algorithms.

Align Resources is where you determine what must be done to actualize your solution. What resources will you need? Who are the people who will help you? Who are the people who will get in the way? What energy will you need? What funds, what time, what environment, what conditions, what materials will you need? This is the step in which you set tasks, align resources, and assign responsibilities. The outcome of this step is a platform for action.

Planning can be quite an eye-opener. It's where you see whether you have enough rubber to meet the road. You'll find this phase of the process particularly revealing if you are working with a group. As you'll

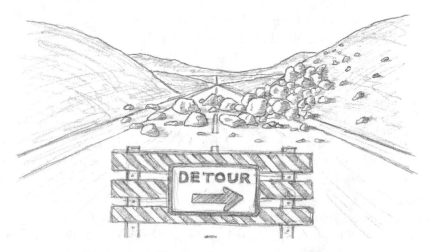

Where plans fail, planning can see you through.

see, one of the most important outcomes of Align Resources is assigning responsibilities and accountabilities for the action steps the group creates. If no one takes responsibility for an action step, there's very little chance it will get done. So whether you are an execution team of 1 or 100, be sure to include *everyone* who might have responsibility for one or more action steps. Unless you make assignments, your plan won't fly.

In Chapters 10 and 11, "Step 4: Generate Answers" and "Step 5: Forge the Solution," you made it rain by generating long lists of ideas, evaluated your ideas against your Success Criteria, and lit a fire underneath it all by powering your ideas into robust solutions. Now you need to capture the steam and transform that power into results. Here's how you do that.

Defining the Tasks

The first step is to conduct a straightforward brainstorm, using divergent, creative thinking to make long lists of the action steps you will need to take to implement your solution. Even if your project involves only you, I strongly recommend doing this with a group. It is much easier to generate a comprehensive list of action steps with a group of people than by yourself. If executing your plan will involve other people, you absolutely *must* do this step as a group. If you expect others to implement some of the tasks in your plan, you'll have a much higher chance of success by involving them in defining those tasks.

The most useful brainstorming technique for this step is a tool I call brainslipping.[2] Brainslipping consists of writing your ideas on sticky notes,[3] one idea per note, and slapping them up on a wall. The purpose is to generate as many possible action steps as you can without judging, without censoring, without differentiating between big steps and little steps, without analyzing dependencies for critical paths, and without worrying about how realistic the ideas are. All you want to produce is a massive brain dump of all the possible action steps that might be required to turn your idea into reality. At the end of this process, you should have a wall full of sticky notes. Some will be major steps, some minor. Some may seem irrelevant. Some may even be silly. But on your wall you will have most of the key action steps for your plan.

Next, you need to use convergent, critical thinking to make sense of all possible action steps. Using a modified version of the C^5 tool (see pages 155–157), cluster the ideas for action steps that relate to one another. Some tasks will be dependent on others, and some will be stand-alone actions. Some tasks may need to be executed in the same physical space or at the same time or rely on common resources. Your aim is not to be perfect. You simply want to begin to understand the spectrum of actions. As you did when you started the productive thinking process in Step 1: What's Going On?, you are sorting the pieces of a puzzle, getting a sense of both the whole and its parts, so you can begin to understand the larger task before you.

As you do this, you will probably discover action steps that need to be combined into a more comprehensive step. You will decide that others make more sense if you divide them into two or more substeps. You will flag numerous slips that are duplicates and should be deleted. You will also note steps you're not sure about or don't understand. Make a separate category for steps that you're unsure about now but that you may want to revisit later.

Once your clusters begin to take shape, you may decide that it's useful to name the clusters and to rewrite the action steps within them for greater clarity. Groups usually find that this is the best time to start thinking about major steps and substeps, to really begin to understand the dependencies between ideas. As you examine your clusters, for each slip on which you've written a step, ask yourself, "Does this step have one or more substeps?" and "Does this step imply a major step?" If you need to add new slips for new steps, do so.

Defining Your Most Important Resources

Now take a look at your emerging plan as a whole. You still haven't put any steps in the right sequence, nor should you. But you do have a sense of the various actions that will be required. If you've been working as a group, all your steps will be on slips clustered on a large expanse of wall or butcher paper.[4] This is a good point at which to start thinking about the two most critical resources in any plan for action: Assistors and Resistors. Assistors are your natural allies: the people who will help you in large and small ways to achieve your plan. Resistors are those who are likely to oppose you or your plan: those who may have something to lose if your plan is accomplished or who are comfortable with things as they are.

Generate a list of Assistors. Whose support can you rely on? How will that support manifest itself? Will it be a contribution of additional resources, of time, of knowledge, of influence? Will it be moral support? Once you've defined who those people are, ask yourself how you might engage your Assistors even more. How might you persuade them to do even more for you and your project? As you list ideas here, they will probably imply additional action steps for your plan. If, for example, you decide that a meeting to explain your project to your Assistors is necessary, list that meeting and your preparation for it as additional steps in your plan. Write new slips for those steps and slap them on the wall.

We think the more detailed and exhaustive our plans, the more likely the future will actually mirror our vision. But it rarely even comes close.

Now list your potential Resistors. Who are they? How might their resistance manifest itself? Will they oppose you actively or passively? What is their motivation? As you did with your Assistors, ask yourself how you might influence them to be more receptive to your plan. How might you persuade your Resistors to be less resistant? How might you covert them from Resistors to Assistors? Again, if influencing your Resistors implies additional action steps, write a new slip for each one and slap it on the wall.

Now, with all or almost all your potential action steps clustered and labeled, you're ready to start putting them in the proper sequence.

The Great Wall of Time

On another wall or length of butcher block paper, preferably facing the wall on which you've clustered your action steps, create either a timeline or a calendar, whichever is more appropriate for your purposes. Make it big, the whole wall's worth, and label your time periods, either with actual days, weeks, months, quarters, or years for calendars or day 1, day 2, . . . day *n* (week 1, week 2, . . . week *n*; Q1, Q2, . . . Q*n*, etc.) for timelines. Separate your divisions with masking or painters' tape. I often refer to this grid as the Great Wall of Time,[5] although a client of mine who works in a very fast-paced industry prefers to call it the Great Wall of Evaporating Time.

The Great Wall of Time—a simple, but powerful scheduling tool.

Now, still working as a group, transfer each slip from the action list to the Great Wall of Time. *Only the person responsible for a given task should physically transfer the slip*, and only after he or she has initialed it. Place the slip on the Great Wall of Time to indicate when the task will be *complete*. As slips are transferred from the action list to the Great Wall of Time, people in the group may begin to shuffle them around to accommodate other tasks that need to be accomplished beforehand. That's fine. Shuffling and juggling are quite appropriate at this stage.

Inevitably, some slips from the action list will not get transferred to the Great Wall of Time. Perhaps they are redundant or unclear. Perhaps they aren't really necessary to the project. It may also be that they *are* critically important to the project but no one has agreed to take responsibility for them. Here is the one incontrovertible law of planning: A *task unclaimed is a task undone*. This law is as fundamental and immutable as Newton's laws of motion. If no one puts his or her name on a task slip, that task will not get done. Period. At this point you have three choices: persuade a member of your group to take responsibility for the unclaimed task, find someone outside your group who is willing and competent to do so, or take it on yourself. You don't necessarily need to find someone who will actually *perform* the task, at least not at this stage. You want someone who will agree to be *accountable* for the task. As the project unfolds, the accountable person may assign the task to a third person, a chain of command, or an entire team. What's important as you align your resources is to ensure that *someone* takes responsibility for the task's completion.

Once your timeline or calendar begins to take shape, there are several more things you need to do.

Producing an EFFECT

By identifying and planning to engage your Assistors and Resistors, you've begun to address your most crucial resource requirements: the human resources. But there are other resources you need to consider as well. To identify and understand the plan's full range of resource requirements, I recommend a simple but effective tool called EFFECT.

EFFECT stands for Energy, Funds, Free time, Expertise, Conditions, and Things. Use this tool as a checklist to determine the resources you'll need to accomplish each step of your plan.

- *Energy*. What levels or types of energy will you need to complete each action step? Will you need high levels of personal commitment, long stretches of intense activity, electricity to run power tools? If you already have the energy resources you need, note where and how you'll access them. If you do not already have the energy resources you need, how you will acquire them? Does acquiring them imply additional action steps? If so, make a new slip for each one, make sure someone has responsibility for it, and place it on your timeline.

- *Funds*. What financial resources will you need to complete each action step? What financial resources do you already have? If those resources are sufficient, note where and how you'll access them. If you do not already have the funds you need, how you will acquire them? Does acquiring them imply additional action steps? If so, make a new slip for each one, make sure someone has responsibility for it, and place it on your timeline.

- *Free time*. How much time will you need to complete each action step? Unlike other resources, time is neither renewable nor elastic. You can't make new time or recapture lost time. The only source from which you can draw time is the pool of time already allocated (explicitly or implicitly) to other things. In this sense, time is fungible; you can't manufacture it, but you may be able to borrow it from somewhere else. How much time will you need to complete each step? If the time required is available, note the amount. If you don't have sufficient free time, how might you borrow it from other activities? Does doing so imply additional action steps? If so, make a new slip for each one, make sure someone has responsibility for it, and place it on your timeline.

- *Expertise.* What type or levels of knowledge will you need to complete each action step? What do you need to know? What skills do you need? If you need to rewire a wall switch and don't know how, you'll either have to find someone who does or learn how to do it yourself. If you already have access to the expertise or knowledge required for a step, note how you will access it. If you need to acquire more, how will you do so? Does acquiring the requisite expertise imply additional action steps? If so, make a new slip for each one, make sure someone has responsibility for it, and place it on your timeline.

- *Conditions.* What conditions you will need to complete each action step? Must there be a contract or agreement in place before you can proceed? Must the outside temperature be mild? Must it be below freezing? What conditions are necessary for each step of your plan? If the conditions required for a step are already in place, note them. If conditions may change (such as the weather), how might you accommodate such a change? Will you need a contingency plan for this step? If so, make a new slip, make sure someone has responsibility for it, and place it on your timeline. For conditions that aren't yet in place, how can you produce them? Does producing them imply additional action steps? If so, make a new slip for each one, make sure someone has responsibility for it, and place it on your timeline.

- *Things*. What things, such as material resources or equipment, will you need to complete each action step? Will you need sticky notes, a laptop computer, a construction crane? If you already have those resources, note them. If you need to acquire them, how will you do so? Does acquiring them imply additional action steps? If so, make a new slip for each one, make sure someone has responsibility for it, and place it on your timeline.

E	F	F	E	C	T
Energy	Funds	Free Time	Expertise	Conditions	Things

As you can see, the EFFECT tool is iterative. Each time you make a new slip, you need to ask the EFFECT questions for that slip. Therefore, applying the EFFECT tool can take time, but once you've gone through it, you will have a very clear idea of the resources you need to complete your plan and what you will need to do to acquire them. In much the same way that the POWER tool from Step 5: Forge the Solution can transform an embryonic idea into a Powered-Up Solution, EFFECT will help you transform a rough sketch of a plan into a robust platform for action.

The final element before you complete your work on the Great Wall of Time is to identify one or more observable outcomes for each of the action steps you've identified. Ask yourself what evidence there will be that the action step has been completed. Write on each slip how you will know the step is complete and note any deliverables for that step.

You should now have a wall with lots of slips on it, each with the name of an action step, all the resources required to accomplish it, how you'll know it's complete, and who's responsible for ensuring that it happens.

The Action Book

The Great Wall of Time is a useful tool for creating your plan, but it's not particularly portable. The best way to boil it down to a practical size is to create a summary spreadsheet of the timeline data as well as detailed task sheets for each action step. Outline each action step on a separate sheet and three-hole-punch it to fit into a binder. Master binders are kept by the project owner, and task-specific binders are issued to each of the project participants. As a preface to each action book, name the project with a complete description of the Powered-Up Solution and a project charter outlining the responsibilities and relationships among the people who will be involved in completing the project.

Here is a generic sheet we use with some of our clients:

Action Sheet	Step #		
Step		**Person responsible**	
Dependent on completion of		**Additional participants**	
Start	**End**	**Duration**	**Notes**
Deliverables or evidence of completion			
Assistors	**Actions to improve support**		
Resistors	**Actions to gain support**		
Resources	**Actions to acquire**		
		Date completed	

A generic action sheet for a single action step.

For small or less complex projects, an action book may be all you need to manage and monitor your work. For larger and more complex projects, you will probably hand off your action book to a project management specialist who in turn will create a detailed project plan, using whatever systems your organization favors.[6]

Whether your plan costs ten dollars or ten million to execute, whether it will be implemented by one person or hundreds, whether it will take one day or several years, remember that *your plan is not the same thing as your project*. You will undoubtedly encounter stumbling blocks and changes along the way. The value of your work lies not in the plan itself but in the planning you've put into it.

Bialystock and Bloom

One of my favorite places to walk and think is Central Park in New York City. On one such walk toward the end of summer in 1967, not far from the park's Columbus Circle entrance, I noticed the lights, scrims, and dollies of a film crew. As I moved in for a closer look, I saw a little old lady sitting on a park bench next to a stout, nattily dressed gentleman. I didn't recognize the lady, but Zero Mostel was unmistakable. Not much was happening in the scene. The two actors just sat there. I was reminded of *Babar and the Old Lady*. About a year later I finally saw the scene on film. It was part of a montage sequence in Mel Brooks's original version of *The Producers*.

I've always loved *The Producers* in its several incarnations. It's funny, it's human, and, for me at least, it's a wonderful little tale about productive thinking and the power of planning despite the failure of the plan.

Mostel's character, Max Bialystock, is a Broadway producer who's had a string of failures. Desperate to turn his fortunes around, Max swears he'll get back on top somehow. In the language of productive thinking, his Target Future is *If only I could find a way to once again be the "King of Broadway"!*

Max seizes on an observation made by his mousy accountant, Leo Bloom, that if you raised a lot of money but spent very little of it to produce an intentional flop, you could make more "profit" than you could with a hit. In the language of productive thinking, Max's Catalytic Question is *How might I produce the worst show of all time?*

Max finds his embryonic answer to that question in Franz Liebkind, a marginally sane neo-Nazi who's written a play called *Springtime for Hitler*. Max then proceeds to Power Up the idea and Align Resources that are absolutely guaranteed to produce the worst show ever:

- He hires the world's worst director and his partner, the world's most outrageous production designer, who want to make *Springtime* into a musical.
- He casts the tone-deaf Liebkind in the lead.
- He sells more than 100 percent of the show to investors.
- To cement the show's failure on opening night, he wishes anyone and everyone "good luck" instead of the Broadway requisite "break a leg."

As it turns out, of course, everything goes wrong. Liebkind actually *does* break his leg just before the opening curtain and must be replaced by the gay director Roger de Bris, whose *Führer* would be at home with the Village People. The show is a huge hit. Max is arrested, and Bloom flies off to Rio with the money.

> *"Plans are useless, but planning is indispensable."*
> —*Dwight D. Eisenhower*

But as with *Apollo XIII*, though the *plan* fails, the *planning* is a success. Bloom, having discovered that there's no business like show business, returns from Rio to take his part of the rap. Together in Sing Sing, based on their experience of producing a successful parody, Max and Leo mount the all-singing, all-dancing, all-convict production of *Prisoners of Love*. So successful is the show in remediating hardened criminals that they are pardoned. They reassemble the entire *Springtime* team and produce a blockbuster Broadway version of *Prisoners*, making Bialystock and Bloom the most successful producing partnership on the Great White Way. Eisenhower was right: Plans are useless, but planning is indispensable.

S U M M A R Y

Align Resources is the step in the Productive Thinking Model that identifies the actions and resources required to implement the Powered-Up Solution you defined in Step 5: Forge the Solution. Whether the project will be executed by one person or many, it is useful to involve a small group of people in identifying, aligning, and scheduling those resources.

- List all the possible action steps required to complete the plan without attempting to prioritize or sequence them. Cluster the action steps to eliminate duplications, group steps and substeps, and clarify individual tasks.

- Assess the big picture to identify potential Assistors and Resistors. Add action steps as necessary, aimed at influencing Assistors and Resistors.

- Ensure that each action step has an owner who is committed to its completion.

- Create a Wall of Time to place clusters of action steps in sequence and rearrange them according to dependencies.

- Conduct an EFFECT (Energy, Funds, Free time, Expertise, Conditions, and Things) analysis of each action step to determine the required resources; determine what resources are already in place and what resources must be acquired. Add action steps as necessary, aimed at acquiring needed resources.

- Identify and list observable outcomes for each action step.

- Transfer the information for each action step onto a single action sheet; insert the sheets in an action book to monitor and manage the project or hand it off to a project management specialist.

The desired outcome of Align Resources is a realistic preliminary plan of action, including people accountable for carrying out each individual action step.

Strategy and Tactics

Align Resources is the step in the productive thinking process in which strategy and tactics come together. Both are critical for success. As Sun Tzu wrote in *The Art of War*, "Strategy without tactics is the slowest route to victory. Tactics without strategy is the noise before defeat." Neither strategy nor tactics will prevail without commitment. Unless each action has a committed owner, even the most carefully considered plan is at risk.

PART 4

PRODUCTIVE THINKING IN
PRACTICE

Productive Thinking Redux

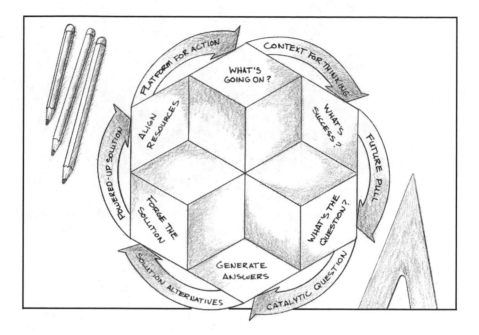

It's déjà vu all over again.

Yogi Berra

The Productive Thinking Model is a framework that will help you think better, think more effectively, think more powerfully. It builds on the work of over 50 years of cognitive research. Productive thinking relies on the overarching principle of separation of thinking: separating and alternating divergent, creative thinking and convergent, critical thinking—in other words, making lists and making choices. The model has six steps, each with a specified outcome. It is comprehensive model rather than a collection of tools or techniques.

The six steps of the model are:

Step 1: What's Going On? In this step you explore your issue and establish a vision for a future you want to achieve. We call this vision your Target Future.

Step 2: What's Success? In this step you define both "soft" and "hard" criteria for success.

Step 3: What's the Question? In this step you articulate, in the form of questions, the problems you need to solve to achieve your target future.

Step 4: Generate Answers. In this step you generate ideas for solving the problems you articulated in Step 3.

Step 5: Forge the Solution. In this step you select and develop the most promising ideas for a solution.

Step 6: Align Resources. In this step you define action steps and resource requirements for implementing the solution.

All models are wrong; some are useful. *George Box*

All models are wrong. At best they are imperfect reflections of reality. Like reflections, they necessarily have fewer dimensions than their subjects do. No painting of a sunset *is* a sunset. No poem of the sea can mist your nostrils with salt spray. Not even the most celebrated scientific explanations of nature are wholly true.

All models are wrong, but some are useful. Newtonian physics may not describe all of reality, but it's a very useful way to understand how the force of a kick transfers to a football as it flies toward a goal.

The Productive Thinking Model is a not a perfect description of the only way to solve a problem. But it *is* a useful way. I have seen it work countless times and in dozens of domains. I have seen it used to solve business problems, clarify sales situations, develop technical solutions, suggest new products, create marketing campaigns, reduce conflicts, map strategies, enhance relationships, reduce frustrations, orient careers, and resolve personal dilemmas. I have seen it help people in finance, manufacturing, engineering, marketing, politics, government, science, medicine, and family life. Occasionally I've seen it fail.

Still, it's just a model. It provides direction and guidance, but it is neither absolute nor immutable. I encourage you to use it flexibly, adapting it to your own needs, circumstances, and thinking styles. In the previous six chapters I described the model in detail from Step 1 to Step 6. In this chapter I will review the basic components of each step, again, from Step 1 to Step 6. In practice, however, you may not need to run through the steps in sequence every time. You may not even need to use them all. As in any discipline, to become good, you need first to learn the rules. To become great, you need to break them. Follow the advice given by Chieh Tzu Yüan Hua Chuan in *The Mustard Seed Garden Manual of Painting*: "Not to have a method is bad; to stop entirely at method is worse still. The aim of possessing method is to seem finally as if one had no method." Productive thinking is an orientation, not a prescription, a discipline, not a straitjacket.

Step 1: What's Going On?

What's Going On? is the central diagnostic foundation of productive thinking. It is one of the more time-consuming parts of the process, but it is critically important.

Regardless of the type of work you do—housework or homework, handwork or headwork, strategic work or tactical work—the better you understand what's really going on, the greater your chances of success. Nevertheless, What's Going On? is always the step that people want to rush through. In our initial conversations, new clients often say something like "I don't want to get into too much analysis. We already know what the problem is. We just need help with the solution." No doubt solutions are important. But how many times have you or your company come up with a great solution that didn't change anything? Sure, it was a great solution—to the wrong problem.

Often we're so anxious to relieve the Itch that we jump at the first idea we think may help. But spending the time to work through Step 1 — to really understand what's going on — can save countless hours, countless dollars, and endless blamestorming later on. I've often seen clients refuse to invest the up-front time to do things right, only to spend even more time doing things over. What a waste!

The board had already decided on its strategy: provide value-added services to members. Why weren't we figuring out how to do that?

Some years ago I ran a strategic planning session for one of the larger North American chambers of commerce. It had thousands of corporate members and high-level relationships with local, state, and federal governments. The chamber's board of directors was concerned about a decline in local membership. Those smaller companies, though not critical to the chamber from a financial point of view, give the organization the grassroots credibility it needs in its representations to governments. The board had decided that a good strategy for stemming the decline would be to offer local members a range of discount services that were often difficult for smaller companies to acquire, such as market research, professional development, and Web consultation. The purpose of our planning session was to figure out which services were most needed by local members and which ones the chamber could credibly provide.

On the day of the session, after outlining the process we would be using, I began with Step 1. Although there was lots of input from the group, I could see the board's president starting to squirm. As the morning progressed, his restlessness became outright agitation. Realizing that we needed to talk off line, I called a break. We huddled, and he expressed his frustration: Not only weren't we getting to any solutions, as he saw it, we weren't even getting to the problem! The board had already decided on its strategy: provide value-added services to members. Why weren't we figuring out how to do that?

I asked for his patience, promising that we would get to the heart of the matter but that it was essential to really understand what was going on with the issues, with the chamber, and with its various stakeholders.

When we broke for lunch, the president came up to me again. His frustration had morphed into gratitude. During the morning session we had discovered that three of the four services the board had considered offering would place the chamber in competition with many of its own members. The fourth was a service the chamber had very little credibility to deliver. A strategy that had seemed promising in theory turned out to be deeply flawed, potentially alienating as many members as it might attract. In the end, on the basis of our What's Going On? analysis, the chamber decided to focus not on providing services but on establishing a clearinghouse through which members could offer services to one another. The reconfigured strategy not only turned the membership trend around but created a new revenue stream for the chamber as well.

It's easy to fool ourselves into thinking we already know what the issues are. Often the true causes of our discomfort are so integral to our environment that we fail to recognize them. The more familiar things are, the easier it is not to pay attention to them.

One morning a few years ago I reached into our fridge for some milk. As I picked up the jug, I realized it was too light. There wouldn't be enough for my cereal, so I decided to go to the local convenience store.

To get there from my house, I went out the front door, walked down the path, turned right, walked a block, turned right, walked down a hill for a block, turned left, walked half a block, turned right, walked a few steps, and entered the store. I then went to the back of the store where the coolers are, got a jug of milk, then walked to the front of the store to pay. To get home, I reversed the process: left the store, turned left, walked a few steps, turned left, walked half a block, turned right, walked up the hill for a block, turned left, walked a block, turned left, walked up the path to the front door, then went to the back of the house and finally to the kitchen.

As I stood in front of the fridge holding the jug of milk, it occurred to me that the only evidence I had that I'd just taken a 15-minute walk was the now-heavy milk jug in my hand. I hadn't noticed the weather, the sounds, the people, the traffic. It was as though it had never happened, as if the light jug had become a heavy jug in an instant.

Like my walk to the store, the details of our business lives, our family lives, even the people we work and live with, can become so familiar to us that we stop noticing them. The only things we see are the patterns we've grown accustomed to. That's why it's so important to invest the time and effort to work through the first step of the process, to force ourselves to look at what's really going on.

In business situations, it can be very seductive to measure ourselves by how quickly we can get things done rather than by the quality of what we do. The seemly unquenchable quest for "productivity" can often undermine our ability to be truly productive. By cheating ourselves of the time it takes to understand what's going on, we run the risk of ending up with great solutions that don't address our real problems.

Taking the time to understand what's really going on is a critically important part of productive thinking. There's nothing productive about solving the wrong problem.

Here's a review of the five substeps in What's Going On?:

What's the Itch?

- List as many ways of expressing the Itch or Itches as time allows.

- Cluster to reveal themes and relationships between the various statements of the Itch.

- Choose the most compelling Itch or cluster of Itches to work on.

What's the Impact?

- List why and how the Itch affects you.

- Choose the most important impacts

What's the Information?

- List all the things you know and all the things you wonder about the Itch.

- Choose the most important items.

Who's Involved?

- List all the stakeholders and potential stakeholders for the Itch and what is at stake for each one.

- Choose the most important stakeholders.

What's the Vision?

- List as many potential Target Futures as time allows.

- Review all the potential Target Futures and select the ones that meet the I^3 (Influence, Importance, Imagination) criteria.

- Select three to five potential Target Futures that are the most important or compelling.

- Select the one Target Future (or combination of Target Futures) to work on now.

- Restate the selected Target Future in a powerful, energizing way that motivates you to achieve it.

As in any discipline, to become good you need first to learn the rules. To become great, you need to break them.

Don't begrudge the time it takes to complete this first step. Often starting slow is the best way to finish fast. What's Going On? is your diagnostic foundation. You will likely return to it again and again as you work through your issues. It will serve you well whenever you need to check your facts, correct your course, or explore additional questions raised along the way. Like a tree, productive thinking is organic: the stronger its roots, the sweeter its fruits.

Step 2: What's Success?

What's Success? has two main functions: first, creating a richly detailed image of a desirable future; second, establishing success criteria for measuring the potential effectiveness of your ideas for reaching that future. Your image of the future needs to be compelling enough to motivate you not only through the productive thinking process but through all the hard work it will take to get you to your goal. Your image of the future should stretch you. As in the game of bocce, it may be impossible to land directly on the target ball, but without the target there is no game. Make your imagined future so compelling that you can't help wanting to get there.[1]

Here's a review of the two substeps in What's Success?:

- First, conduct an Imagined Future (IF) excursion (see page 130) to project yourself into a future in which the issue has been resolved. Review the IF exercise and highlight the items that seem most important or have the most emotional impact.

- Second, using the DRIVE tool (see page 136), list as many potential Success Criteria as possible in terms of what an eventual solution must do, what it must avoid, what you are prepared to invest, the values you must live by, and any essential outcomes. Review the DRIVE exercise and highlight the most important observable success criteria.

Like the first step, What's Going On?, What's Success? provides a foundation for the rest of your work. Unless you take the time to clearly articulate what success will mean both emotionally and practically, you may find that some members of your team think of your goal as one thing while others think of it as something else entirely. It's unlikely that you'll come up with a satisfactory outcome if people have different understandings of success.

In some cases you may already be clear about your measurable Success Criteria; perhaps they were defined in your mandate. Even so, it's still useful to conduct an Imagined Future exercise. If you want to be able to maintain the energy you will need to complete your plan, you may well need to anchor your efforts in a compelling image of the future, especially when the going gets rough. Military leaders throughout history have known the power of the Imagined Future. When facing deprivation, pain, and even death, soldiers are a lot more likely to fight for a cause than for a paycheck.

As you work through a productive thinking session, you will return periodically to the work you did in What's Success? You will use your key Success Criteria for your Evaluation Screen (see pages 180-181) in Step 5: Forge the Solution. You may also find them useful when Powering-Up your idea, also in Step 5. And as you Align Resources for your preliminary plan of action, you will almost certainly refer back to and possibly modify your Success Criteria.

Step 3: What's the Question?

In Step 1 you asked yourself, "What's going on, and where do I want to go?" In Step 2 you asked, "What will it be like when I get there?" Step 3 is where you ask, "What problems do I need to understand and solve to get where I want to be?"

Clients sometimes ask, "Didn't we already define our problem when we described our Target Future?" The answer is: probably not.

Think of your Target Future as where you want to go, your vision. *It would be great if we were the best company in our industry! I wish I got more recognition for the contribution I make to this company! If only we could develop a category-killing product! Let's increase sales by 25 percent! I wish I could retire rich!*

Problem Questions are different. They're the questions that ask how you might get there. They uncover the strategies you'll need to achieve your vision.

Of course, it is possible that after all your analysis, you will decide to restate your Target Future as a Problem Question, but let's analyze a hypothetical case to see what happens if you were to do so. Let's say your Target Future is "It would be great if we could increase sales!" and you transform that statement into "How might we increase sales?" Your answers might be "Find better ways to motivate our sales force," "Establish a more effective sales pipeline," "Get marketing on board to support our sales efforts better," "Develop better advertising," and so on.

These may sound like answers, but on closer inspection they're pretty empty. For each of these "answers" you now have to ask yourself how you're going to do that. "Develop better advertising" isn't a solution. It's not much more than a "we should" statement. You've probably been at hundreds of meetings that have ended with a list of "we should" statements that ultimately never got implemented. Although they sound enough like solutions to allow everyone in the meeting to feel they have addressed the problem, "we should" statements are rarely actionable because no one has thought them through.

Now look at the same scenario from the productive thinking perspective. The Target Future is "It would be great if we could increase sales!" That's the vision: where you want to go. Now you list a series of Problem *Questions*. "How might we find better ways to motivate our sales force?" "How might we establish a more effective sales pipeline?" "How might we get marketing on board to support our sales efforts better?" "How might we develop better advertising?" These are questions that if answered well may get you to your Target Future. The fact that we've posed them as questions implies that we have to answer them. You can't leave a meeting thinking you've solved a problem —*when you haven't* — *if* you've stated it as a question. "Develop better advertising" lets everyone off the hook. "How might we develop better advertising?" demands an answer and propels you forward.

Here's a review of the substeps in What's the Question?:

- Using divergent, creative thinking, list as many Problem Questions as possible in the form How Might I . . .? (HMI) or How might we . . . ? (HMW).

- Using convergent, critical thinking, select one or more Problem Questions that if answered will create the potential to lead to your Target Future. These are your Catalytic Questions.

It's not uncommon to end up with more than one Catalytic Question in this step. You won't be able to answer them all at once, so you will have to structure the rest of your productive thinking session to accommodate each one. The best way to do that is to prioritize the questions in terms of their urgency or importance, any dependent relationships that may exist among them, or simply the energy you have for working on them. Once you've prioritized, select one question and work it through Step 4: Generate Answers. Then come back and work on your other Catalytic Questions in turn.

"Often the true causes of our discomfort are so integral to our environment that we fail to recognize them."

If you are working through a productive thinking session as a team, you may want to split into subgroups to generate answers to different Catalytic Questions and then reconvene to work through the final steps of the model.

Step 4: Generate Answers

Generate Answers is the part of the productive thinking process that most people think of as brainstorming. You brainstorm to find ideas that might address the Catalytic Question or Questions you identified in the previous step.

Here's a review of the substeps in Generate Answers:

- List to many ideas for answering the Catalytic Question as possible.

- Converge on three to six ideas that, when fully developed, may result in useful solutions.

You can use a variety of idea-generating tools for the divergent, creative phase of this step. There are literally hundreds of such tools, ranging from the cognitive to the kinesthetic, from music to meditative, and from visual to visceral. I have listed a number of useful resources in the bibliography.

Many of these thinking tools are a lot of fun to use. As people get to third third ideas, you often hear a lot of laughter, especially as crazier and crazier ideas are called out, written on sticky notes, and slapped onto the wall. Sadly, however, when it comes time to converge—to choose which ideas to develop further—those energizing, crazy ideas often end up in the wastebasket.

Third third ideas are powerful, but they are also vulnerable. Because they don't feel safe or sound "reasonable," these off-the-wall ideas are often left on the wall and forgotten. What a shame. To plumb their potential, it is essential to use a tool such as What's UP? to identify the underlying principles behind those zany ideas—to see if they can be tamed into something workable. As Alex Osborn said, "It's a lot easier to tame a wild idea than to invigorate one that has no life to begin with." Honor these third third ideas. More often than not, they will be the source of your *tenkaizen*.

Step 5: Forge the Solution

The essential questions answered in Forge the Solution are "How well do the ideas we've selected meet our Success Criteria?" and "How can we develop them to be as powerful and effective as possible?"

Here is a review of the two substeps in Forge the Solution:

- First, using the Evaluation Screen (see pages 180-181), compare the most promising ideas from Step 4: Generate Answers with the key Success Criteria from Step 2: What's Success? Review the first pass comparison, using the principle of Generative Judgment (see page 182) to improve each idea as measured against each Success Criterion. Then select the most promising ideas for further development.

- Using the POWER tool, evaluate, stress-test, improve, and refine each selected idea to create robust Powered-

Up Solutions. Then rewrite each Powered-Up Solution in a way that clearly communicates its essence and can form the basis of a preliminary action plan: an executive summary that tells the story of the idea

Forge the Solution is one of my favorite steps in the Productive Thinking Model. Its strength lies in its flexibility. In working on client issues, we often use Forge the Solution as the only step in the model. You can use POWER to evaluate any idea that comes across your desk, whether it's a formal proposal, an embryonic idea for action, a résumé, or even a casual suggestion. Many productive thinking sessions end with Forge the Solution, especially in larger organizations where project planning (Step 6: Align Resources) is often handed off to dedicated project managers.

Step 6: Align Resources

Align Resource is where you explore the tactics required to convert your strategy into action. In this step you ask, "How will I transform the ideas I've developed into action?" You identify the actions and resources required to implement the solutions defined in the Step 5: Forge the Solution. It is one of the more time-consuming parts of the process.

Here is a review of seven substeps of Align Resources:

1. List all the possible action steps required to complete the plan without attempting to prioritize or sequence them. Cluster the action steps to eliminate duplications, group steps and substeps, and clarify individual tasks.

2. Assess the big picture to identify potential Assistors and Resistors. Add action steps as necessary, aimed at influencing Assistors and Resistors.

3. Ensure that each action step has an owner who is committed to its completion.

4. Create a Wall of Time to place clusters of action steps in sequence and rearrange them according to dependencies.

5. Conduct an EFFECT (Energy, Funds, Free time, Expertise, Conditions, and Things) analysis of each

action step to determine the required resources. Determine what resources are already in place and what resources must be acquired. Add action steps as necessary, aimed at acquiring the needed resources.

6. Identify and list observable outcomes for each action step.

7. Transfer the information for each action step onto a single action sheet; insert the sheets in an action book to monitor and manage the project or hand it off to a project management specialist.

The processes and tools available in Align Resources offer a great way not only to plan a project but to understand it. When you are aligning resources, you will naturally find yourself revisiting other steps in the model to check and double-check the assumptions that have gone into a project, to better understand stakeholder concerns, and to ensure that the Success Criteria are clearly understood.

Productive thinking is specifically for those times when you need new ideas to address challenges.

Align Resources is also an excellent way to prepare for the work you will do as you advance your project through your organization. If your organization is like most, you'll have to do a fair bit of presenting to people in authority before your project gets the go-ahead. Working through Align Resources will provide you with invaluable information and insights that will help you answer the inevitable questions from those in a position to approve or reject your ideas.

To Think or Not to Think

Productive thinking isn't for every situation. How can you tell when it is appropriate to use the model? There are three parts to the answer.

1. Productive thinking is specifically for those times when you need new ideas to address challenges. Not all challenges require new ideas. There are many circumstances in which a new solution may be

useful but you are satisfied with a quick fix. There may be nothing wrong with such a decision. There may be other circumstances in which the solutions you need have already been devised. By all means use them.

Imagine that you've been working on a report for work. The report is due on Monday. You've decided to do your final polish at home on the weekend. Halfway through your final edit, the fuse for your home office trips. That fuse is touchy. It controls the circuits for both the laundry room and your office. So when someone else in the house turns on the clothes dryer, the fuse can get overloaded. It's happened before.

You don't need a productive thinking exercise to solve your problem. The problem is clear: no power. The solution is clear too: Go down to the basement and reset the fuse. The solution works fine even though it's not the optimal solution. Clearly, the *optimal* solution would be to change things to avoid overloading the fuse in the future. You might rewire the panel, add a circuit, or even move your office to a different part of the house. But you're perfectly willing to live with the nonoptimal solution to get your report done. You may even make a note to yourself to think about the problem in the future. And, like many people, you may forget to do so until the next time the breaker pops. But for now your nonoptimal, reproductive thinking solution is just fine.

Remember the I^3 test. The mnemonic I^3 stands for Influence, Importance, and Imagination. Although I usually employ I^3 to determine whether the model will be useful for finding ways to achieve a Target Future, you can also use I^3 earlier in the process to evaluate your original issue.

- Do you (or your group) have Influence over the issue? If the challenge is completely out of your control or authority, it may not be worth spinning your wheels on.

- Is the issue of Importance to you (or your group)? Are you motivated to address it? Will you have the energy to carry your solution through? If your interest is peripheral or academic, you may not be prepared to invest the time or energy to resolve it. Some issues are small and go away by themselves. Some are linked to circumstances that can change. Some you may just be prepared to live with.

- Does the challenge require Imagination? Will it be served by an innovative solution? If the challenge is

can be addressed with an off-the-shelf solution, you
may simply want to go to the shelf. Not every problem
needs an original solution. But if you can improve on
an existing solution, by all means go for it.

If you can answer yes to all three I^3 questions, you will probably
benefit by applying the Productive Thinking Model. If your answer to
any of these questions is no, you may not need to use the model at all, or
you may want to think about restating your issue in a way that does meet
the I^3 criteria.

In the blown fuse example, you could answer yes to the first I:
Influence. Yes, it's a problem you can fix. You might also answer yes to
the second I: Importance. You need to finish the report. You need power
for your computer and printer. But you would likely answer no to the
third I: Imagination. A long-term solution might require an imaginative
approach, but the short-term solution is clear: Go downstairs and flip
the breaker.

2. Sometimes, you may not be willing to invest the effort to go
from good to great. We often settle for a good solution that is well executed over a great solution that costs more than the benefit it might provide. In the best of all possible worlds, we'd probably all like to participate
in brilliant plans that are brilliantly executed, but that's not always practical, either because of time, financial, or other resource constraints.
Sometimes it's just not practical to go through the effort of creating a new
solution when an existing solution will do the job almost as well. In other
words, sometimes the answer to the second I question—Is it important?—is no. The issue simply isn't worth fussing or fighting over.

Think about the last time your computer's operating system was
scheduled for an upgrade. Although the new OS would probably provide
more functionality, work faster, and crash less, many people put off such
upgrades. For them it isn't worth the hassle to change. They're reasonably
comfortable with the way things work now, and until the operating system becomes obsolete, they'll keep going with what works.

A few years ago I learned an acronym from a brilliant leader
whose great skill was to know just when to take the time to think and just
when to move. He used to say GEPO: Good Enough, Push On! We all
need to know when to say GEPO.

3. Sometimes you don't have the influence. The issue is important and yes, an innovative solution would make a difference. But you

may not be the person to effect it. You may not have the resources. You may not have the power. You may not have the authority.

Some years ago I was involved in a massive project for two large financial institutions that were exploring a merger. I had been contracted to help develop the strategic plan that would go first to the CEOs of both companies, then to their boards, and finally to the regulators. The regulators had serious concerns that the merged megabank would stifle competition, so it was important to make a powerful case for the public as well as the private benefits of the merger. I was working with a team of senior executives from both organizations. Two of them developed the following Target Future: *It would be great if the merged organization could form a special small business bank to fund microbusinesses throughout the country to stimulate community growth and local job creation!*

One of the CEOs was intrigued, but the one from the larger and more powerful of the two organizations was adamantly opposed. The plan for a microfinancing bank was scuppered.

The two business unit heads and their staffs worked for months researching, designing, and fine-tuning their plan. What emerged was a concept for creating a completely new kind of bank within a bank, an entity that could offer a transformative social service while at the same time meeting profit targets. As the plan began to take shape, the people working on it became more and more excited about its possibilities both as a business case and in terms of countering regulatory concerns.

About a month before the submissions were to go before the regulators, my two clients presented their plan in an informal meeting with their CEOs. One of the CEOs was intrigued, but the one from the larger and more powerful of the two organizations was adamantly opposed. He had built his career on the mantra of increased shareholder value, and he believed that the microfinancing bank would stunt returns. He was also convinced that he could address the regulatory concerns in other ways.

The plan for a microfinancing bank was scuppered: It would not be presented formally to the executive team; it would not be presented the board; it would not form part of the submission to the regulator.

Two months later the regulator rejected the merger proposal on the grounds that it would unduly diminish competition and consumer choice, specifically in smaller rural communities. My clients had a great idea. They were rightly convinced that the issues they were addressing were important. They knew that an innovative solution was called for. But ultimately they didn't have sufficient influence.

A footnote to this story is that 10 years later the concept of a microfinancing bank investing in community-level entrepreneurs won the Nobel Peace Prize for its founder and chief officer, the Bangladeshi economist Muhammad Yunus. My clients were ahead of their time. They were brilliant. They were dedicated. But they didn't have the influence to get the job done.

I know that the Influence dimension of the I^3 approach may sound jaded. Ten years ago my clients might have been tilting at windmills. But in the intervening years the winds had changed. They were working in a highly industrialized country whose gross dometic product dwarfed that of the third world countries on which Yunus focused his efforts.

Perhaps, ultimately, there is another I: Inspiration. Clearly, there are issues that are worth tackling even though your influence seems pitifully small. The I of Importance may be so large that it more than makes up for the very small I of Influence. Gandhi once said. "Whatever you do will be insignificant, but it is very important that you do it." If you are driven by a passion to change the world or your workplace or your marriage even though the odds are stacked against you, go for it. The I of Inspiration may well trump the other I's.

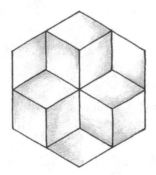

CHAPTER 14

Training vs. Entraining

*In theory there's no difference between
theory and practice.
In practice there is.*

Yogi Berra

T hinking better can change lives. This book was designed to give you a taste of the productive thinking process. Its principles are straightforward: Separate your thinking, stay in the question, strive for the third third, look for unexpected connections. The model is fairly simple, consisting of six interlocking steps. Its tools are powerful. Knowing the principles, steps, and tools, however, is not enough. To really understand them, you have to use them.

In think^x seminars and workshops around the world, I've introduced productive thinking to people in a wide range of businesses and cultures. To give the participants a sense of how they can use the model, my colleagues and I usually end each workshop with a Galeforce: an abbreviated version of the full process through which participants can work on a challenge of their own.

Almost inevitably, a few days after a workshop, we receive e-mails from participants who have started to apply their Galeforce solutions to business and personal challenges. Here's a sample of the kinds of comments they send:

I've finally cracked a problem that has been intriguing and terrifying me for weeks.

I thought I had gone through all the angles on my problem, so I was more than impressed with what your approach was able to do for me in such a short time.

If only everyone who feels confused and overwhelmed could know that a process like this exists.

On the basis of the results of our work with organizations and individuals, we have some pretty good evidence that productive thinking works. But old habits are hard to break. For most of us, those old habits are *not* to think productively, *not* to separate critical thinking from creative thinking, and definitely *not* to push ourselves to the third third. We've practiced unproductive ways of using our minds all our lives. Is it any wonder that we tend to fall back into our habitual ways of thinking even after we learn a better way? Anyone who has ever tried to change a golf stroke or move a cutlery drawer knows how easy it is to slip back into the habitual and less effective patterns we've spent so long reinforcing. It's the same with thinking: No matter how powerful the new technique you've learned is, as soon as you relax your attention, you inevitably slip back into the old ways.

When it comes to developing new skills *of any kind*, the major challenge is generally not learning them but making them stick. Think back to the last corporate training program you attended. It might have lasted a day and a half or been compressed into a single day. You might have been expected to learn a new skill in just a half-day session or even in a so-called lunch and learn. However long the program, you were probably given some sort of overarching principle, presented with a set of tools, and given a pep talk about how you and your company would be better off once you applied your new skill back on the job.

Training, as practiced in much of corporate America, is an astonishing waste of resources.

Now fast-forward to your next day at work. First, you're behind. You have to catch up on the work you missed while you were at the training program. That means you're probably under pressure. Second, nothing has changed. You're still facing the same issues you faced the day before the training program. Given these two circumstances, what are the chances you'll apply your new skill? Pretty slim. You'll do things the way you've always done them because that's easier than trying to change. You may still be enthusiastic about the new learning, but right now you have to get your work done. Old habits have a strong gravitational pull. You don't have time to experiment. Within a few days, your training program may not be much more than a memory of having felt good. Within a week, even that may have faded. Your company invested money, you invested time, and in the end very little changed. Sound familiar?

Training, as practiced in much of corporate America, is an astonishing waste of resources. The fact is that you cannot train someone in a day. You may *teach* people something, but you can't *train* them. Training is about creating behavioral change, and that doesn't happen overnight. Ideally, the training seminar is the front end of a process that will take time and continual reinforcement to embed a new set of skills. Unfortunately, in many organizations that front end is the only end there is. *Training*, like so many other bizspeak words, has lost its meaning. Because it is now more commonly used to refer to information transfer rather than skill development, I prefer the word *entraining*. In chemistry, to entrain means to trap suspended particles in a solution and carry them along. This concept is an apt metaphor for skill development. We introduce new skills and try to trap them in our way of being.

Entraining results in a new and different workflow. Keeping those new skill particles suspended in your workflow requires behavioral change. Behavioral change in turn requires the forging of new synaptic connections, new neural pathways. A one-day program can open doors, but to foster real behavioral change, you have to reinforce new skills on a regular basis. In the same way, though this book may have introduced you to some useful concepts, if you put the book down and do nothing with them, very little will change for you. If you want to benefit from productive thinking, you have to make a commitment to using it. If you want it to stick, you need to understand the four requirements for entraining a new skill set:

1. Proof

2. Approbation

3. Language

4. Practice

Proof

To want to try something, you need evidence that applying the new skill will be worth your while. In the case of productive thinking, that's fairly easy. The first time you apply the model as a whole or even some of its components, you will notice a difference. You will generate more ideas, and more useful ideas, more of the time.

You don't have to start out with the full model. You can start small. Try the POWER tool described in Chapter 11 (see page 185). Take any simple idea: It could be your plan for dinner or your next vacation, your ideas for how to approach your day tomorrow, even the habitual route you take to work each morning. Power it up, using the POWER tool to ask what's good about the idea, what's wrong with it, what else might be in it, how you can enhance what's already good, and how you can remediate its weaknesses. I guarantee you'll have a better idea at the end of the exercise than you had going into it.

Once you've proved the POWER tool to yourself, try some of the other parts of the model. Analyze your next dilemma with What's Going

On?, which was described in Chapter 7. You will arrive at a much more robust understanding of your issue. Take a relatively small project at work and conduct Imagined Future and DRIVE exercises on it. These exercises are described in detail in Chapter 8. You'll be amazed at how your perception of your issue changes. Once you've used several of the steps independently, find a challenge on which you can run the complete model. Put it to the test. You may encounter frustrations as you challenge your assumptions and old habits, but you won't be disappointed.

I'm passionate about the power of productive thinking. As a result, I talk about it often. But I've discovered that no words can replace having people actually experience the model for themselves. Imagine trying to tell someone how wonderful Mozart is, how beautiful a Mattisse can be, or how exhilarating love is. No matter how articulate you are, your explanation will be only a shadow of the thing itself. To appreciate productive thinking, you have to experience it. So the first step in entraining is to test the model and prove it for yourself. The more you use it, the more you will reinforce its value.

Approbation

Introducing and entraining new ways of thinking in organizations requires an overt commitment by senior management: approbation. Approbation means approval. It's a rather formal word and implies official sanction rather than merely a passing nod. It's exactly the word I mean.

Goran Ekvall, a professor at Lund University in Sweden, reports that 67 percent of the creative environment in any organization is directly attributable to the attitude and behavior of the leader.[1] To paraphrase the old joke, what that means is the lightbulb has to want to change. If the leadership in an organization doesn't make productive thinking an expectation, it will necessarily be seen by employees as a threat. Creativity and innovation can be messy. Creative thinking is often ambiguous. It can't be easily analyzed or measured. New ideas often challenge old orthodoxies. If it's just "nice to have," productive thinking will fade away. Imagine your company merely "supporting" ethical behavior rather than requiring it. It's the same with productive thinking. It's not good enough to simply tolerate it or pay lip service to it: Leadership must demand it and all the messiness that goes along with it.

Creating the conditions necessary for entraining productive thinking in an organization requires the explicit approbation of senior management. The best way to get that is to demonstrate quick wins. If leaders see that productive thinking can truly enhance a company's innovative edge, streamline its operations, or help in the creation of new products, the task becomes much easier. Quick wins can be powerful persuaders.

Language

The words we use have a powerful transformative influence on the way we think and act.

The third step is language. As you've seen throughout this book, the Productive Thinking Model has its own vocabulary. We talk about Itches and Imagined Futures. We use tools called DRIVE and AIM and POWER (these tools are described fully on pages 136, 152, and 185, respectively). We strive to create the conditions necessary for *tenkaizen*, or "good revolution," as opposed to *kaizen*, or "good change." Creating the productive thinking vocabulary was not done just to be idiosyncratic. I wanted a vocabulary that could describe the concepts, steps, and tools of productive thinking precisely. I wanted to facilitate communication between people and groups using the model.

Training, as practiced in much of corporate America, is an astonishing waste of resources.

After many years of working in marketing, I know how important vocabulary can be in fostering change. When people in organizations begin to share vocabularies that describe particular concepts, they are more likely to embed those concepts in both their individual and their collective thinking. For example, when people start saying things like "Let's POWER this up," both the tool and the notion of Generative Judgment (see page 182) become embedded in the behavior of the group. The more people say "Did you do a DRIVE on this before you wrote it up?" the more likely it is that people will begin using this simple tool to establish Success Criteria. The more people use the language of productive thinking, the more likely productive thinking is to become the norm.

Practice

The fourth step is practice. No skill can be mastered overnight; you start out small and get better each time you practice. One of the great negative reinforcers in personal development is the naive notion that there's a magic bullet, that we can learn something and then change everything overnight. We tend to overestimate what we can do in the short term and underestimate what we can do in the long term. Various studies comparing performers in different disciplines demonstrate a direct relationship between cumulative hours of practice and excellence of performance. Chess players, runners, and musicians who practice more tend to be better at what they do than those who practice less.[2]

Productive thinking is no different from any other skill. You have to do it to get good at it. Fortunately, unlike music or chess or running, you don't need expensive equipment or a special environment in which to practice productive thinking. You can use it as easily at home as at work, as easily in your garage as in your lab, as easily alone as in groups. Any time you have to analyze a problem, think about a possible future, generate ideas, or evaluate potential solutions, you can apply the principles and tools of productive thinking.

You'll also find that if the first three steps of entraining, or skill development, are in place, practicing becomes easier. If you've established some quick wins for yourself or your organization, you're likely to want to use the process again. If the leaders in your department, team, or organization are fully committed, you won't have to battle for the time it may take to think a problem through. And if it's easy to talk about productive thinking with your colleagues because you have a shared vocabulary, you're more likely to use the process when working with others.

Remember too that along with all other living creatures, human beings are subject to the effects of stimulus and response. No matter how well developed a behavior is, no matter how good you get at it, unless you *continue* to reinforce it, it will die. You never truly finish developing anything. You need to create a positive feedback loop to keep it happening. We often do this with periodic reinforcements such as celebrations, retreats, keynote speeches, and ongoing refresher courses to keep the skills alive and sharp. After all, doctors, engineers, and airline pilots are all required by their licensing bodies to take ongoing training. Why shouldn't thinkers?

No skill can be kept at peak level without constant reinforcement.[3] There's no magic bullet. It takes work. Would any athlete assume that after reaching a certain level of performance he or she could keep it up, let alone get better, without practice? Would a musician? A chess player? Of course not. A single day's training or reading a book like this won't do the trick. Nor will calling in a consultant every time you need to solve a problem or develop a new product. Entraining is about doing the work yourself. Then doing it again. If you want to change your behavior, the biggest investment you have to make is in yourself. Those who are willing, benefit. Those who aren't, don't. It's that simple.

● ● ●

Productive thinking is a model and a discipline, but perhaps even more, it's an attitude. Through it, we look at problems and convert them into opportunities. We look at the world and see that we can always do better. We look at challenges and see that nothing is impossible. We look at obstacles and see that there is always a way through.

If you can identify an area in which your world might be improved, put productive thinking to the test. The more you use it, the more natural it will become for you, the better you'll get, and the more benefit you'll get out of it. I promise you that if you make productive thinking part of your life, you'll find you get better at just about everything you do.

Productive thinking can help you think better, work better, and do better in every aspect of your life. The sooner you begin, the sooner you will benefit.

What you can do, or dream you can do, begin it;
Boldness has genius, power and magic in it.

Johann Wolfgang von Goethe

APPENDIX

Productive Thinking in Action

JetWays, a hypothetical company, is a successful regional airline that focuses on the business market. As part of its plan to expand nationally, JetWays is looking for ways to differentiate itself from other carriers. One area of exploration is how to add value to the middle seats on JetWays planes. The following is an abbreviated version of how this initiative might be developed using the think^x productive thinking model.

Step 1: What's Going On?

Step 1 consists of five substeps, each phrased as a question, and each with a divergent, list-making phase and a convergent, choice-making phase. The five substeps are What's the Itch?, What's the Impact?, What's the Information?, Who's Involved?, and What's the Vision?. For a complete explanation of Step 1, see Chapter 7.

This is the long list of itches the group generated through answering, What's wong with the middle seat?.

What's the Itch? (make a list)	
• Uncomfortable	• Awkward when window seat passenger has to go to bathroom
• Not good for big people	
• Claustrophobic	• Middle seats are stinky
• No leg room	• Too cramped
• Hard to get up from middle seat	• Inadequate computer room
• Forces you to share arm rest	• Middle seats seem narrower
• Space invasion	• No room to maneuver
• Too hot	• Middle seats get spilled on
• Low status	• Disgusting to have someone fall asleep on your shoulder
• Same price, worse seat	
• No view	• Less personal space
• Inconvenient	• Enclosed on two sides

These are the clusters the group made to sort out its long list, and the itches (circled) that they selected as the most significant through critical thinking.

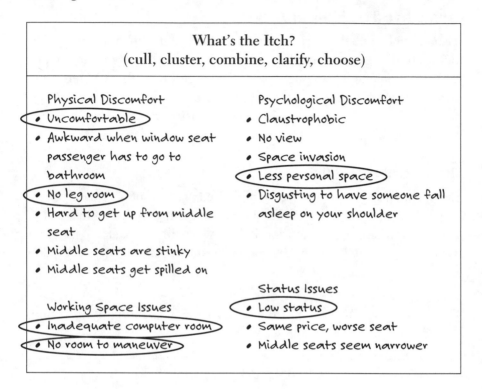

What's the Itch?
(cull, cluster, combine, clarify, choose)

Physical Discomfort
- Uncomfortable
- Awkward when window seat passenger has to go to bathroom
- No leg room
- Hard to get up from middle seat
- Middle seats are stinky
- Middle seats get spilled on

Working Space Issues
- Inadequate computer room
- No room to maneuver

Psychological Discomfort
- Claustrophobic
- No view
- Space invasion
- Less personal space
- Disgusting to have someone fall asleep on your shoulder

Status Issues
- Low status
- Same price, worse seat
- Middle seats seem narrower

First the group used creative thinking to list the answers to the question, What's wrong with the middle seats? Then they used critical thinking to circle the items that are most significant.

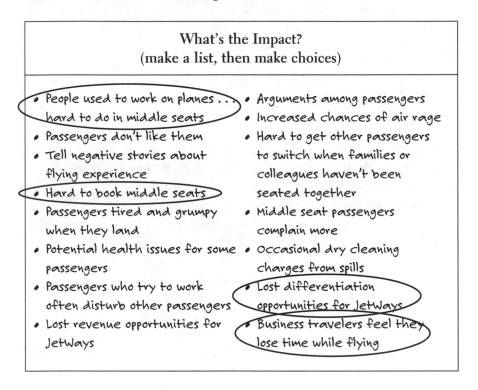

What's the Impact?
(make a list, then make choices)

- People used to work on planes . . . hard to do in middle seats
- Passengers don't like them
- Tell negative stories about flying experience
- Hard to book middle seats
- Passengers tired and grumpy when they land
- Potential health issues for some passengers
- Passengers who try to work often disturb other passengers
- Lost revenue opportunities for JetWays

- Arguments among passengers
- Increased chances of air rage
- Hard to get other passengers to switch when families or colleagues haven't been seated together
- Middle seat passengers complain more
- Occasional dry cleaning charges from spills
- Lost differentiation opportunities for JetWays
- Business travelers feel they lose time while flying

This is the long list of information the group listed by using creative thinking and the KnoWonder tool to answer the question, What do you know about the middle seats? The circled items are those the group then selected as the most significant or that they needed to know more about.

What's the Information?
(make a lists, then make choices)

Know
(what do you know about the issue?)

- Almost all solo passengers prefer aisle or window seats
- Couples and families often choose middle seats
- 76% of JetWays traffic is business traffic
- Middle seats actually same width as others
- JetWays needs to average 70% load factors to be profitable
- Middle seats are necessary for adequate load factors
- No major success stories from airlines that have tried business class only experiments
- Discounts and price breaks are ineffective competitive solutions in the long term
- Special mileage rewards may also be ineffective in that they are easy to copy
- Airlines have been struggling with this issue for years without a good solution

Wonder
(what do you wonder about the issue?)

- Would people pay a premium for better seats?
- Are there configurations that provide more room in less space?
- Would anything really make enough of a difference?
- What have other carriers tried?
- Will our business traffic ratio be the same on a national basis?
- What are passengers not getting that they would value?
- How much of the negative around middle seats is purely psychological?
- Is this true?
- Do economy passengers want more than just cheap flights?
- Is length of flight a factor?
- At what length of flight does the middle seat become an issue for passengers?
- Who are the experts in seating ergonomics?

This is the long list of stakeholders the group generated through answering the questions, Who influences or is affected by the middle seat and What's at stake for these people? The circled items are the key stakeholders the group they selected as the most important through critical thinking.

Who's Involved?
(make a list, then make choices)

Stakeholders (who influences or is affected by the issue?)	What's at Stake? (what's at stake for these people?)
• JetWays	Profitability, competition
• Business travelers	Often need to work, also to feel fresh on landing
• Marketers	Need unique selling proposition
• Seat suppliers	Capable of real change?
• Travel agents	Want to please customers
• Airplane manufacturers	Want to offer suitable configurations for clients
• Interior designers	Need to work within weight, materials, and safety constraints
• Shareholders	Want return on investment
• Competitors	Will want to copy success
• Staff	Want minimal hassle or negative interactions with passengers
• Regulators	Safety concerns

This is the long list of potential Target Futures the group generated through creative thinking to finish the phase, I wish . . . The circled items are the two Target Futures the group then, selected through critical thinking.

What's the Vision?
I wish . . . It would be great if . . . If only . . .
(make a list of target futures, then make choices)

- we could eliminate middle seats but not give up revenue
- we could have luxury middle seats
- everyone had the comfort of first class
- people weren't so picky and looked at travel as a means to an end
- the competition would go away!
- we knew the future needs of customers
- middle seat passengers didn't show up
- middle seat passengers didn't complain
- passengers actually wanted to sit in our middle seats
- we had hyper speed flights so it didn't matter
- passengers came in uniform sizes
- we could sell full capacity on all flights
- the competition had even bigger problems
- the competition had more middle seats than we do
- middle seats had more legroom
- all our planes were like Air Force One
- we didn't shove so many people on that we had to have middle seats

- we had satisfied clients and customers
- we could design more comfortable planes
- there were no middle seats
- people would take what they were assigned
- airplanes were less expensive!
- airplane operation was less expensive
- all passengers were happy in their seats
- we could find low cost solutions
- people could work on planes in comfort
- we were the only airline in the universe
- we had invisible seats
- there were no middle seats
- we cared more about passengers than profit
- there were no middle seats at all
- middle seats could be marketed as premium seats
- our customers could afford only first class
- passengers didn't complain
- we came up with something so cool that it would blow the competition away
- people could always sit with people they knew and liked

The group then chose to combine the two statements they had selected to create a Target Future they were motivated to work toward. The group finished Step 1: *What's Going On?* with a comprehensive context for further thinking and a Target Future that was stated as:

> It would be great if we blew the competition away with middle seats so fantastic that passengers actually wanted to sit in them!

Step 2: What's Success?

Step 2 consists of two substeps. The first consists of robustly imagining an ideal future in which your issue has been resolved, creating a powerful motivation to reach your Target Future. The second consists of using the DRIVE tool to establish clear, observable success criteria that can be used in subsequent phases of the productive thinking process to evaluate potential solutions. For a complete explanation of Step 2, see Chapter 8.

Imagined Future

When people think of flying, they think of JetWays first. One of the reasons is that JetWays offers the best middle seats in the world. Many of our customers consider them to be the best seats on the plane. Seasoned travelers always ask to be booked in JetWays middle seats. They are so good that people often compete for them. When customers choose JetWays, they always feel they've made the best choice. Some won't fly any other airline. In fact, people often fly our planes just for the pleasure of it, even if they have nowhere to go.* Our middle seats offer business travelers an experience like no other.

---

*See Chapter 8, page 134 for why this sentence in the most important one in JetWays Imagined Future.

This is the long list of potential Success Criteria the group generated by using the DRIVE tool and creative thinking. The circled items are the key Success Criteria the group selected through critical thinking as the most promising.

DRIVE (make lists of potential success criteria, then make choices of key success criteria)				
Do	**Restrictions**	**Investment**	**Values**	**Essential outcomes**
Sales up	No safety compromise	6-month max to proof of concept	Safety	50% more requests for middle seats
Profit up	No other regulatory issues	100,000 max to proof of concept	Sustain-ability	7 point increase in customer satisfaction
Morale up	Do not reduce average load factor	Maintain 70% load factor	Customer satisfaction	
Complaints down			Best working conditions	20% decrease in complaints
Customer satisfaction up			Airline of choice	
Employee satisfaction up	Do not compete on price alone		"Your business is our business"	7-point increase in business market share
Repeat customers up	No offering that can be easily copied		On time	70%+ load factor
Brand differentiation				10% increase in sales
Unique offering				10% increase in profit
Passengers happy when they land				10 point increase in business airline of choice

Step 3: What's the Question?

Step 3 is a pivotal step in the productive thinking model. In it you generate as many problem questions as possible, then converge to focus on one or more Catalytic Questions that, if answered, will create the potential to get you to your Target Future. For a complete explanation of Step 3, see Chapter 9.

This is the long list of problem questions the group generated through answering the questions, How might we . . . . The circled items are the problem questions the group selected as most promising through convergent, critical thinking.

What's the Question?
How might we . . .
(make a list, then make choices)

- get people to ask for middle seats?
- change the perception of middle seats?
- make the middle seat more comfortable?
- ask our customers for a solution?
- eliminate cost constraints?
- make travel more pleasurable?
- encourage people to travel more?
- have people book middle seats?
- make the middle seat more inviting?
- make JetWays more profitable?
- market middle seats effectively?
- make employees happier?
- get special revenue streams from the middle seat?
- add value to the middle seat?
- reduce fares and retain profitability at the same time?
- pay for improving the middle seat?
- make the middle seat pleasurable?
- make preferential treatment available to everyone?
- provide more services on planes?
- differentiate ourselves from the competition?

- make the middle seat more attractive?
- keep customers satisfied?
- get rid of middle seats?
- find a partner?
- make the middle seat seem wider?
- only have skinny passengers?
- inspire people to work for our company?
- give a financial reward for sitting in the middle?
- redefine the load factor?
- differentiate ourselves from the crowd?
- make the middle seat not be seen as the middle seat?
- look at value vs cost of flying?
- change the mindset of our passengers about the middle seat?
- persuade airplane manufacturers to partner with us?
- ensure customer loyalty?
- inspire passengers to bid for the middle seat?
- Make sitting in the middle seat a sexy thing to do?

After reviewing all these potential Catalytic Questions, this is the question the group chose as the one it had the most interest in working on now:

Catalytic Question

How might we change the mindset of our passengers about JetWays middle seats?

Step 4: Generate Answers

Step 4 is the step in the productive thinking model that generates potential answers to each of the Catalytic Questions selected in Step 3: *What's the Question?* For the purposes of this example, we have focused on a single Catalytic Question. These answers are not yet full-blown solutions. Rather, they are embryonic ideas that, if developed, may lead to solutions. For a complete explanation of Step 4, see Chapter 10.

This is the long list of answers to the Catalytic Question that the group generated through creative thinking.

Generate Answers (make a list)	
• Pay people to sit in middle seat	• ObusForm seat
• Make middle seat fashionable	• Stagger middle seats
• Only gorgeous people in middle seat	• Rotate seats for family groupings
• Assign middle seat first	• Make it wider
• Use middle seat for speed dating	• Middle seats adjustable or movable
• Only single people in middle seat	• Tell passengers it is safest seat
• New name for middle seat	• Only svelte people get middle seat
• Price middle seat higher	
• Price middle seat lower	• Market as networking opportunity
• Bum warmers	• No middle seat: 3 sections of 2
• Choice of movie	
• Double arm rest	• No seats on plane: lying room only

Generate Answers
(make a list) *Continued*

- Premium service on ground
- Future upgrades
- Middle seat gets extra airline miles
- Big ad campaign
- Don't call it middle seat
- Eliminate middle seat
- Change seat direction
- Bench seat, love seat
- Make it higher
- Middle seat appears larger
- Redesign as standing position seat
- Adjustable height
- Make clusters
- Make it a cot
- Divide plane into three aisles
- No reserved seats
- Every seat is a middle seat
- Remove every other middle seat
- Middle seats more comfortable
- Swiveling middle seats
- Prize, lottery ticket under seat
- Better meal
- Free drinks
- First class service in middle seat
- Middle seat is wider
- Seat middle seat passengers first
- Let them off plane first
- Special reclining middle seat
- Middle seats for sales people so they can talk to <u>two</u> other passengers
- Can slide back and forth
- Floor window on middle seat
- Space foam middle seat
- Mandatory for staff passes
- Kid-designed middle seats
- Make middle seat your flying office
- Market as premium seat
- Premium service on the ground
- Middle seat cheaper
- Upgraded meals for middle seat
- First class is only middle seats
- Lots of activities to distract
- Board window, middle, then aisle seats
- Wing chairs
- Speakers on both sides of wings
- Make it a leather seat
- Removable DVD player
- Bring spouse for free
- Reinvent middle seat
- Call it the throne
- Turn it around
- Make it more ergonomic
- Access to play center
- Access to work center
- On and off first

These are the clusters that the group made to sort out their long list, and the embryonic ideas for solution that the group selected as the most promising through critical thinking.

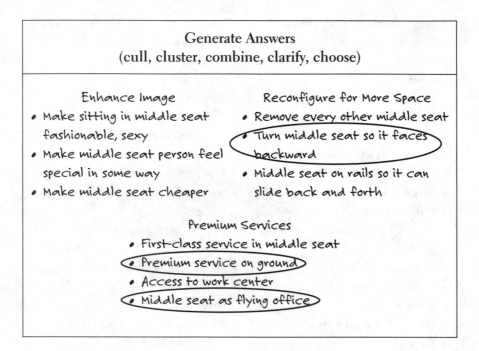

Generate Answers
(cull, cluster, combine, clarify, choose)

Enhance Image
- Make sitting in middle seat fashionable, sexy
- Make middle seat person feel special in some way
- Make middle seat cheaper

Reconfigure for More Space
- Remove every other middle seat
- Turn middle seat so it faces backward
- Middle seat on rails so it can slide back and forth

Premium Services
- First-class service in middle seat
- Premium service on ground
- Access to work center
- Middle seat as flying office

Step 5: Forge the Solution

Step 5 consists of two substeps, both of which may be iterated several times, depending on the complexity of the issues and the time available. The first is to use an evaluation screen to compare the ideas selected in Step 4: *Generate Answers* to the key Success Criteria developed in Step 2: *What's Success?* and then choosing the most promising idea to develop further. The second is to use the POWER tool to analyze, improve and refine an embryonic idea into a robust solution. For a complete explanation of Step 5, see Chapter 11.

Evaluation Screen

(Evaluate column by column and mark intersections "+" if the idea meets a given criterion, "−" if the idea does not meet a criterion, or blank if the idea neither meets nor does not meet a criterion)

Note: to simplify this illustration, only three of the selected Success Criteria in Step 2: *What's Success?* are shown here

	Differentiates	No safety issues	Hard to copy
Turn middle seat to face backward	+	−	
Premium service on the ground		+	−
Make middle seat a flying office	+		+

On the basis of this evaluation, the group selected one embryonic idea for further development.

This is the long list of possible positives, objections, and potential improvements to the original idea that the group generated by using the POWER tool and creative thinking.

POWER Make the middle seat a flying office				
Positives	Objections	What else?	Enhancements	Remedies
Elevates status of middle seat

Good differentiator

Hard to copy first in

Passengers can stay connected | Could still be copied

Not enough room to fit it in

Privacy concerns while working

Will cannibalize business class | Test market for receptivity

A flying office club?

Add premium ground service?

Partnership opportunities? | Partner with Herman Miller?

Trademark a name

Offer tools, connectivity

Sleep convertible | Brand and make central to image

Remove alternate seats

Create blinders, special lighting

Enhance business class |

This is an abbreviated example of how the group refined their POWER exercise to create a robust idea for solution.

**Powered-Up Solution
What we see ourselves doing is . . .**

We will create a special class in our airplanes, and call it the JetWays Flying Office. To do this we will remove every other middle seat, and place the remaining middle seats on sliders so that they can be adjusted. The new configuration will provide space, ease of access, productivity tools, special lighting, privacy barriers, and special ground services through the JetWays Flying Office Club. We believe we can charge a premium for this service. In order not to cannibalize our existing business class, we will enhance current Business Class offerings, keeping for example, its wider chairs. By removing only every other middle seat we can maintain our average load factors. We will pilot test the reconfigured middle seat in selected markets.

Step 6: Align Resources

Step 6 is the step in the productive thinking model that identifies the actions and resources required to implement the powered-up solution defined in Step 5: *Forge the Solution*. For a complete explanation of Step 6, see Chapter 12.

This step consists of seven substeps:

1. Using sticky notes, write one action step per note and list all the possible action steps required to implement the solution. Place the sticky notes on a large wall. Do not prioritize or sequence the action steps. Once all the action steps have been defined, cluster the sticky notes to eliminate duplications, group steps and substeps, and clarify individual tasks.

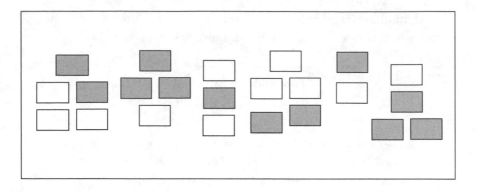

2. Identify potential Assistors (those people who will help the plan) and Resistors (those people who will hinder the plan). Add action steps, using one sticky note per action step, aimed at influencing Assistors and Resistors.

3. Ensure that each action step has an owner who is committed to its completion. Label each sticky note with the name of the action step owner.

4. Create a Wall of Time (in calendar or timeline format) to place clusters of action steps in sequence and rearrange them according to dependencies.

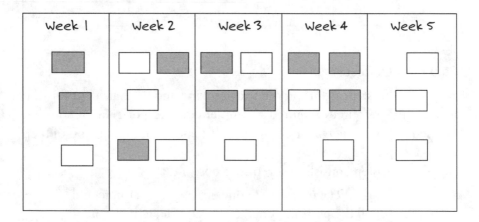

5. For each action step conduct an EFFECT (Energy, Funds, Free time, Expertise, Conditions, and Things) analysis to determine the required resources. Determine what resources are already in place and what resources must be acquired. Add action steps,

using one sticky note per action step, aimed at acquiring the needed resources.

6. Identify and list observable outcomes for each action step. Add those outcomes to each sticky note.

7. Transfer the information for each action step onto a single action sheet; insert the sheets in an action book to monitor and manage the project or hand it off to a project management specialist.

○ **Action Sheet**	Step #
Step	**Person responsible**
Dependent on completion of	**Additional participants**
Start　　　**End**　　　**Duration**	**Notes**
Deliverables or evidence of completion	
○ **Assistors**　　**Actions to improve support**	
Resistors　　**Actions to gain support**	
Resources　　**Actions to acquire**	
	Date completed
○	

GLOSSARY

AIM   A tool designed to stimulate questions in Step 3: What's the Question? AIM is an acronym that stands for Advantages, Impediments, Maybes. Its purpose is to generate a list of all the Advantages of achieving a given Target Future, all the Impediments to achieving that Target Future, and all the additional unknowns, possibilities, or spin-offs (the Maybes) that might arise if the Target Future were achieved. The resulting list is rephrased as a series of "How might I . . ." or "How might we . . ." questions.

Align Resources   Step 6 of the Productive Thinking Model. In this step, preliminary action plans and responsibilities are determined. The outcome of this phase is a platform for action.

Assistors and Resistors   Assistors are people who can be expected to assist, help, or support the realization of a plan or goal. Resistors are people who can be expected to resist, oppose, or obstruct the realization of a plan or goal. Assistors and Resistors is a tool used to help generate action steps in Step 6: Align Resources.

Brainslipping   A tool designed to help people generate long lists of ideas. Brainslipping is distinguished from brainstorming in that it is not vocal: People write down their ideas rather than calling them out. Brainslipping can be more productive than brainstorming because it encourages contributions from people who are less comfortable calling their ideas out publicly.

Brainstorming   A term coined by colleagues of the advertising executive Alex Osborn in 1941 to describe a thinking methodology he had developed "by which a group attempts to find a solution for a specific problem by amassing all the ideas spontaneously suggested by its members." Over the years Osborn developed and refined a series of rules for brainstorming meetings. His original rules were: (1) Criticism is ruled out. Adverse judgment of ideas must be withheld until later. (2) Freewheeling is welcomed. The wilder the idea, the better; it is easier to tame down than to think up. (3) Quantity is desirable. The greater the number of ideas, the more the likelihood of useful ideas. (4) Combination and improvement are sought. In addition to contributing ideas of their own, participants should suggest how the ideas of others can be turned into better ideas or how two or more ideas can be joined into another idea.

C⁵   A tool used in several steps of the Productive Thinking Model. Its purpose is to help organize and filter a large number of ideas to identify and develop the most promising ones. C⁵ stands for Cull, Cluster, Combine, Clarify, and Choose.

Catalytic Question   The outcome of Step 3: What's the Question? One or more Catalytic Questions is selected from the long list of questions generated in this step. The Catalytic Question then becomes the starting point for Step 4: Generate Answers.

Convergent thinking   A thinking mode that evaluates ideas in terms of predetermined criteria and attempts to select those that best meet such criteria. This mode of thinking is judgmental and focused so that promising ideas can be selected from long lists of possibilities. Each phase of the Productive Thinking Model employs alternating convergent and divergent phases. See also *Critical thinking*.

Creative thinking   A thinking mode that explores new meanings, new connections, and new perspectives. This mode of thinking is nonjudgmental and expansive so that it can generate long lists of possibilities. See also *Divergent thinking*.

Critical thinking   A thinking mode that evaluates ideas in terms of predetermined criteria and attempts to select those that best meet those criteria. This mode of thinking is judgmental and focused so that it can select promising candidates from long lists of possibilities. See also *Convergent thinking*.

Divergent thinking   A thinking mode that explores new meanings, new connections, and new perspectives. This mode of thinking is nonjudgmental and expansive so that it can generate long lists of possibilities. See also *Creative thinking*.

DRIVE   A tool designed to identify Success Criteria in Step 2: What's Success? DRIVE is an acronym that stands for Do, Restrictions, Investment, Values, and Essential outcomes. Its purpose is to generate lists of what a successful solution must do, what it must avoid doing, what investment limits it must adhere to, what values it must sustain, and what measurable outcomes it must achieve.

EFFECT A tool designed to identify resource requirements in Step 6: Align Resources. EFFECT is an acronym that stands for *E*nergy, *F*unds, *F*ree time, *E*xpertise, *C*onditions, and *T*hings. Its purpose is to generate lists of the resources that will be required for all the action steps in an eventual project plan.

Elephant's tether A metaphor for habitual thinking patterns. The metaphor is derived from the traditional practice of Indian mahouts, who train elephants by chaining their legs to stakes as calves so that they will learn not to try to escape. Even when they grow strong enough as adults to break their tethers, they don't.

Entraining The process of integrating new knowledge, attitudes, beliefs, or behaviors through repetition, practice, and reinforcement.

Evaluation Screen A tool used in Step 5: Forge the Solution to test two or more different solutions against predetermined Success Criteria.

Excursion A tool that helps people see their challenges from a variety of different perspectives. Excursions can be real (visits to museums, parks, or shopping malls) or imaginary (guided imagery exercises to remote locations, fantasy worlds, or even microscopic biological processes). Excursions can be useful for imagining the future in Step 2: What's Success?, listing "How might I . . ." questions in Step 3: What's the Question?, listing ideas in Step 4: Generate Answers, and listing action steps in Step 6: Align Resources.

Forge the Solution Step 5 of the Productive Thinking Model, in which the solution alternatives (the outcome of the preceding phase) are evaluated to create Powered-Up Solutions.

Future Pull The notion that a compelling, richly imagined future plays a powerful motivational role in helping people generate novel and powerful ideas for solving problems and developing opportunities.

Galeforce A condensed version of the full Productive Thinking Model designed primarily for use by individuals in a private setting. It moves the user through the various phases of the productive thinking process by means of a series of questions that serve as prompts. Groups can also use the Galeforce technique to address challenges that may not require longer productive thinking sessions. An effective Galeforce session may last from 50 to 180 minutes.

Gator brain   An informal reference to the primitive or stem brain, which is responsible for fight, flight, and other primitive responses in animals and human beings. Notwithstanding the influence of the much more complex, cortical brain structures with which people logically process information, recent research suggests that the stem brain governs significant areas of human behavior.

Generate Answers   Step 4 of the Productive Thinking Model, in which long lists of ideas are generated. From these lists one or more solution alternatives are selected.

Generative Judgment   An evaluation technique designed to improve ideas while evaluating them. Generative Judgment is a central principle in Step 5: Forge the Solution. It poses the question "How might this idea be modified to better meet Success Criteria?" This is in contrast to establishing a "hurdle test" for an idea, which the idea either passes or fails.

GEPO   An acronym that stands for Good Enough, Push On. GEPO is used in various steps of the Productive Thinking Model to move to the subsequent phase.

HMI/HMW   Acronyms that stand for "How might I . . ." and "How might we . . . ," which are used in generating lists of Problem Questions in Step 3: What's the Question?

H(E)MI / H(E)MW   Acronyms that stand for "How else might I . . ." and "How else might we. . . ." These slightly rephrased Catalytic Questions are used to help generate ideas in Step 4: Generate Answers. The addition of *else* is designed to provoke long lists of potential ideas for a solution.

I³   A tool primarily used in Step 1: What's Going On? designed to help select Target Futures for which the model is appropriate. I³ is a mnemonic that stands for Influence, Importance, and Imagination. It purpose is to determine whether a given Target Future is something over which the individual has influence, is important enough to spend time and energy on, and warrants an imaginative or novel approach.

Imagined Future (IF)   A tool primarily used in Step 2: What's Success? designed to create Future Pull by describing a powerful and compelling future. See *Future Pull*.

Incubation   A phenomenon proposed by Graham Wallas, who described the creative process as having five stages (preparation, incubation, intimation, illumination, and verification). Wallas noticed that many people report that creative ideas and solutions come after they have spent time away from a problem, forgetting it for a while. Incubation is the period in which the problem is internalized and processed by the subconscious.

Itch   The essential discontent, imbalance, or frustration that motivates the desire for new, imaginative thinking.

Kaizen   Literally, "good change," from the Japanese *kai* ("change") plus *zen* ("good"). *Kaizen* characterizes reproductive thinking, in contrast to *tenkaizen* ("good revolution"), which characterizes productive thinking.

KnoWonder   A tool for analyzing issues, concepts, or conditions. Its purpose is to ask what is known and what is yet to be known about the thing being examined. KnoWonder is particularly useful in assessing where different people may have consistent or conflicting perceptions about things.

Mindmapping   A graphical method of organizing ideas and information that was developed by Tony Buzan. Mindmapping is an excellent method for generating and capturing ideas and understanding the relationships between them.

Monkey mind   The tendency for seemingly random thoughts to fly through the mind, unbidden and uncontrolled by the mind's owner. The term is used in Buddhism, where it describes one of the difficulties in meditating: the meditator's mind being filled with seemingly random thoughts, like monkeys playing in the trees.

POWER   A tool designed to evaluate ideas in Step 5: Forge the Solution. POWER is an acronym that stands for *Positives*, *Objections*, *What else?*, *Enhancements*, and *Remedies*. The outcome of using the POWER tool is a detailed statement of what the new idea looks like: the Powered-Up Solution.

Powered-Up Solution   The outcome of Step 5: Forge the Solution, often expressed as a statement beginning with "What I see myself doing is. . . ."

Problem Question   One of a list of questions, generally starting with "How might I . . ." or "How might we. . . ." It is used in Step 3: What's the Question? Problem Questions are designed to explore the true nature of the problem to be solved or the opportunity to be addressed. Productive thinking poses Problem Questions rather than making traditional problem statements because questions invite answers, whereas statements tend to be static.

Productive thinking   The kind of thinking that generates new, often challenging ideas that may or may not be useful. Productive thinking is important for innovation, growth, capacity building, and differentiation.

Reproductive thinking   The kind of thinking that follows familiar patterns to achieve high levels of efficiency and minimal error. Reproductive thinking is important for quality control, consistency, speed, and efficiency.

Resistors   People who can be expected to resist, oppose, or obstruct the realization of a plan or goal. See *Assistors and Resistors.*

Satisficing   A term coined by Herbert Simon to describe the human tendency to stop thinking once the most obvious solution to a question or dilemma has been identified.

Solution alternatives   The outcomes, usually in the form of embryonic ideas, of Step 4: Generate Answers.

Stakeholders   People who have or could have an interest in the issue being worked on during the productive thinking process.

Success Criteria   One of the outcomes of Step 2: What's Success? Success Criteria are used to evaluate the effectiveness of various alternative solutions that may be generated in Step 4: Generate Answers.

Target Future   The vision or goal for a productive thinking exercise, "the place you would like to arrive at." The Target Future is established by first generating long lists of desirable futures and then selecting the most powerful or compelling one.

Tenkaizen   Literally, "good revolution," from the Japanese syllables *tenkai* ("revolution, turnaround") and *zen* ("good"). *Tenkaizen* is a characteristic of productive thinking, in contrast to *kaizen* ("good change"), a characteristic of reproductive thinking.

Third third   The final third of a productive idea-generating session. In the most productive ideation sessions, the first third of ideas generated tend to be safe and/or obvious, the second third more unusual, and the third third the most original. These are the ideas that have the greatest creative potential.

What's Going On?   Step 1 of the Productive Thinking Model, in which an issue is identified and explored in terms of its causes, effects, stakeholders, and other defining characteristics. This information is then used to generate a series of possible Target Futures for further work in subsequent steps of the model.

What's the Question?   Step 3 of the Productive Thinking Model, in which a long list of possible problem questions are articulated.

What's Success?   Step 2 of the Productive Thinking Model, in which criteria for evaluating potentially successful resolutions to an issue are determined.

What's UP?   A tool for finding the practical value in what appear at first to be ideas that are too strange or way out to be of any use. The method consists of asking, "What is underlying principle (UP) behind this idea?"

NOTES

Chapter 1

1. J. H. Fabre, *The Life of the Scorpion*, trans. Alexander Teixseria de Mattos and Bernard Miall. New York: Dodd, Mead and Company, 1923.

2. The description of Fabre's experiment is from J. Henri Fabre, *The Life of the Caterpillar*, transl. Alexander Teixeira de Mattos. New York: Dodd, Mead and Company, 1914.

3. Ainsworth-Land is the author of *Grow or Die: The Unifying Principle of Transformation* (New York: Random House, 1973), in which he explores his transformational theory of change, which has been adopted by businesses, governments, and academic institutions around the world.

4. This is not the real name of the initiative; I've changed the name to protect the organization's identity.

Chapter 2

1. William H. Calvin, "The Emergence of Intelligence," *Scientific American* 271(4): 100–107, 1994.

2. Steven Pinker, *How the Mind Works*, New York: Norton, 1997.

3. Selfridge's illusion can be found in Michael Michalko, *Tinkertoys: A Handbook of Business Creativity for the '90s*, Berekely, CA: Ten Speed Press, 1991.

Chapter 3

1. It used to be explained as the persistence of vision, or the phi effect, but more recent experiments favor an explanation that incorporates the way in which the brain processes information relating to movement in the real world. See Joseph Anderson and Barbara Anderson, "The Myth of Persistence of Vision Revisited," *Journal of Film and Video* 45(1): 3–12, 1993. For an explanation of the phi phenomenon, see Lloyd Kaufman, *Sight and Mind: An Introduction to Visual Perception*, New York: Oxford University Press, 1974, p. 368.

2. Interestingly, though their effects were profound, those experiments were not particularly original. By 1912, when Wertheimer had completed his initial experiments, the film industry was already a reality. Georges Méliès produced *A Trip to the Moon* in 1902, Edwin S. Porter made *The Great Train Robbery* in 1903, and D. W. Griffith's *Birth of a Nation* and *Intolerance* were less than four years away.

3. Robert Sternberg, *Cognitive Psychology*, 4th ed, Belmont, CA: Wadsworth, 2006.

4. J. P. Guilford was a U.S. psychologist, who developed a series of psychometric tests of human intelligence. He was the first scientist to make the distinction between convergent thinking and divergent thinking. E. Paul Torrance was an American psychologist best known for his pioneering research in the study of creativity. Torrance developed a benchmark method for quantifying creativity and invented the Torrance Tests of Creative Thinking. Alex Osborn was an advertising executive who developed the concept of brainstorming. Together with Sid Parnes, he developed the Osborn-Parnes Creative Problem Solving Process, on which the Productive Thinking Model is based.

5. Ellen Langer, *Mindfulness*, Reading, MA: Addison-Wesley, 1989.

6. Between 1995 and 2005, 16,742 Americans died from such complications. See Ryan Singel, "One Million Ways To Die," *Wired*, September 11, 2006.

7. Atul Gawande, *Complications: A Surgeon's Notes on an Imperfect Science*, New York: Metropolitan Books, 2002.

8. R. Bendavid, "The Shouldice Technique: A Canon in Hernia Repair," *Canadian Journal of Surgery* 40: 199-207, 1997.

9. G. Chan and C. K. Chan. "A Review of Incisional Hernia Repairs: Preoperative Weight Loss and Selective Use of the Mesh Repair," *Hernia* 9(1):37–41, 2005.

10. In Japanese the syllables *tenkai* can be written with different Kanji characters meaning either something like evolution or expansion as in 展開, or turnaround as in 転回. I have been assured by several Japanese friends and colleagues that although it is not a word that exists in the language, most Japanese people, upon hearing the syllables in *tenkaizen*, would think of the kanji characters for "turnaround," followed by the notion of "good," "right," and "virtue," in other words, "good revolution".

11. It's a happy coincidence that you also can think of *tenkaizen* as 10 times more powerful than the plain vanilla variety.

12. See the entry on Netflix in Wikipedia.

13. Although this example is apocryphal, recent research suggests that the leading political science journals are "misleading and inaccurate due to publication bias." Rebecca Skloot, "Spurious Correlations," *New York Times Magazine*, December 10, 2006.

14. The information on the *Journal of Spurious Correlations* is drawn from the journal's Web site, jspurc.org, and from Skloot, op cit.

Chapter 4

1. Mark Kingwell, *Practical Judgments: Essays in Culture, Politics, and Interpretation*, Toronto: University of Toronto Press, 2002.

2. Quoted in John Briggs, *Fire in the Crucible: The Alchemy of Creative Genius*, New York: St, Martin's Press, 1988, p. 105.

3. Sylvia Wright, "The Death of Lady Mondegreen," *Harper's Magazine*, November 1954.

4. Gavin Edwards, '*Scuse Me While I Kiss This Guy, and Other Misheard Lyrics*, New York: Fireside, 1995.

5. W. Mischel, "Convergences and Challenges in the Search for Consistency," *American Psychologist* 39:351–364, 1984.

6. Marvin Minsky, *The Society of Mind*, New York: Simon & Schuster, 1986, page 42.

7. Fons Trompenaars and Charles Hampden-Turner, *Riding the Waves of Culture: Understanding Cultural Diversity in Global Business*, 2d ed. London: Nicholas Brealey, 2006.

8. Lewis Kamb and Mike Barber, "Police Were Told Years Ago of Pig Farm," *Seattle Post-Intelligencer*, February 9, 2002.

Chapter 5

1. Much of the information about W. L. Gore is from Alan Deutschman, "The Fabric of Creativity," *Fast Company* 89, December 2004.

2. Osborn originally called his method thinking up. The term *brainstorming* was coined by his colleagues.

3. Alex F. Osborn, *Applied Imagination: Principles and Procedures of Creative Problem-Solving*, New York: Scribner, 1963.

4. Research supporting the third third, or "extended effort," hypothesis can be found in: S. J. Parnes, "The Creative Studies Project," in Scott G. Isaksen (ed.), *Frontiers of Creativity Research: Beyond the Basics*, Buffalo, NY: Bearly Limited, 1987, pp. 156–188; S. J. Parnes and R. B. Noller, "Applied Creativity: The Creative Studies Project: Part II: Results of the Two-Year-Program," *Journal of Creative Behavior* 6:164–186, 1972; C. W. Wang and R. Y. Horng, "The Effects of Creative Problem Solving on Creativity, Cognitive Type and R&D Performance," *R&D Management* 32:35–45, 2002; and, Gerard J. Puccio, Mary C. Murdock, and Marie Mance, *Creative Leadership: Skills That Drive Change*, Thousand Oaks, CA: Sage, 2007. Anecdotal evidence supporting the hypothesis can be found in Osborn, *Applied Imagination*, cited in footnote 3.

5. As you might imagine, often third third ideas seem ridiculous at first and therefore not worth exploring. The actual idea that came up during this session was "Let's use magnifying glass in our booths and roast the buggers out!" In Chapter 11 I will discuss the concept of What's UP: extracting useful underlying principles from ideas that may at first seem too wild to merit further development. In this case the result of looking for the underlying principle in "roast the buggers out" was "make it uncomfortable for people to stay in the booths."

Chapter 7

1. I³ was inspired by the work of Bill Shephard, Roger Firestein, Don Treffinger, and Scott Isaksen.

2. Piet Hein, *Grooks*, Gylling, Denmark: Narayana Press, 1993.

3. One of the tenets of productive thinking is to steep yourself in your issue and let your subconscious mind do the work for you. The phenomenon is called incubation and was proposed by Graham Wallas in *The Art of Thought* (New York: Harcourt Brace, 1926). Wallas identified what he referred to as the four stages of the creative process: (1) preparation: gathering relevant information and narrowing the problem until obstacles are visible, (2) incubation: during which unconscious processes of mind seem to work on the problem; during this time it's okay to think occasionally about problem as long as there's no pressure

for solution, (3) illumination: spontaneous or as result of conscious effort; in this stage intuition and insight produce possible solutions, and (4) verification: logical testing of intuitive and insightful potential solutions for validity, followed by organization and elaboration into finished product. My think[x] colleagues and I frequently employ the concept of incubation in our client work. When facilitating groups through the productive thinking process, we will often schedule a break of one or more days after an intensive What's Going On? session. The participants can sleep on the work they've done, allow the ideas they've generated to settle for a while, and return with renewed energy and insights. There's no one right way to use the model. One of the beauties of productive thinking is that you can fit it to the way you work, to the circumstance of the issue, and to the time available.

Chapter 8

1. Stephen Lucas and Martin Medhurst. "'I Have a Dream' Leads Top 100 Speeches of the Century," *University of Wisconsin–Madison News*, December 15, 1999. Available at www.news.wisc.edu.

2. "A Dream Remembered," *OnlineNewsHour*, August 28, 2003. Available at www.pbs.org.

3. The velocity required to escape from the surface of the earth is about 11.2 kilometers per second, or just over 25,000 miles per hour. The velocity required to escape from Jupiter is about 59.5 kilometers per second, or over 130,000 miles per hour. Theoretically, the velocity required to escape from the past may be greater than the speed of light.

4. If you decide to have someone to interview you, make sure it's someone you feel comfortable expressing your thoughts and feelings to. Sometimes that may mean a close friend. Sometimes it may mean someone completely neutral.

5. The French name for the game, pétanque, derives from the *pieds tanqués*, which in the Marseilles dialect means "stuck feet," because the players' feet have to remain fixed together within a small circle outside the target area.

Chapter 10

1. In 1989, Rose was banned from Major League Baseball after allegations that he had violated Rule 21(d), which prohibits gambling on

baseball games. In 1991, the Hall of Fame voted to exclude all players on baseball's ineligible list from consideration for election to Cooperstown.

2. Baseball statistics define official at bats as all complete batting appearances, not including bases on balls, being hit by a pitch, sacrifices, and obstruction

3. James Gleick, *Genius: The Life and Science of Richard Feynman*. New York: Pantheon, 1992.

4. See Roger von Oech, A *Whack on the Side of the Head: How to Unlock Your Mind for Innovation*. New York, Warner Books, 1983; Arthur B. VanGundy, *Brain Busters for Business Advantage*, San Diego, CA: Pfeiffer and Company, 1995; Robert Alan Black, *Broken Crayons: Break Your Crayons and Draw Outside the Lines*. Dubuque, IA: Kendall/Hunt, 1995.

5. John Biggs, "The Alarm Clock as a Moving Target. Catch It if You Can", *New York Times*, February 9, 2007.

Chapter 11

1. Kokan Nagayama, *The Connoisseur's Book of Japanese Swords*, Tokyo: Kodansha International, 1997. See also the article on katana in Wikipedia.

2. The Evaluation Screen is based on the work of Sidney Parnes in *Creative Behavior Guidebook* (New York: Scribner's, 1967) and *The Magic of Your Mind* (Buffalo, NY: Creative Education Foundation, 1981).

3. The halo effect refers to a cognitive bias we all display in which we give a special value to the items we judge at the beginning of lists. We tend to confer a "reference" status on those early items. In other words, our perceptions of items later in the list are colored by what we thought of the items early in the list. Brand marketers often use the halo effect to enhance the image of their entire line of products by creating a single product with special qualities. You have probably experienced this effect when shopping for a car. Even though you may not buy the top-of-the-line model, you transfer some of the value of that premium car onto the one you eventually purchase. The contrast effect refers to a cognitive bias in which we tend to evaluate items in a list not by independent criteria but by how we subcon-

sciously believe they compare to other items in the list. We have a natural tendency to enhance or diminish evaluations when comparing items with other recently observed contrasting objects. You probably experience this effect in the way you evaluate other people—more often in comparison to each other rather than by benchmarking them against individual character traits.

4. Daniel Kahneman, Paul Slovick, and Amos Tversky (eds.), *Judgment under Uncertainty: Heuristics and Biases*, Cambridge and New York: Cambridge University Press, 1982; Daniel Kahneman and Amos Tversky, *Choices, Values, and Frames*, New York: Russell Sage Foundation, 2000.

5. Piet Hein, *Grooks*, Gylling, Denmark; Narayana Press, 1994

6. To respect the confidentiality of the client organization, I haven't used Scott's real name.

Chapter 12

1. Details of the *Apollo XIII* mission and rescue are from an article by Stephen Cass, "Apollo 13, We Have a Solution," *IEEE Spectrum*, April 2005.

2. Brainslipping is based on the work of Horst Geschka, Scott Isaksen, and Don Treffinger.

3. For this task, I recommend 3- by 5-inch sticky notes.

4. If you are working alone or with a smaller group, another good option is to use mindmapping software. Two excellent products that we use at think[x] are NovaMind for the Mac platform and MindManager for the PC platform.

5. The Great Wall of Time is based on a strategic planning technique developed by Frank Prince.

6. Independent of the productive thinking process, my think[x] colleagues and I also use this action planning approach in helping organizations structure their annual operational plans. The procedure is almost identical: Gather a team of managers, have them brainstorm the actions required to meet the plan over the next year, transfer the actions to a timeline, resource them appropriately, and consolidate them into a tracking system. The process is fast (often taking less than half a day), simple, transparent, and it works like gangbusters.

Chapter 13

1. Occasionally, in our think^x training programs, participants will ask why we define the Target Future in the final substep of Step 1: What's Going On? rather than in the beginning Step 2: What's Success? Indeed, the Target Future makes sense either as a culmination to Step 1 or as a kickoff to Step 2 (all models are wrong; some are useful). If you work through the model in a single session, it doesn't much matter where you consider Step 1 to end and Step 2 to begin. Often when we're working with groups, however, we break up our thinking sessions over several days and sometimes even longer. In these cases, it is useful to conclude each session with a powerful result. We've found that ending an exploration of What's Going On? without resolving it into a Target Future can be demotivating for groups, whereas ending with a compelling Target Future can produce excitement and enthusiasm for the next step. Ending with a Target Future also allows ideas about a desirable future to incubate until the next session. I've mentioned the power of incubation several times in this book. So the answer is yes, the Target Future can reasonably be in What's Success? If it makes sense to you to deal with it there, by all means do so. Make the model work for you. Follow the advice in the *Mustard Seed Manual*: "One should at first observe rules severely, then change them in an intelligent way." First learn the rules, then break them.

Chapter 14

1. G. Ekvall and Y. Tangeberg-Anderson, "Working Climate and Creativity: A Study of an Innovative Newspaper," *Journal of Creative Behavior* 20(3): 215–225, 1986.

2. Atul Gawande, *Complications: A Surgeon's Notes on an Imperfect Science*, New York: Penguin, 2002.

3. K. Anders Ericsson, *The Road to Excellence: The Acquisition of Expert Performance in the Arts and Sciences, Sports, and Games*, Mahwah, NJ: Lawrence Erlbaum Associates, 1996.

BIBLIOGRAPHY

Adams, James L. *The Care and Feeding of Ideas: A Guide to Encouraging Creativity.* 1986. Reading, MA: Addison-Wesley.

Adams, James L. *Conceptual Blockbusting.* 1986. London: Penguin.

Ainsworth-Land, George. *Grow or Die: The Unifying Principle of Transformation.* 1973. New York: Random House.

Amabile, Teresa M. *Creativity in Context.* 1996. Boulder, CO: Westview Press.

Black, Robert Alan. *Broken Crayons: Break Your Crayons and Draw Outside the Lines.* 1998. Dubuque, IA: Kendall/Hunt.

Bohm, David. *Thought as a System.* 1992. London: Routledge.

Bohm, David (ed. Lee Nichol). *On Creativity.* 1998. London: Routledge.

Boorstin, Daniel J. *The Creators: A History of Heroes of the Imagination.* 1992. New York: Random House.

Briggs, John. *Fire in the Crucible: The Alchemy of Creative Genius.* 1988. New York: St. Martin's Press.

Claxton, Guy. *Hare Brain, Tortoise Mind.* 1997. Hopewell NJ: Ecco Press.

De Bono, Edward. *Parallel Thinking.* 1994. London: Viking.

De Bono, Edward. *Practical Thinking.* 1971. London: Penguin Books.

Dennett, Daniel C. *Consciousness Explained.* 1991. Boston: Back Bay Books.

Ericsson, K. Anders. *The Road to Excellence: The Acquistion of Expert Performance in the Arts and Sciences, Sports, and Games.* 1996. Mahwah NJ: Lawrence Erlbaum Associates.

Flesch, Rudolf. *The Art of Clear Thinking.* 1951. New York: Harper and Brothers.

Focault, Michael. *The Order of Things: An Archaeology of the Human Sciences*. 1970. New York: Random House.

Fritz, Robert. *Creating*. 1991. New York: Fawcett Columbine.

Gardner, Howard. *Changing Minds: The Art and Science of Changing Our Own and Other People's Minds*. 2004. Boston: Harvard Business School Press.

Gardner, Howard. *Creating Minds*. 1993. New York: Basic Books.

Gawande, Atul. *Complications: A Surgeon's Notes on an Imperfect Science*. 2002. New York: Penguin.

Gelb, Michael J. *How to Think Like Leonardo da Vinci*. 1998. New York: Dell.

Gleick, James. *Genius: The Life and Science of Richard Feynman*. 1992. New York: Pantheon.

Gordon, William J. J. *Synectics: The Development of Creative Capacity*. 1961. New York: Collier Books.

Guilford, J. P. *Way Beyond the IQ: Guide to Improving Intelligence and Creativity*. 1977. Buffalo, NY: Creative Education Foundation.

Hadamard, Jacques. *The Psychology of Invention in the Mathematical Field*. 1949. New York: Dover.

Hein, Piet. *Grooks* (vols. 1, 2, 3, and 4). 1969. Garden City, NY: Doubleday.

Hirschberg, J. *The Creative Priority*. 1998. New York: Harper Business.

Hofstadter, Douglas R., and Daniel C. Dennett (eds.). *The Mind's I: Fantasies and Reflections on Self and Soul*. 1981. New York: Bantam.

Howard, Pierce J. *The Owner's Manual for the Brain: Everyday Applications from Mind-Brain Research*. 2000. Atlanta: Bard Press.

Isaacs, William. *Dialogue and the Art of Thinking Together*. 1999. New York: Doubleday.

Kahneman, Daniel, and Amos Tversky. *Choices, Values, and Frames*. 2000. New York: Russell Sage Foundation.

Kahneman, Daniel, Paul Slovic, and Amos Tversky. *Judgment under Uncertainty: Heuristics and Biases.* 1982. Cambridge and New York: Cambridge University Press.

Kaufman, Lloyd. *Sight and Mind: An Introduction to Visual Perception.* 1974. New York: Oxford University Press.

Kingwell, Mark. *Better Living: In Pursuit of Happiness from Plato to Prozac.* 1999. Toronto: Penguin Books.

Kingwell, Mark. *Practical Judgments: Essays in Culture, Politics, and Interpretation.* 2002. Toronto: University of Toronto Press.

Koestler, Arthur. *The Act of Creation.* 1989. London: Arkana.

Kosko, Bart. *Fuzzy Thinking: The New Science of Fuzzy Logic.* 1993. New York: Hyperion.

Lakoff, George, and Mark Johnson. *Metaphors We Live By.* 1980. Chicago: University of Chicago Press.

Langer, Ellen J. *Mindfulness.* 1989. Reading, MA: Addison-Wesley.

May, Rollo. *The Courage to Create.* 1975. New York: Bantam Books.

Michalko, Michael. *Thinkertoys: A Handbook of Business Creativity for the '90s.* 1991. Berkeley, CA: Ten Speed Press.

Minsky, Marvin. *The Society of Mind.* 1986. New York: Simon & Schuster.

Neethling, Kobus, and Raché Rutherford. *Am I Clever or Am I Stupid?* 2001. Vanderbijlpark, South Africa: Carpe Diem.

Osborn, Alex F. *Applied Imagination: Principles and Procedures of Creative Problem-Solving.* 1963. New York: Scribner.

Parnes, S. J. *Creative Behavior Guidebook.* 1967. New York: Scribner's.

Parnes, S. J. *Optimize: The Magic of Your Mind.* 1978. Buffalo, NY: Creative Education Foundation.

Pinker, Stephen. *How the Mind Works.* 1997. New York: Norton.

Pinker, Stephen. *The Language Instinct: How the Mind Creates Language*. 1995. New York: HarperPerennial.

Ramachandran, V. S. *A Brief Tour of Human Consciousness*. 2004. New York: Pi Press.

Ratey, John J. *A User's Guide to the Brain*. 2001. New York: Pantheon.

Ristad, Eloise. *A Soprano on Her Head: Right-Side-Up Reflections on Life and Other Performances*. 1982. Moab, UT: Real People Press.

Ruggiero, Vincent Ryan. *The Art of Thinking: A Guide to Critical and Creative Thought*. 1998. New York: Addison-Wesley.

Shank, Roger C. *Tell Me a Story: Narrative and Intelligence*. 1990. Evanston IL: Northwestern University Press.

Sternberg, Robert. *Cognitive Psychology*, 4th ed. 1999. Belmont, CA: Wadsworth.

Sternberg, Robert. *Handbook of Creativity*. 1999. Cambridge, MA: Cambridge University Press.

Sternberg, Robert J. (ed.). *Wisdom: Its Nature, Origins, and Development*. 1990. Cambridge, MA: Cambridge University Press.

Taylor, Warren. *Models for Thinking and Writing*. 1966. Cleveland: World Publishing.

Thompson, Charles "Chic." *What a Great Idea! The Key Steps Creative People Take*. 1992. New York: HarperPerennial.

Torrance, E. Paul. *The Search for Satori and Creativity*. 1979. Buffalo, NY: Creative Education Foundation.

Trompenaars, Fons, and Charles Hampden-Turnder. *Riding the Waves of Culture*, 2d ed. 2006. London: Nicholas Brealey.

VanGundy, Arthur B. *Brain Boosters for Business Advantage*. 1995. San Diego CA: Pfeiffer and Company.

VanGundy, Arthur B. *Idea Power: Techniques and Resources to Unleash the Creativity in Your Organization*. 1992. New York: Amacom.

von Oech, Roger. *Expect the Unexpected (Or You Won't Find It)*. 2001. New York: Free Press.

von Oech, Roger. *A Kick in the Seat of the Pants*. 1986. New York: Harper & Row.

von Oech, Roger. *A Whack on the Side of the Head: How to Unlock Your Mind for Innovation*. 1983. New York: Warner Books.

Wenger, Win. *Discovering the Obvious*. 1998. Gaithersburg, MD: Project Renaissance.

Wenger, Win. *The Einstein Factor*. 1996. Rocklin, CA: Prima Publishing.

INDEX

ABOUT THE AUTHOR

Tim Hurson is passionate about productive thinking: the ability people have to use their creative intelligence as an effective tool for change. He is deeply committed to the belief that creative intelligence is a set of skills *everyone* can learn and cultivate.

Throughout his career Tim has worked with organizations of all sizes—from Fortune 500 giants to small nonprofits—to create innovation, marketing, and new product initiatives. In his work Tim has seen how barriers to creativity and productive thinking are also barriers to financial and personal success.

He travels extensively, consulting and speaking about how companies and individuals can use productive thinking to remove these barriers to success. He shows how organizations can foster a creative working environment that generates innovation daily and enables them to adjust to rapid changes in technologies, markets, and mandates.

Tim is a founding partner of think^x intellectual capital (www.thinkxic.com), a firm that provides global corporations with training, facilitation, and consultation in productive thinking and innovation. He's both a faculty member and a trustee of the Creative Education Foundation and a founding director of Facilitators without Borders.

Born in South Africa and raised in Manhattan, Tim attended Oberlin College and now lives in Toronto, where he shares his passion for creativity with his wife and four children.